P9-CRT-334
COMING SOON, FROM MYS
Cutting Edge
Blackjack
by
Richard Harvey
Contains the powerful
results of Richard Harvey's
latest research project!
Includes the groundbreaking
"How To Count Cards At 1- & 2-Deck Tables"
Ask your favorite bookseller to carry it!
Tell them to call Mystic Ridge Books at:
1-877-977-2121.
ISBN#: 0-9672182-4-1
SEE OUR WEB SITE FOR FREE
BLACKJACK TIPS AND INFORMATION!:
www.blackjacktoday.com

Blackjack The SMART Way

The Millennium Edition

by

Richard Harvey

MYSTIC RIDGE BOOKS

ALBUQUERQUE, NEW MEXICO

Blackjack The SMART Way – The Millennium Edition
by Richard Harvey

MYSTIC RIDGE BOOKS
P.O. BOX 66930
ALBUQUERQUE, NM 87193-6930
(505) 899-2121
Find us on the World Wide Web at:
http://www.blackjacktoday.com
MYSTIC RIDGE BOOKS is a division of Mystic Ridge Productions, Inc.

First Edition Printed February 1999.

Library of Congress Catalog Card No. 00-090888

ISBN: 0-9672182-3-3

Legal Disclaimer:
This book's purpose is to prepare you to deal well with the blackjack environment, and to make you a smart, *conservative,* winning player. NO book should guarantee winnings every time – because you're dealing with the randomness of cards and other uncertainties. This includes your personality, your abilities and the differing rules and restrictions of the different casinos at which you will choose to play. There are rarely huge jackpots to be won at any one sitting, and blackjack is unlikely to make you a millionaire. For the average player — for whom this book is written — any winnings at the casino will be amply satisfying but will NOT make you rich. You must never go to the casino hoping for and expecting huge, Lottery-sized riches, nor should you bet or play beyond your limit. ONLY play if you can keep it in the realm of a fun activity, NOT an obsession. Those who are inclined to ignore my advice and become addicted to gambling, please contact Gambler's Anonymous or a similar help group and AVOID casinos entirely.

PRINTED AND BOUND IN THE UNITED STATES OF AMERICA.

Contents

Publisher's Note For The Millennium Edition

All of us at Mystic Ridge Books are very proud to bring you The Millennium Edition of *Blackjack The SMART Way*. With its additions, the breakthrough book you have chosen is now even better! Among other things, Richard Harvey has expanded the popular section on his fabulous invention, **Card Observation**. There's some material from his national seminars. His unique card strategy has been fine tuned, to reflect the startling results of his ongoing research. Also, the Dangers In Doubling & Splitting chapter has been expanded.

If you are seeking a book based upon what it can do for your game, look no further! No other comparable book has so much going for it!:

✔ This book gives you a comprehensive and uniquely successful system. *It is jam-packed with information that you will find nowhere else*. The author will teach you skills few players even know they must possess to become consistent winners.

✔ It is NOT — like many books — a rehash of others' ideas. It is based upon original research and totally fresh new concepts of the author's own creation. You will acquire money-making tools and benefit from Richard Harvey's unique insights.

✔ The author will explain in detail *every* move he recommends. He doesn't ask you to take his word for it — he shows you *why* you should want to follow the *Blackjack The SMART Way* system. Read this book and you will come to a greater understanding of the logic behind the moves you will want to make.

✔ The author is a regular blackjack player, whose win rate is in the 80-percentile range — he knows of which he speaks, and puts his money where his mouth is.

- ✔ This system has been field-tested at many different casinos and has been *proven* highly successful. The results can be duplicated by you — as others have done before you.
- ✔ *Blackjack The SMART Way* is designed specifically for the realities you'll face at today's modern-day casinos — it's cutting edge stuff.
- ✔ This is the system he has taught to hundreds of players around the nation, at countless workshops and seminars which have received overwhelming acclaim.

It's all of this and more!

Now, once you've mastered all of the information in this book — be sure and check out *Cutting Edge Blackjack*, Richard's latest book, which should be out by the time this edition is released.

Not only does it contain the breakthrough method of "How To Count Cards At 1- & 2-Deck Tables," but it also unveils powerful new concepts and information you can use to great profit, from the author's original research projects!

Enjoy!

Preface to The Millennium Edition

Since the First Edition of *Blackjack The SMART Way* was published, there have been many fantastic happenings — nationwide book signing events, workshops, seminars, talk show appearances and newspaper interviews.

The nicest thing to come from these events is wonderful feedback from countless readers and seminar-goers. Many have told me that this book and my audio book, *Preparing YOU To WIN,* have given them a fuller understanding of the game, enabling them to win as they never have done before. That makes me very proud of these books, and my system.

♣

Now, this book was designed with the typical blackjack player in mind. The player who prefers the low stakes tables. The player who cannot or does not want to bring a lot of money to the casino. The player who wants to win most of the time and have fun, without risking the house payment. The player who wants a system that's comprehensive, current, highly successful, and easy to understand.

After years of teaching players my system and turning them into winners, I am looking forward to doing the same for you.

♦

I'd like to tip my hat in recognition of the great blackjack authors who have come before, especially those who laid the foundation of modern Blackjack strategy: those involved in the computer studies at MIT, Los Alamos and IBM in the 1960s who revolutionized the game — most notably, Dr. Edward O. Thorp and Julian Braun.

While my approach to the game differs from theirs, every modern blackjack player owes those folks respect. They belong in the Blackjack Hall of Fame, if such a thing existed.

♥

Blackjack The SMART Way will improve your game, no matter what level your playing skill or ambition. I'm also excited about my follow-up to this book — *Cutting Edge Blackjack*. It contains exciting new concepts, methods and information that have resulted from my latest studies, from which you can really profit once you have absorbed all of the material in this book.

Players who have learned how to win regularly are much happier players. My ambition is to make you a successful, winning player, who achieves maximum results while having a maximum amount of fun.

It's no fun if you lose!

♠

By the way — be sure to surf the Mystic Ridge Books web site regularly. There, you'll find frequently updated blackjack tips, that will help make you a better player. You will also find my calendar of events that you won't want to miss!

Go to:

www.blackjacktoday.com

Enjoy!

Richard Harvey
June 2000
New Mexico

A
YOUR MONEY
IS
ON THE LINE
A

Blackjack is a great game.

I mean, shouldn't you jump at the chance to have someone *pay* you to have a good time? ...Pay you $50, $150, $250 or more, to have two hours of fun playing cards?

The beauty of blackjack is that that kind of return is achievable on most occasions, playing at the tables most players prefer – the low stakes tables; specifically, the $5 or $10 minimum bet tables. *IF* you are a good player.

Now, it's unlikely that you will ever become a millionaire from blackjack, if you play the low stakes tables. However, the rewards of learning how to play properly are such that you can have a great time playing, while making a tidy profit.

By the end of the year those "little returns" from each trip to the casino can add up to a substantial total — *thousands* of dollars. That is, *if* you are a good student of *Blackjack The SMART Way*.

Nothing Comes From Nothing

Blackjack is deceptive, in that it seems like a simple game, but it is most definitely NOT. Casinos have been effective in conning great numbers of otherwise smart people into believing the line that "if you can count to 21, you can play blackjack." That popular casino come-on has led many down the road to disaster.

No – blackjack is a *challenging* game, much like the game of Bridge. If it weren't, casinos would be packed with wealthy, happy winners.

But I will make your job simple, by giving you the tools and the rules you need to win. I will make it as easy as possible for you to understand the ins and outs of blackjack, from a *winner's* perspective. You hold in your hands the key to fun and profit.

The First Principles Of Winning at Blackjack

Do you want to know what the First Principle of Winning at Blackjack is? *Be happy with your gains – no matter how modest*

they might be. Never throw back your winnings.

The Second Principle of Winning at Blackjack is the flip side of the First: *Know when it's one of those times when you should cut your losses and leave.*

If you keep your losses on any one occasion below what you usually win on average on any one trip to the casino, you won't wipe out the winnings you've earned in the majority of your trips to the casino.

Makes sense, right? Well, these principles might sound, on the surface, *obvious* to you – perhaps even unnecessary to mention – but they are obviously NOT. If these principles alone were that easy to implement, casinos would be loaded with winners.

What I'm talking about here is *knowing when to leave*. You need more than a vague recognition of this necessary skill, in order to put it into action at the casino. Many players say they understand this principle, but they then go out and either throw back any winnings they might have made, or they accrue huge losses, because *they play too long*.

In later chapters, you will acquire the necessary skills such that you will never again throw back your winnings, or leave a big loser.

This is NOT Your Father's Blackjack Game

There are many things you must know if you want to win at casino blackjack. First, you must realize that the game *has* changed since the father of modern Blackjack strategy, Edward O. Thorp, wrote his brilliant book *Beat The Dealer* in the early 1960s, and Lawrence Revere wrote his wonderful book *Playing Blackjack As A Business* in the early 1970s.

In fact, the complexion of the average casino has changed in just the past *10* years alone, and — some of those I've met at my workshops say they have noticed this — it *is* a bit harder to beat the house now. That is, playing the *old* way.

Don't worry. *Blackjack The SMART Way* will get you through the morass that is the modern casino environment.

New Challenges

Why the radical change over the years?

Number one — there has been a veritable explosion in the construction of new casinos in recent years (almost all of the 50 states now allows casino gambling in some form or another). Unfortunately, many of these casinos are either unregulated or under-regulated. That is, many lie in regions where there is little or no governmental oversight. (In fact, there have been Congressional hearings investigating this shortcoming, with an eye toward possibly imposing Federal regulation.) This presents a possible danger the player should be aware of.

Number two — casinos have gotten very sophisticated about targeting winners for countermeasures. Countermeasures include a whole host of actions — such as frequent shuffling and dealer changes, which can spoil your game. (We'll discuss this in detail later on.)

And, finally — aside from casino countermeasures, which are legal but unfair, there are a small minority of casinos and dealers who are resorting to dirty tricks that make winning all but impossible. By dirty tricks I mean casino cheating. While this is not the norm by any means, I estimate that you might run into this about 10 percent of the time, if you play at as many casinos as I do.

That's why you especially need to read this book from cover to cover — you need to understand the modern challenges you're facing at today's casinos, and learn how to respond to them, to protect yourself against losses that might be caused not by your card strategy, but by outside forces. Many times you will find that you are playing not just against the game, but against the house as well.

An Object Lesson

You can lose a lot more than your money if you are unaware of all of this. For instance, there was a tragic story I became aware of while being interviewed on a Las Vegas talk show. On the wall, behind the interviewer, was an article with a headline that read "High Roller Shoots Dealer" — or something to that effect.

It seems this high roller was playing at a casino somewhere in Asia (I don't remember where — Singapore?) and he was losing hand after hand. Yet, he continued to play! HE WENT ON TO LOSE NEARLY 50 HANDS IN A ROW! Convinced he had been cheated, he then pulled out a revolver and killed the dealer! Later on, he told a reporter he regretted killing her, but he "couldn't help himself."

There are a number of lessons to be learned here (other than the fact that being a "high roller" doesn't necessarily mean being a smart player). First — yes, there is some cheating going on out there. Second — you need to know how to detect and avoid it. Finally — shooting the dealer is not an acceptable option!

Blackjack Is Still Fun and Profitable

Given all of this, it should be obvious that today's blackjack player must be much more aware and much more skilled than the player of the past. Knowing only a good card strategy just won't cut it.

And so I will teach you the extra skills you will need, to avoid falling victim to any unfair modern blackjack practices.

I win the great majority of times with my method, and you can too — that is, if you know what I've learned. That's why I can write this book in good conscience. If I can win, so can you.

Good players can still win consistently, but they need a new approach.

Blackjack is still a great game. It offers the excitement of uncertainty and possible risk, and yet, with the right method and awareness of minefields to avoid, it can be approached with the confidence of one who knows he or she will beat the house on most occasions, and make a nice bit of money over time. It's a game of wits, and requires a lot of thinking, which is exhilarating to those of us who like card games and the thrill of winning.

The Concepts Today's Blackjack Player Needs to Learn

There are a number of important concepts a player needs to understand in order to come out a winner:

♣ CARD STRATEGY: This is the process of choosing which of the options available to you would give you the best odds of winning, in any given card situation. (Actually, in some cases, where you are facing a losing situation no matter how you cut it, you will want to choose the move that loses a lesser percentage of times than other possible moves.) *Blackjack The Smart Way* is special in that it explains the mathematical reasoning behind each recommended move — so you come to understand the WHYs behind the game. Plus, the winning card strategy found here is unique to this book.

♣ MONEY MANAGEMENT: This includes deciding how much you should bet on a particular hand; how much money you need to bring to the table; how to keep any losses to a minimum; and, how to leave with your winnings intact. Having a good money management system is as important as having a good card strategy. My **3-Level, Notch-Up, Notch-Down Bet Management System** tips the odds in your favor. It gets your bet up to a good level when the cards are good for you, and lowers your bet to a mininum amount when the cards are not, so that – even if you win only about 50% of the hands played – it greatly increases the odds of your coming away a winner.

♣ KNOWING HOW TO PICK A GOOD CASINO: This is an essential skill you must perfect. Few players seem aware that there are good and bad casinos. Learning this often-neglected skill will spare you many a heartache. *The more discriminating you become, the higher your win rate will become.*

♣ KNOWING WHEN TO LEAVE A CASINO: Whether you are winning or losing, you need to know when to call it quits.

Staying too long is one of the most common habits of the perpetual loser. This might just be the most important concept you must learn.

- KNOWING HOW TO PICK A GOOD TABLE WITHIN A CASINO: This crucial skill will save you hundreds, if not thousands of dollars, in unnecessary losses. All tables are not alike, as you will learn.

- KNOWING WHEN TO LEAVE A TABLE: This is immensely important, giving you a lot of power in counteracting losing streaks and possible dirty tricks.

- THE **X FACTOR:** This isone of my inventions. It's a measure of how well the cards are breaking for you, versus the dealer. Getting a handle on this is essential to making crucial decisions, such as how much money to put on the table. You will use the **X Factor** to assess, in quantitative terms, whether the table you are playing at is bad, neutral, good or great.

- KEEPING TRACK OF THE CARDS: By paying attention to what cards have been played, you can take advantage of the predictability of the game. You can do this either by card counting, or by using my invention, **Card Observation**. (Or, you can use them BOTH!) This skill – similar to one used effectively by Bridge players – is based on easy-to-understand mathematics, and will enable you to maximize your winnings.

- KNOWING HOW TO DETECT CASINO COUNTERMEASURES: This will protect you when you have been targeted for unfair practices designed to make you lose, and will enable you to leave with your winnings intact.

- KNOWING HOW TO SPOT THE ROGUE "DIRTY DEALER": This will keep you from falling victim to a cheater that, although not common, is out there. This will spare you huge losses.

- KNOWING HOW TO DETECT RIGGED CARDS: This will keep you away from the minority of casinos who play dirty.

- KEEPING TRACK OF YOUR FELLOW PLAYERS: This will enable you to respond to the threats posed by: players who sit out some bets, or who vary the number of bets they place; players who enter the game before the shuffle, or who leave during play; and, people who pretend to be players but who are actually casino employees!

I will teach you all of this and more.

Who Should NOT Play Blackjack

It is *not* a game, however, for those without the determination, the desire and the patience to learn how to play correctly. You cannot simply sit down at a Blackjack table and magically win consistently on your hunches. And, since it involves real money, YOUR money, promise me right now that you will treat this "game" with respect and study what I am about to teach you.

Dumb Luck

By the way, there IS such as thing as DUMB luck – that is, players winning without having a clue as to what they're doing, or how the game is played. I have witnessed it.

I was at a casino in a popular winter resort town that seemed chock full of loud drunkards – tourists on vacation – who were the WORST Blackjack players I'd ever run into. One guy was splitting 10s (I'll explain this faux pas later). The gal next to me was putting a fortune on bets regardless of how well she was doing. In fact, everyone at the table seemed intent on impressing the rest with how much money they had to waste.

Miraculously though – and you won't see this very often – the dealer busted and lost more than is normal, and some of these fools actually were ahead when I got up to leave (I was ahead by about $75 after an hour of choppy action)! That's *dumb luck!*

Another time, I was at a casino in Atlantic City where a very pretty young woman was making such hopelessly stupid moves everyone at the table groaned aloud, but in spite of herself, she was winning time and time again! Of course, I didn't see how much money that woman actually left the casino with. Like most others who go unprepared, she undoubtedly played for hours, until all her money was gone, or threw her winnings away the next time she played.

I promise you, YOU won't win through dumb luck. Maybe in a blue moon, but not in a string of trips to the casino. You certainly don't want to rely on it, because then you WILL find out why they affix the word "dumb" to it.

Don't Be A Big Shot

And – please — don't try to compete with one of those reckless big shots that "grace" every casino. You know the type: the boisterous players who try to impress everyone with how many black chips ($100 chips) or pink chips ($1000 chips) they can shower the table with. You might see them make one impressive "win," but, make no mistake. These are the people you ultimately read about, who take thousands of dollars to the casino, bet wildly and extravagantly, only to lose everything and then jump off the casino roof without even checking out of their hotel.

It's YOUR money. Treat it with respect, and forget about trying to "impress" anyone. (No one is really impressed by big shots, anyway. Suckers stand out no matter how they fool themselves into thinking the smiles that they see are admiring smiles.) The smart players never make a show of it. They win quietly, and only make bets that won't set them back terribly if they lose.

Learning My Strategy Requires Practice

If you decide you want to learn how to play intelligently, and try my strategy, you must first study not just this text, but the charts as well, AND THEN PRACTICE, PRACTICE, PRACTICE.

PRACTICE at home – preferably with decks of cards, or, if you prefer, on a good computer game, which is how I perfected my system, without subjecting myself to risk. Make your mistakes at home. You can make it fun by inviting friends over to play with you, players taking turns being the dealer. There's no reason why practice can't be fun!

Some of the more recent computer games are great because they give you a good feel for the casino action and let you master your memorization of all the card situations you'll need to remember. Some games even give you a taste for the casino atmosphere, subjecting you to distracting slot machine bells, crowd noises and other annoying sounds you have to deal with at the table. THAT will teach you to concentrate!!!

When I was starting out, testing my theories, I used a fun computer game, where the dealer spoke to the players, as they would at a casino – you know, "Bets, please!" I couldn't wait to see how much I could win, even though no money was involved! But, then, I love the game itself!

Blackjack Requires an Analytical Approach

Now, let me explain something you need to understand. Three things in particular make blackjack winnable:

❶ Its relative predictability – much like the game of Bridge.
❷ Its adherence to mathematical principles.
❸ The **personality of the dealer up cards**.

Your job is to learn everything you can about those keys to winning.

By predictability, I mean your ability to guesstimate what type of card might be coming next, or what type of card the dealer's hole card (hidden card) might be. By mathematical principles, I mean all of the factors I will teach you that enable you to get a handle on the probability of your winning a particular hand. By the **personality of the dealer up cards**, I am referring to the

unique behavior of each of the up cards – each has a different propensity toward reaching a winning score and busting.

I will give you the tools you need to win, but then you need to apply that knowledge in a constantly changing environment. Your ability to use these concepts to think through the various challenges that come your way will make you a very good player.

How you handle your bets, for instance, cannot be scripted beforehand. With the information I will give you, you must then analyze what's going on at your table at a particular point in time and adjust to that reality to maximize your gains. I will give you guideposts, concepts, methods and strategies developed through years of research and experience playing blackjack, but, in the end you still must be able to apply what you've learned.

You might run into a difficult table, or casino, and then you have to decide whether it's time to change tables, or casinos, or hang in there and battle it out. You will encounter card situations where you must think it through – above and beyond basic strategy. No one else can do that for you. There's no getting on a cell phone and calling for advice.

I'm not trying to scare you – far from it. I'm going to make everything as simple to understand as possible. What I'm trying to say is – you need to do your homework. It's a fun, winnable game, but it's not simple, like tic-tac-toe. You must study this book fully, and then practice, practice, practice, until you are confident you are able to use this system and win.

It's a Game of Ups 'n Downs

Now, one thing you must understand is that blackjack is a game of swings — up-and-down cycles. Like the wind, the **flow of the cards** sometimes blows hot and then cold, with no one holding up a sign to let you know how long the current breeze, good or bad, will last.

Many times down cycles will right themselves. Sometimes they won't. I will give you a great concept – the X Factor – to help make it easy for you to figure this out.

But, in the end, you are on your own, and how quickly you respond to changes in the cards and the casino environment will determine how well you do.

You must pay attention to the cards, the players around you, the dealer, and the casino pit bosses. You will learn all about these important aspects of the game in this book.

Beware the Loser's Traps

Whatever you do — never, never throw good money after bad. My advice on money management and words to the wise on when to leave a table or casino will protect you from real harm – IF you practice what I'm about to preach.

Willpower is also part of the equation. I've seen way too many otherwise good players get greedy, or obsessed, and throw all their winnings away because they don't know when to stop. I'll give you very effective guidelines, that are easy to follow, to help you avoid the major pitfalls.

Playing The Percentages

Now, before I teach you Basic Strategy, there's something you must know. You will sometimes lose hands in spite of making the proper moves.

So, don't get blown away by the times that my successful, tested and proven strategy doesn't work with a particular hand in a particular card situation. Losing a certain number of hands is part of the game.

Understand this – you are going to ***play the percentages.*** There is no way to play any card situation such that you will win 100% of the time, nor any player that has ever come close to doing this. *What you must do is choose the move that will cause you to win a higher percentage of times than it causes you to lose.* That's a very important concept to understand. I'm going to call this the Third Principle of Winning at Blackjack.

It's not winning every hand that makes a great player a win-

ner. It's the player's ability to pick the move that, *over time*, wins the most, or makes the most mathematical sense (by that I mean that sometimes it even involves choosing a path that simply limits your losses, in a no-win situation).

(Even when you have a great hand – let's say, a two-card hand of 20 points – one that requires no thinking – you will still lose a certain minority of times!)

Playing the percentages means, for instance, if you consistently double on an 11 against the dealer's 6, you will win more money than you lose, over the course of your playing experiences.

DON'T BE INTIMIDATED IF AND WHEN A BULLY TELLS YOU "SEE, YOU LOST THAT HAND, YOU WERE *WRONG* IN THE WAY YOU PLAYED IT!" You know better. After I explain the underlying math to you, you won't have any doubt that my system will work for you. You will see the results.

Don't Waffle – Stick To This Strategy

The corollary to this is: You must play each card situation consistently — the same way — every time. If, for instance, you know you should take a card when you have a 13 against the dealer's up card of 10, but you sometimes get so overwhelmed by fear that you shake off that extra card, you're going to wind up betting on the *losing* side of the percentages and, inevitably, your chips will disappear.

Think about it: If I tell you to play a hand a certain way because it wins, let's say – if you HIT a certain hand, you'll win 62% of the time (conversely, *losing* 38% of the time, of course) — do you really want to be scared or cajoled instead into STANDING, when that choice would put you on the 38% side of that equation, therefore causing you to LOSE 62% of the time? Yes, if you stand on 13, you'll win a small minority of times against the 10. That does NOT make it a wise move, however.

NO! *So, don't get upset about the hands you lose, in the normal course of the game* (unless you're sitting at a horrible

table – that's a different matter). That's part of the game. *How you come out when it's time to leave is what we're concerned about.*

My Warnings Come from Observations

I recently met a seemingly intelligent fellow who, upon seeing my book, told me he was a recreational Blackjack player. He then related some very astute observations about situations he'd run across, but then drew the wrong conclusions.

For example, he noticed that, at one particular casino, the dealer didn't seem to ever lose when he showed weak up cards. So what did this recreational player do? He changed his playing strategy! He began to take cards when he knew he shouldn't! Not only that – he told me he now tends to do that at ALL casinos!

That's akin to changing your golf stroke to a ridiculous one because, the last time you hit the ball, you lost your balance, made a faulty swing, and lucked out, getting a hole in one.

Would you really want to try to repeat that experience? Don't fall into this common trap! It will lead to disaster!

Don't Play 'Til You Drop!

Another example of faulty thinking is seen everyday at every casino: witness the players who play until they drop from exhaustion or, finally, the lack of money.

One of my friends once said to me, "your system doesn't address the situation where someone might want to play for 3, 4 or more hours at a time." He's right. Because that's a good way to become a perpetual loser.

This bears repeating. Please – especially at first – *limit the amount of time you play. Don't play for more than one or two hours at any one casino.* You'll be tired and you'll make costly mistakes if you start playing marathons. There are other reasons this is bad strategy, which will be made clear to you, in detail, in

later chapters.

There will, in fact, be times when you should leave a casino *before* an hour or two is through – being either up or down in chips. I will teach you how to recognize these situations.

That reminds me of the very first time I went to a casino. It was in Atlantic City. Playing at a $25 minimum bet table, I won more than $450 in 20 minutes!

I had driven nearly four hours to get to there, and so I had to "pry" myself away from that table, but I had the foresight to know the situation was such that it was time to leave. That's why I came away a winner, and continue to do so.

Debunking Cherished Myths

I expect this book to be somewhat provocative, because I debunk some cherished myths. For example – in a later chapter, I argue strenuously against your tying your betting strategy to what card counting tells you. AND, I warn you not to subscribe to the dangerous "when the count is positive, put the maximum allowed bet down" mentality.

The card strategy you will learn is also at odds in many ways with what the old school has taught for years. (I will explain to you what's behind it, so that you too will be sold on how much more accurate and successful it is!)

That's understandable – new theories, inventions, products, etc., are usually the focus of some skepticism from those intent on following the old way of doing things.

Those who have no interest at stake, however – the players who have read my book and come to my seminars – have greeted *Blackjack The SMART Way*, with its new concepts and methods, with overwhelming praise and acceptance.

When You Should Choose NOT To Play Casino Blackjack

One last thing – and please keep this in mind – there are times when you should not even consider playing.

NEVER go to a casino when:

- You're ill and can't concentrate.
- You've forgotten the rules, or much of your card strategy.
- You've had alcohol. You'll make big mistakes! Why else do some casinos love providing you with free booze? You should hear the stories I hear of players who dropped thousands of dollars after having one too many.
- You're depressed, pessimistic or worried. You're not in the right frame of mind.
- You've gotten obsessed and you've lost your perspective of blackjack being a form of *entertainment*, to be played in moderation. You play too often, when you know you shouldn't.
- You've gotten "greedy" and it's no longer fun. I can't quite explain it to you, but you will tend to *lose* when you find you have lost the "fun," and the normal gains from blackjack no longer seem to please you. Plus, it's a sign that you're entering dangerous psychological territory.
- You've just come off a losing session, and you're upset. Your emotions are clouding your thinking. Take a day or two off.

You can only win at blackjack if you stay disciplined. Yes, blackjack is a game, but it's an adult game, and your money is on the line.

OK – that being said — let's talk about smart blackjack card strategy!

You are not ready yet to enter a casino.

2
BASIC
CARD
STRATEGY
2

Before I explain the basics to you, I need to debunk yet another popular myth that has become an obstacle to many players becoming great players. *There is NOT one "Basic Strategy" floating around that we all would be wise to follow.*

Players who believe the myth of the one, simple Basic Strategy are often under the misapprehension that blackjack is a simple game, and that one ubiquitous chart is all you need to become a winner. That's why I need to make this clear.

Every book has a different angle on what "Basic Strategy" should be. That being said, let's look at what makes *Blackjack The SMART Way* Basic Strategy such a good starting point.

It's Simple, Really: Win, Lose or "Push"

In casino blackjack, you're playing against the dealer — not the other players.

You win in one of two ways:

❶ If you get a higher point total than the dealer without "busting" (losing by going OVER 21).
❷ If the *dealer* busts (loses by going over 21) and you haven't busted.

If you beat the dealer, the dealer will pay you the same amount of chips as you placed as your bet. If you lose, the dealer will take your bet. If you "push" (tie), you will not make any money, but you won't lose any, either — you get to keep your bet.

There's one special situation that works differently, from whence comes the name of the game:

If you have an Ace with a 10 or face card — which is called *a Blackjack* — you're paid one-and-a-half times your bet. You're usually paid immediately. (That is, UNLESS the dealer ties you with a Blackjack. Then, as with any tie, you make no money, but you don't lose your bet, either.)

If the *dealer* has a Blackjack, all players who don't have a Blackjack too lose instantly — without benefit of playing out their

cards.

The best situation, of course, is when the dealer busts; then, *everyone* wins (UNLESS a player busted first). Boy is that great!

The trouble is — *you* have to play your cards BEFORE the dealer plays his or hers. You don't have the luxury of waiting to see if the dealer is going to bust before deciding whether or not to draw an extra card that might make your hand bust. Therefore, there will be times that you won't want to risk taking an extra card, if the dealer is likely to bust. In this and following chapters, you will learn the mathematical logic that will enable you to make wise decisions in that regard.

The Ace Has A Powerful Advantage

An Ace, in the game of blackjack, can count as either 1 or 11 points. Dealers have certain restrictions in how they must count their Aces, but you don't.

Dealers must count their Aces as 11 points if that creates *a winning total of 17 to 21 points* (with one possible exception — some casinos require their dealers to continue taking cards if they have an Ace-6).

Unlike the dealer, you can often choose what you want your Ace to be. You might choose to stand on a hand of Ace-7, counting your Ace as an 11, which gives you a score of 18. Or, you might choose in some situations to chance it by taking more cards, which will often necessitate counting your Ace now as 1 point. Of course, if you draw an Ace to a hand that totals 11 points or more, you will have no choice but to count that Ace as 1 point (otherwise, you'd bust).

(FYI: Because, in blackjack, the face cards count simply for 10 points, like the 10s, they are not any more special to you than the 10s — they hold an equal position. Therefore, we will not have to refer individually to the Jacks, Queens or Kings when taking them into consideration. They are, for all intents and purposes, just 10s. And so, I will lump them together and simply refer to them *all* from now on — the 10s, Jacks, Queens and Kings — as either the "10s" or "10-pointers.")

Everything Starts With The Dealer Up Card

OK. Now, *Blackjack The SMART Way* Basic Strategy is based upon two things: *what the dealer's up card indicates about the strength of his or her hand (what his or her eventual point total is likely to be); and, how dealers must play their cards.*

(Later, as an advanced player, your strategy will also be based on what the dealer's hole card and your hit card are likely to be.)

Dealers give themselves one face-up card (their up card) and one face-down card (their *hole* card).

Now, blackjack dealers are required to pull cards until they get to a total of at least 17. (Except, as noted before, at the casinos where dealers must draw a card to their hand of Ace-6, also known as a "soft 17," because of the Ace's ability to count either as a 1 point or 11 point card. This is a move that favors the house, by the way. It tends to lead to stronger dealer scores.)

This reality of how dealers must play their cards means that YOU SHOULD ALWAYS STAND ON HANDS THAT TOTAL 17 OR MORE (assuming your hand doesn't include an Ace, which, as you'll see soon, you might want to count as 1 point in some situations).

Here's How Your Strategy Will Work

One of the many ways *Blackjack The SMART Way* is unique is that card strategy is based upon the different **personality of the dealer up cards**.

The up card gives us very important information. Depending on its point value, every dealer up card behaves differently. By that, I mean they exhibit different tendencies toward arriving either at a particular winning score, or busting.

If, for instance, you have a hand that totals less than 17 points and you know the up card you're playing against is very strong for the dealer, you'll usually choose to take more cards until you

score a winning total (17 through 21 points).

If, instead, you're facing one of the dealer's weakest up cards, one that is likelier to make the dealer bust, you might then choose to stand pat with your original two cards — even if you have a non-winning point total of 12, 13, 14, 15 or 16. It depends on what the dealer up card is, how weak it is. We'll examine that in a second.

The point is, if you have a hand known as a "stiff" (a hand of 12 through 16, which puts you in danger of busting if you take one more card), you are will sometimes want to STAND, to avoid the risk of busting, in the hope that you'll win simply because the dealer might bust.

The only times you'll have no decision to make are when you get a Blackjack, or when you have achieved a total of 17, 18, 19, 20 or 21 points, upon which you would always stand.

HARD and SOFT Hands

The first thing you should do when your first two cards are dealt is assess whether your point total makes your hand HARD or SOFT.

A HARD hand is one that contains no Ace.

This is most significant when your hard hand totals more than 12. Then, it poses the danger of your going over 21 to "bust" or lose if you need to "hit" those cards — that is, take another card to improve your score.

Examples of hard totals of 12 or more are shown on the following page, in **Illustration 2-1** (these are by no means the only possilbe hard hand combinations, however).

A SOFT HAND is a hand that contains at least one Ace.

Since an Ace can count for either 1 point or 11 (your choice), a hand with an Ace cannot bust (go over 21) if you decide to hit it -- that is, if you ask the dealer for another card in the hope of bettering your point total. In this sense, some of these hands might seem somewhat more desirable than their counterparts above, especially if you are in a possible doubling down situation.

Illustration 2-1: Some Examples of Hard Hands

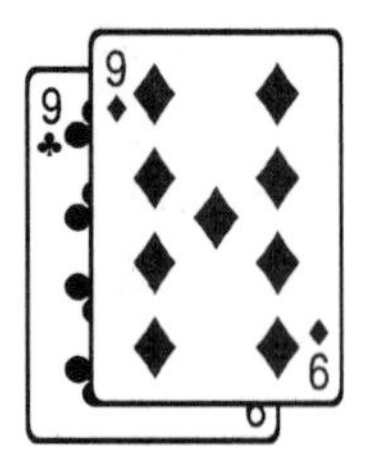

On the next page, in **Illustration 2-2**, you will see some examples of SOFT HANDS.

SOFT HANDS are great because they often give you some very lucrative options.

You'll soon see that you'll have to play your hard hands differently than your soft hands.

Hard And Soft Totals

Now, a ***hard total*** is a bit different than a hard hand. A hard total *can* contain an Ace, but the Ace would be counted as 1 point. Put another way, a hard total is the sum of a player's or dealer's cards, usually where there is no Ace. If there is an Ace, it's in a situation where the other cards total more than 11, and the Ace then can only be a 1-point card.

A ***soft total*** is a total always made with one or more Aces, and those Aces can count either as 1 point or 11 — a total which has the ability of accepting another card without busting. This distinction will be important to you, when deciding how to play your cards.

A Word About "Stiffs"

Many players moan when they get anything less than a Blackjack or two 10s. That's just the nature of the beast. Yes, those are marvelous. But, on occasion, even those 10s might only give you a "push" (a tie with the dealer, without gain), or, the two 10s might even *lose,* if the dealer has 21 points total, or a Blackjack.

Invariably, there are those that audibly groan when they are dealt a stiff (a hand of two cards that totals between 12 and 16 points, which is in danger of busting with an extra card). But, let me point something out — those hands often look like losers, yet you'd be surprised at how many times they combine with hit cards to achieve a strong score.

What I'm cautioning you against is getting emotional with every hand that is dealt. Often, the results will turn out far

Illustration 2-2: Some Examples of Soft Hands

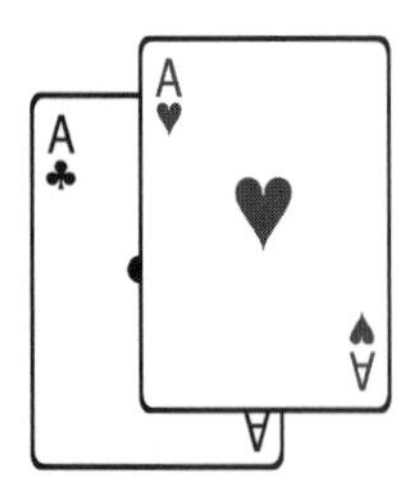
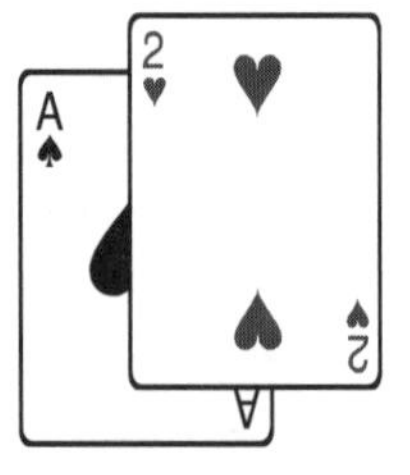
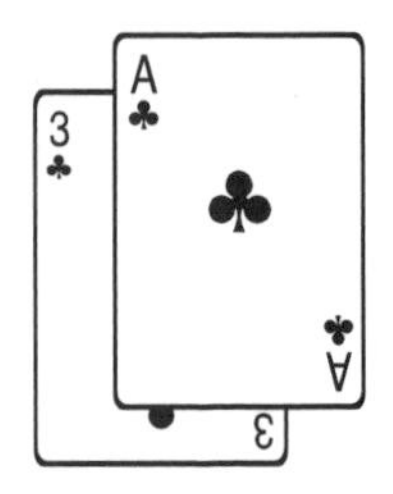

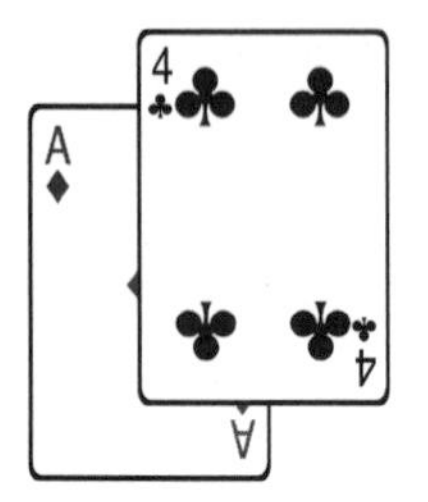
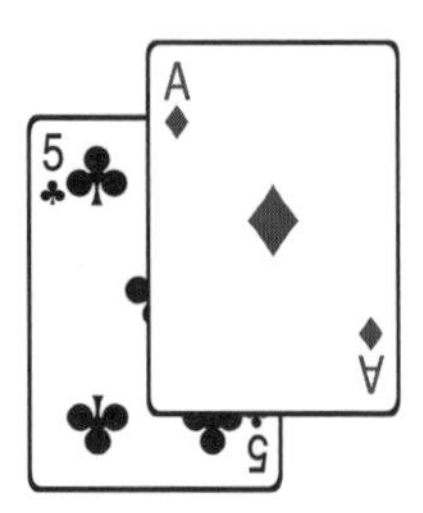
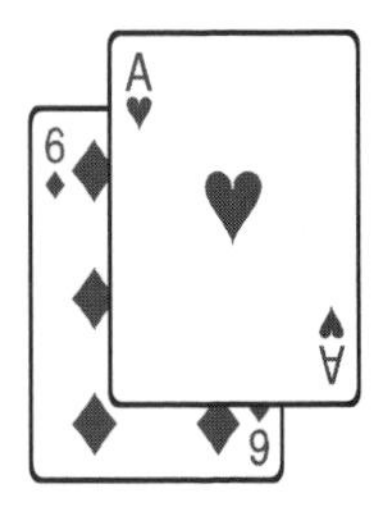

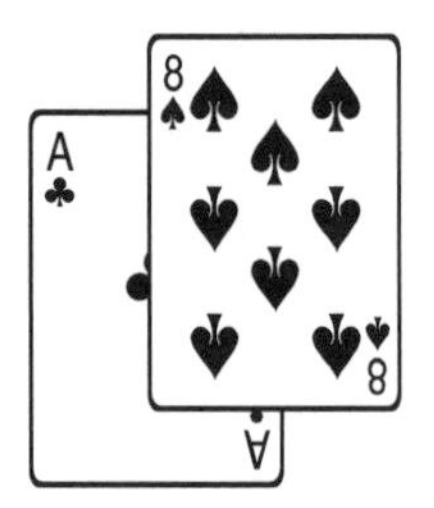
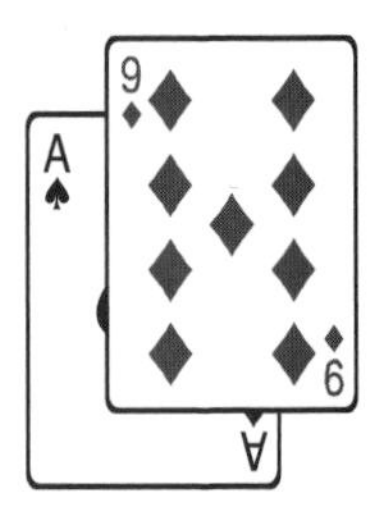

differently than you had expected. More than anything else, letting your feelings get the better of you — especially negative feelings — will only hurt your game. Negative emotions will only cloud your thinking and wear you out.

Your Options

OK, now, in playing your hands, let's look at the options you have. You may choose to do any one of the following:

HIT — That means to take another card. (HIT is denoted by an "H" in the strategy charts.)

STAND — That means you don't want to take another card; you want to stick with the cards you have. (Denoted by an "S" in the strategy charts.)

DOUBLE DOWN or DOUBLE — This is where you're allowed to raise your initial bet by up to the same amount of chips you placed as your original bet, and then you're given just one extra card. You might do this in two situations: first, if your initial hand of 2 cards has a lot of potential to draw to a strong winning total with just one more card, so you want to get more money on the table; or, second, if you're pretty certain the dealer will bust, and you have a hand that won't bust with the acceptance of one more card. You have the option in most casinos of "doubling" with an extra amount of chips that's *less* than your original bet, but, hey, if it's a situation where it's worth doubling down, go *all* the way. *Double* your bet. (See **Illustration 2-3** on page 27, for a demonstration of how to double down.) (Denoted by a "D" in the strategy charts.)

SPLIT — This is where you have a pair of cards of the same point value and you want to separate them, to play them out as two individual hands (or more – if the dealer places a card on top of the split cards that's the same point value, you can RE-split *those* too, in most casinos, into two separate hands; many casinos allow this to be done until you reach

a limit of four hands). The dealer then places a card upon one of your split cards, which you then play out like a normal hand. After you're through playing out the first of the two split hands, you do the same, then, with your second split card. The one *exception* to this is when you split a pair of Aces. Then, you have a limitation — you only get one extra card upon each. Aces are such strong cards, however, producing a wide range of winning totals in combination with 8 of the 13 cards (the 6s through the 10s) that you shouldn't mind that limitation. (See a demonstration of this practice in **Illustration 2-4**, on page 28.) (Denoted by "Sp" in strategy charts.)

SURRENDER — This option allows you to give up your hand without playing it out if you think it's a definite loser. The dealer then gives you half of your bet back, while taking the other half. What do you gain? You spare yourself the loss of half your bet. Surrender, unfortunately, is not offered at every casino. And surprisingly, while it gives a big advantage to the player, few players avail themselves of it when it is offered! They're either unaware of it, too shy to do it, or not certain how and when to do it! If you're not allowed to surrender, by the way, you should do the alternative move I suggest — either HIT (indicated by "Sur/H") or SPLIT (indicated by "Sur/Sp" in the charts).

INSURANCE OR EVEN MONEY — If the dealer has an Ace as the up card, the dealer will ask "Insurance?" That means, you can place an amount of chips equal to HALF your initial bet in the Insurance section of the table, and, if, after the dealer checks the hole card and it's a 10, for a Blackjack, you will get all of your money back (Insurance pays 2-to-1). If the dealer does NOT have a Blackjack, you lose your Insurance bet and play on. Instead of Insurance, I suggest beginners and intermediates *ask for "Even Money". That means, when the dealer says "Insurance?" you say "Even Money" and the dealer instantly pays off your Blackjack. You won't get 1-1/2 times your bet, as usual with a Blackjack, but an amount equal to your bet.* (Denoted by "Even" in the strategy charts.)

Illustration 2-3: HOW TO DOUBLE DOWN

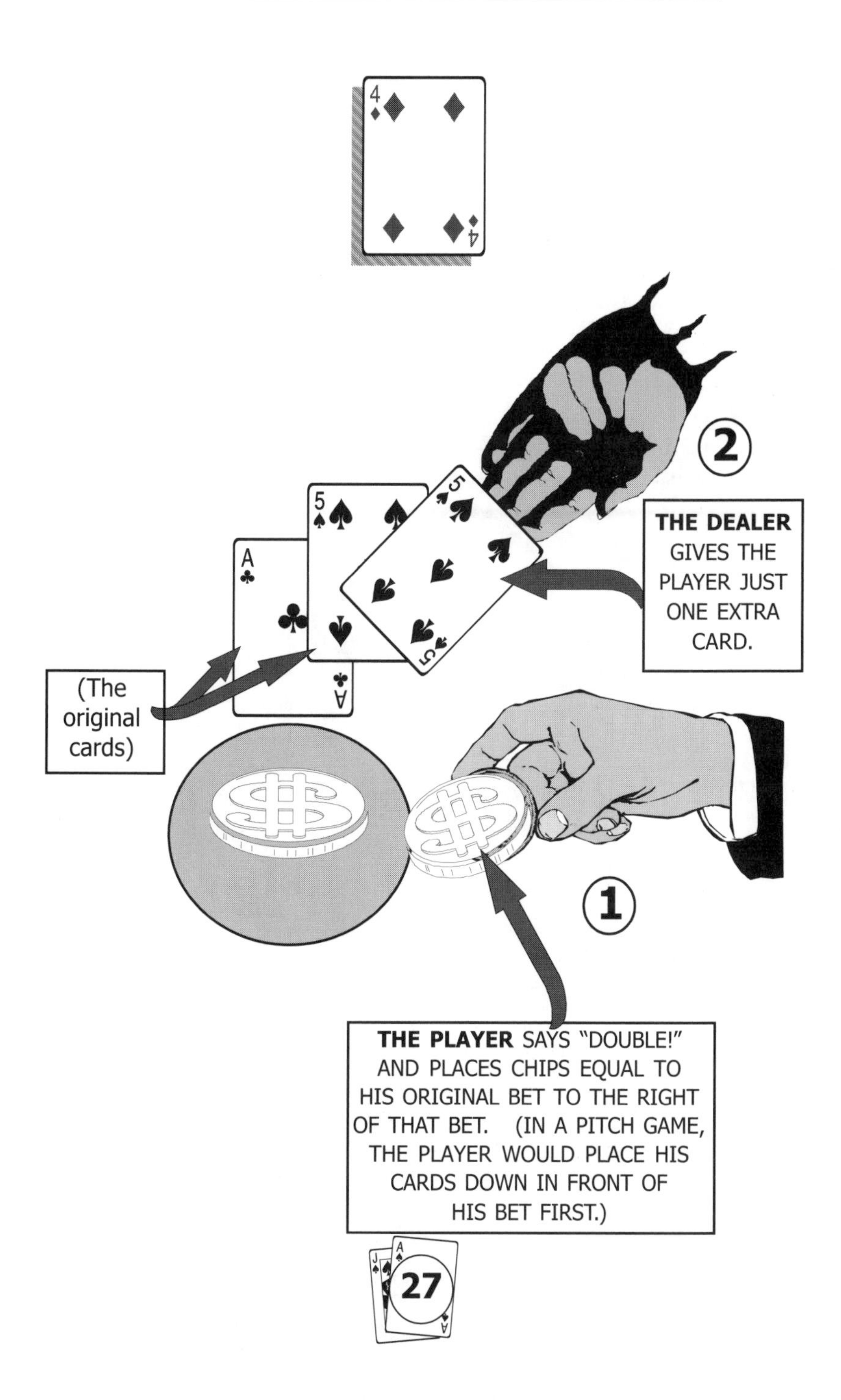

Illustration 2-4: HOW TO SPLIT YOUR CARDS

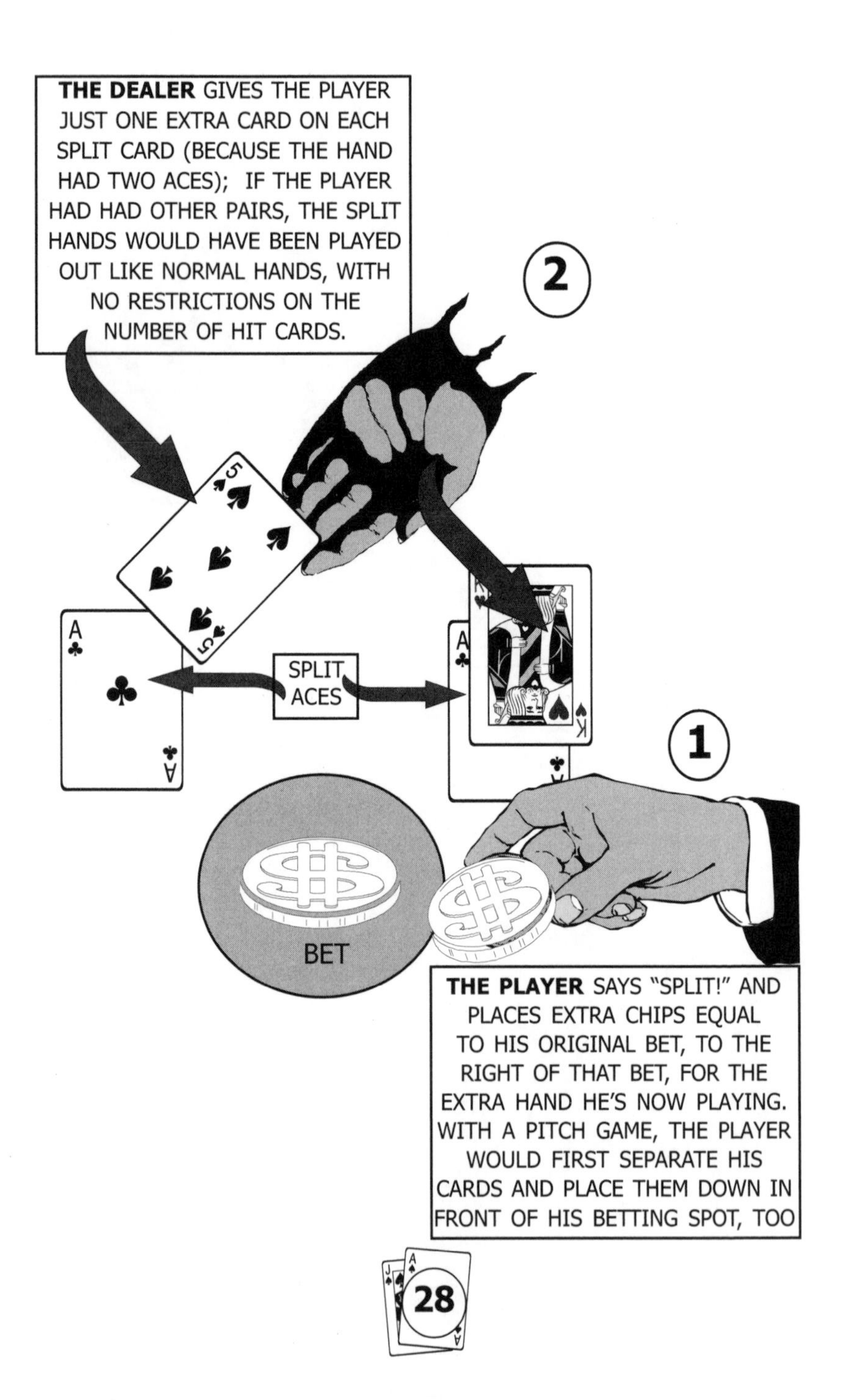

How To Signal The Dealer

To do any of these moves, you must usually use hand signals. (Your moves are being recorded by the "eye in the sky" — a hidden camera above the table — in case disputes arise later.) Let's review how this is done.

Signaling is done a little differently at the 1– and 2-deck tables, where you hold your cards in one hand, versus the other tables, where cards are placed, face-up, in front of you and you're not allowed to touch them.

Signaling At 1- & 2-Deck Tables

At 1- & 2–deck tables — also known at "pitch game" tables, because the cards are pitched, or tossed to you — here's how you do it. (First, wait for your turn to arrive!)

To HIT, gently stroke or scratch your cards on the table, toward you. The dealer will give you a card, face up. If you want yet another card, repeat this process.

To STAND, slip your cards face down under your bet. You can do this as soon as you decide to stand — you don't have to wait until it's your turn. The dealer will simply pass by you when he or she sees your cards under your bet, and move on to the next player.

To DOUBLE DOWN, gently lay out your cards, face up on the table, on the dealer side of your betting spot. Then, place an amount of chips equal to your bet to the right of your betting spot, and say "double!" The dealer will then give you one extra card, face down under your bet. (You may peek at it if you like, but then leave it where it was placed.)

To SPLIT, as with doubling, put your cards down in front of your bet, face up. Then, place an amount of chips equal to your bet to the right of your betting spot, and say "split!" The dealer will then separate your cards into two new hands, and place one card upon the card to your right. If you want to HIT that hand, hit the table gently or make a rubbing motion on the table, toward

you. To stand on that hand, wave your hand back and forth in a "no thank you!" motion. The dealer will then place a second card on the other card you split, and you will play out that hand similarly.

(By the way, if your second cards on either of those split cards are the same point value, you can split those, too, at most casinos. Place another pile of chips equal to your original bet on the table and once again say "split!")

To SURRENDER, lay down your cards, face up, and say "surrender!" The dealer then takes half your bet, and leaves the other half in your betting spot for you to take, or to use in the next round.

For EVEN MONEY, place your cards down face up in front of your bet and say "Even Money!" The dealer will usually pay off your Blackjack immediately (with an amount equal to your bet).

For INSURANCE, place an amount of chips equal to half your bet in the circular zone that says INSURANCE, and, if you have a Blackjack, lay down your cards, face up, in front of your bet at the same time. You will LOSE that Insurance bet if the dealer checks and finds that he or she does NOT have a Blackjack. The dealer will then pay off your Blackjack, however. Or, if the dealer checks and indeed has a Blackjack, you essentially will be paid even money for your bet — your Insurance bet wins (it pays 2-to-1), but you push with your Blackjack, and so you'd not make any money there.

(By the way — Insurance is a separate bet from your original wager, and can be made even if you do NOT have a Blackjack, but I recommend that move only for advanced players. We'll talk about that in Chapter 10.)

Be very careful when you want to double, split or surrender, by the way. DO NOT move your hands when you verbally tell the dealer what you want to do. You might end up with an unwanted card that will create controversy at the table, if not wind up against your favor. If the dealer gives you that extra card by mistake, he or she will then have to interrupt the game and call for a casino boss to come to the table to resolve the dispute.

Often, they'll resolve the dispute in your favor. Sometimes not.

Signaling At Multi-Deck Tables

OK — here's how you signal at tables with more than 2-decks, where the cards are dealt face up.

(You're not allowed to touch your cards at these tables. The casinos are afraid of cheaters who, if allowed to touch the cards, might "mark" them for the purpose of cheating.)

To HIT, either gently hit the table with your open hand, or stroke the table lightly with a short motion that is directed toward you. The dealer then gives you one more card. Repeat this process for every extra card you want.

To STAND, wave your hand back and forth in a standard "no thank you!" signal.

To DOUBLE DOWN, place an amount of chips equal to your bet to the right of your betting spot while saying "double!" The dealer then places one card, face up, on your hand.

To SPLIT, place an amount of chips equal to your bet to the right of your betting spot, while saying "split!" The dealer will then separate your cards into two new hands, place one card upon the split card to your right, and you will play that hand first, and then the other. At most casinos, you can split again if you're dealt a like card on either of the split cards. To do that, follow the same procedure as before.

To SURRENDER, don't move at all (careful!) — simply say "surrender!" The dealer then takes half your bet, and leaves the other half for you to use as you'd like.

For EVEN MONEY, simply say "Even Money!" and the dealer will usually pay off your Blackjack immediately (with an amount equal to your bet).

For INSURANCE, all you need do is place an amount of chips equal to half your bet in the circular zone that says INSURANCE.

Blackjack The SMART Way Basic Strategy

OK. How do you know how to play your cards? *How you play your cards has less to do with what you have than what the dealer's up card is, and therefore, what you assume the dealer's point total will be.* For example, if this is your hand (a soft total of 18 or 8):

you might want to STAND, HIT, or DOUBLE DOWN. *It depends upon what the dealer has.*

The dealer's strongest up cards — the ones that will beat you the most — are the 9, 10, and Ace. Upon seeing those, you should assume they will achieve a winning score — and a high winning score at that. As you will see shortly, you should then HIT your Ace-7 combination (seen above) against the dealer's 9 and 10, to try to improve your score. Your 18 won't beat the dealer's anticipated 19, 20 or 21.

However, against the dealer's Ace, strange though it may seem, you'd be wise to STAND. Follow my thinking here — if the dealer doesn't have a Blackjack, you now know the hole card is not one of the four 10-point cards. The dealer, therefore, only has a 2 in 9 chance (a small, 22% probability) of having a card in the hole that would beat you (of the 9 possible non-10 cards, only an 8 or 9 would give the dealer an immediate win over you). That leaves your 18 looking pretty good, and so you STAND.

(See how probability rules the game? See how *Blackjack The SMART Way* strategy is based upon a rock-solid mathematical foundation? This is just one example of how you'll be weighing the probabilities affecting each of your moves. You will soon

understand that there are often other considerations that will affect your odds of winning any one hand, which you will need to factor into your probability calculations.)

OK, now, against the dealer's 2, 7 or 8, you would also be wise to STAND. The dealer's 2, as you'll see shortly, doesn't bust enough for you to risk doubling down on with your Ace-7; but your 18 will beat or push with the 2 more than not. With the up card of 8, my studies have shown the dealer's resultant score will most often be 17 or 18, or a bust. If the dealer has a 7 showing, you'd assume the dealer to have just 17 points, because my research shows that, more than not, that's the total the dealer usually arrives at with that up card. So, with the dealer's 2, 7 or 8, you'll STAND, because your 18 will do well against the dealer's 2 and 8 — at least holding its own, a majority of times — and will beat the dealer's anticipated 17 most times.

If the dealer has up cards of 3 through 6, however, you'd DOUBLE DOWN holding that hand of Ace-7. That's because they're the dealer's weakest up cards, often causing the dealer to bust. So, you'd want to double, to get more money on what will probably be a winning hand for you.

"Your" Cards vs. the "Dealer's" Cards

The dealer's up card tells you your relative likelihood of winning any hand.

We'll call the dealer's 3 through 6 YOUR CARDS (for now — we'll add one more card later):

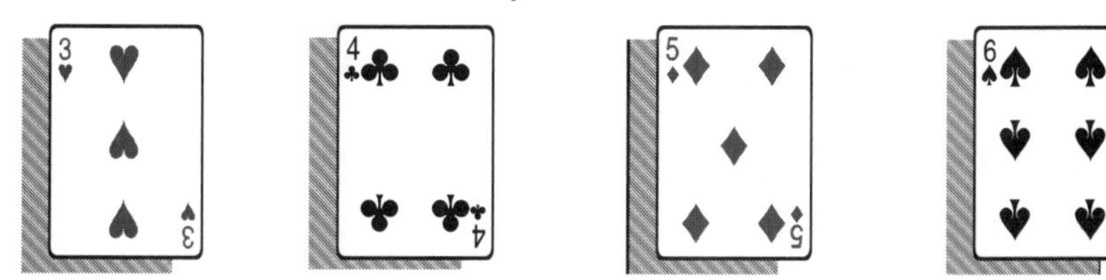

That is, if the dealer shows these cards, you should quietly get excited. These are the cards that most often cause the dealer to bust (typically in the range of 40% to 60% of the time!). With

these cards showing, since you believe the dealer is likely to bust, you'll do most of your doubling down and splitting. These are your "money" cards.

You should stay sharp to take notice of these cards — a bell should go off in your head, so you can take advantage of every opportunity these cards afford you to double down and split your cards when appropriate. That way, you'll get as much money on the table as you can in probable winning situations.

We'll call the dealer's up cards of 9, the 10s and Ace the DEALER'S CARDS (for now — we'll add one more card later):

(Notice how dealers seem to have more up cards in their favor than players do. Another thing you might notice is that the 8 is not included here. This is because, contrary to popular thinking, it is not such a strong card for the dealer, nor is it such a bad card for the player, as you will see later. You will come to understand, later on, that the 8 is off in its own category.)

As indicated before, the dealer wins more than not with the up cards of 9, 10 and Ace, and so you must play more cautiously when they appear.

Now, about the dealer's up cards of 2 and 7 — about which there will be a chapter, called "The Tricky 2s & Silent 7s:"

You will see, with regard to these up cards (contrary to what most of you have been taught), that the dealer's 2 behaves much more like a "dealer's card" and player's enemy, and the dealer's 7

often behaves like a "player's card." Let's save this discussion for Chapter 4.

Why Three Different Charts?

To learn how to play each of your hands, you will start by referring to charts on pages 50-54 that spell out your recommended Basic Strategy moves. You will want to memorize these moves, so that they are second nature to you by the time you choose to go to the casino. (You should be able to think through how to play your hand in the event you momentarily forget a particular move from these charts in the heat of action at the blackjack table, however, because I will now *explain* what's behind each move. Hopefully, you will then at least remember what the reasoning is for each move, if you blank out, and will be able to figure out how to proceed. That's the benefit of being taught the WHYs behind the *Blackjack The SMART Way* system.)

As is standard, I've divided up the game into three different charts, for the three different types of hands and card situations you will encounter, based upon the first two cards you will be dealt: The first chart will tell you how to play your first two cards, if they are HARD hands (hands which contain no Aces or pairs of like cards). The second chart will tell you how to play your first two cards if they are SOFT hands (hands with at least one Ace). The last chart will tell you how to play hands with *two like cards* — for instance, two 2s, two 3s, etc.

Basic Strategy: How To Play HARD HANDS

OK. Let's cover all the card combinations you will encounter, if your first two cards are hard hands, and what you should do (please refer to CHARTS 1A & 1B on pages 50 and 51):

♣ **With totals of 4 through 8, you always HIT.**
You cannot bust here; pulling extra cards can only improve your position.

- ♥ **With a total of 9, you should DOUBLE DOWN if the dealer has a 3 through 6 as the up card. Otherwise, you should HIT.**
  Your 9 card is just large enough to make a nice total if you get a 10-point card or an ACE (which accounts for 38% of the cards). You want to DOUBLE here, to get more money on the table in situations where the dealer is most likely to bust.
- ♠ **With a total of 10, DOUBLE DOWN against the dealer's 2 through 7; HIT against the dealer's 8 through Ace.**
  Since you have a greater than 50% chance of improving your 10 to a winning point total with one hit card, and the dealer's 2 through 7 statistically don't achieve as many high winning scores as the 10 and tend to bust more, here's where you want more money on the table, to capitalize on your mathematical advantage. You're playing the probabilities. (See Chapter 5 for more details.)
- ♦ **With a total of 11, you DOUBLE against everything except the dealer's 9, 10 and Ace, against which you should HIT.**
  Oh boy! Eleven is a great total, because my research indicates it tends to draw to high winning scores and causes you to bust rather infrequently. Plus — eight of the 13 possible hit cards you might get in *doubling* will produce a winning score — the 6, 7, 8, 9, and 10-pointers. So, with a strong total like that, by all means, get more money on the table by doubling — EXCEPT against the dealer's strongest cards of 9, 10 and Ace, against which you should simply HIT your 11. This might be controversial in some circles, but — those cards produce strong winning totals for the dealer. In fact, the dealer is likely to outscore you, on average, if you restrict yourself to taking just one card upon your 11. (See Chapter 5 for details.)
- ♣ **With a total of 12, HIT against the dealer's 2, 3, 7, 8, 9, 10 and Ace; STAND if the dealer's up card is 4 through 6.**
  A hand of 12 is tricky. You have to hit against the dealer's stronger cards and try to better your score. The only

cards that will cause your 12 to bust are the 10s, which make up about 31% of the deck. So, 69% of the time — the great majority of the time — you'll do well to hit your 12. If the dealer shows a 4 through 6, though, the dealer is most likely to bust, so you'll STAND to avoid the 31% risk of busting. Let the dealer bust.

♥ **With a total of 13, it's similar to a total of 12, except you STAND on the dealer's 3 and SURRENDER against the dealer's Ace.**
Since 5 possible cards — the 9s through the 10-pointers, or approximately 38% of the possible hit cards you might draw will cause you to bust on this total, you'll want to STAND when you think the dealer is most likely to bust. Since the dealer's ACE is such a strong, likely winner, however, and 13 not such a good total, SURRENDER and get back half of your bet so as to avoid a probable loss.

♠ **With totals of 14 through 16, STAND against the dealer's 2 through 6. HIT against the dealer's 7 and 8. SURRENDER against the dealer's 10 and Ace. Against the dealer's 9: HIT your 14; SURRENDER your 15 and 16.**
When your total is up in this range, you are very likely to bust when taking another card to better your score (around 50% or better). So STAND when the dealer is most likely to bust. You must HIT when the dealer is most likely to score a winning total, EXCEPT when the dealer has such a strong up card that your best option is to surrender (if allowed) and take the least possible loss (while at the same time getting half your bet back). This is smart when you have totals of 15 or 16 against the 9; 14-16 against the 10; and 13-16 against the Ace, because, in those cases, you will lose more than half of the time. Surrender is a very advantageous option for you. Don't be too shy to use it! If SURRENDER is not allowed by the casino, HIT those hands.

♦ **With a total of 17 or more, you should always STAND.**
Since the dealer must stand on all 17s and above, you are

now in winning territory. The odds are very high you'll bust if you draw another card if you hold a hard hand total of 17 or greater, so you should never ever even consider doing so. (Of course, the only way you can *beat* the dealer with a 17 is if the dealer busts — it's the lowest winning total. So, if you get a score of 17, don't be unhappy if you simply push — tie — with the dealer.)

♣ **With a Blackjack (an Ace and a 10-point card), you win instantly, and you are paid 1.5 times your bet, UNLESS the dealer has a Blackjack too. Then, you'd make no money, you'd push. In that isolated instance, I recommend that beginners and intermediates ask for EVEN MONEY when the dealer asks "Insurance?"** As you saw earlier, that means you only get paid an amount equal to your bet, *but*, you *win* even if the dealer indeed has a Blackjack. For beginners and intermediates, who lack advanced skills, whose win rate is lower than advanced players', and who might be disappointed if they push here, this is best.

(NOTE: Some casinos have restrictions on what cards you can double down on, and some do not allow surrendering. This varies from location to location. In most places you can find a casino that offers these very desirable options without restrictions! Avoid casinos that DON'T! See Chapter 3 for more information on how to pick a good casino.)

What To Do After You've Hit Your Hand

OK. Now, what if you've HIT your first two cards, as recommended above, but your total is still below the magical total of 17 (above which you never take cards)?

Easy. Just refer to CHART 1B (page 51).

Find your total on the left column, move your finger to the column that's below the up card number the dealer has, and the chart will tell you what to do. Your totals are listed in the left-most column, the dealer's up cards are shown in the top row.

Basic Strategy: How to Play SOFT HANDS

When your hand is SOFT, that is, it contains at least one Ace, here's how you should play it (please refer to CHART 2, page 52):

♠ **If you have an Ace-2 through Ace-5, you DOUBLE DOWN only when the dealer has a 4 through 6. Otherwise, you HIT.**
Since you're dealing with weak point totals of 16 (or 6) or less, you want to play it safe and only double here when you're pretty certain the dealer will bust. If you HIT and your total is still below 17, refer to CHART 1B (page 51) for what to do.

♣ **If you have an Ace-6, DOUBLE DOWN against the dealer's 3 through 6. Otherwise, HIT.**
Although you always stand on a HARD 17, that's ***not*** true of a SOFT 17. You NEVER stand on a soft 17 (and that includes 3-, 4- or more-card soft 17s.) There are two reasons for this. First — since 8 out of 13 possible hit cards (Ace, 2, 3, 4, 10, J, Q, and K) would give you winning totals — you have extremely favorable odds in DOUBLING DOWN against the dealer's weakest cards (when the dealer is most likely to bust) and in getting a good card when HITTING against the dealer's stronger cards, with the hope of beating the dealer's likely strong total). Second — 17 is the weakest winning score possible, and, with the flexibility of the Ace (to be a 1-point card if necessary), the odds are in your favor if you hit this hand with the hope of improving it. Refer to CHART 1B if you've hit and your total is below 17 points.

♥ **If you have an Ace-7, DOUBLE only when the dealer shows a 3 through 6. STAND on a 2, 7, 8 or Ace. HIT against the 9s and 10s.**
This is the most complicated Ace combination in terms of remembering what to do. Since Ace-7 is 18, a pretty good total, you want to STAND against the dealer's Ace or 2, rather than risk ruining your respectable total of 18 by doubling down (nor would you want more money down

against those cards, which don't bust very much). (The Ace here is not as strong as the dealer 9 or 10 because — don't forget — you're not making this move when the Ace is at its strongest, when it couples up with 10s to form a Blackjack. Those hands have been removed from consideration; you won't have a choice of what move to make if the dealer makes a Blackjack!) You should also stand against the dealer's 7 and 8, but for a different reason — you expect to win or push here. However, when faced with the dealer's 9, and 10, which will usually produce very strong winning totals of 19 through 21, you must try to better your score. You cannot stand on your Ace-7 and expect to beat those up cards most of the time. Plus, more than half of the time, you will get a hit card that will either improve your Ace-7 (if it's an Ace, 2 or 3), or, at the very least, not hurt you (if it's a 10, J, Q or K).

♦ **ALWAYS STAND with your Ace-8 and Ace-9.**
These point totals — 19 and 20 — are too good to HIT or DOUBLE on. They're often winners. You don't want to risk making these weaker, with a hit card.

♠ **Ace-10 is a Blackjack. The only time you'd do something other than take your winnings here is if the dealer has an up card of an Ace. Then, take EVEN MONEY if it's allowed, or, if it's not, take INSURANCE**.
As mentioned before, I recommend beginners and intermediates ask the dealer for EVEN MONEY in this case instead of risking the lack of a win here. Taking Insurance, — if EVEN MONEY isn't allowed — means putting 1/2 the amount of your bet in chips in the INSURANCE circle above your bet. Then, no matter what, you're given even money in winnings. (Insurance pays 2-to-1. So, if the dealer has a Blackjack — which they usually check for before letting players play their hands — you'd get an amount equal to your original bet for your Insurance bet, and you'd push on the original bet itself. Once again, Insurance is considered a 2nd, independent bet. You're betting the dealer will have a Blackjack. If it turns out

that the dealer DOESN'T have a Blackjack, then you LOSE the Insurance bet, but get paid 1-1/2 times your original bet for your Blackjack. The net result is you get even money as if you had won a non-Blackjack hand.)

♣ **If you get two Aces, ALWAYS SPLIT THEM.**
The great thing about splitting Aces is that 8 of the possible 13 cards you might get upon each of those Aces would provide you with *two potentially winning hands* (the 6, 7, 8, 9 and the 10s would help each of the Aces achieve nice scores — 62% of the cards). Go for it! You will have a restriction here, though, that you should be aware of — at nearly all casinos, you will only be given one card upon each of your split Aces. Unlike other splitting situations, you may not draw any more cards to those two new hands. We will take this into consideration, in Chapter 10, on Advanced Strategy.

The Rules of Splitting

Splitting your hand into two new hands when you have a pair of same-point cards is often a good thing to do. Sometimes the cards add up to a poor total, and, by splitting them, you create the possibility of getting two hands with winning totals; plus, you get more money down in a winning situation (and, by the way, you should DOUBLE after splitting if your new hand is a total worth doubling on; most casinos allow this).

Please refer now to CHART 3A (page 53). This shows you the method you'll use in most casinos at which you'll play — where you can DOUBLE DOWN after splitting, and re-split if you get another like card upon one of the original cards. (Review CHART 3B, on page 54, on your own. You should never play at casinos with the restrictions referred to there; they work against you and require you to use a new strategy, as you can see.) OK, so:

♦ **If you have a pair of 2s, SPLIT them against the dealer's up cards of 2 through 7. Otherwise — HIT. With 3s, SPLIT them against the 3 through 7. Otherwise, HIT.**

Two 2s equals 4, and two 3s equals 6, which are not great point totals. Against the 4 through 6, it's a no-brainer — those are the dealer's weakest cards. Plus, my research shows the dealer's 2, 3 and 7 outperform your un-split hands of 4 and 6 points. If you split them, you create two new hands that are less likely to bust, and more likely to achieve winning point totals. But, against the dealer's stronger up cards of 8 through Ace, you'd be smart to HIT your pairs of 2s and 3s, because you're likely to lose whether or not your split them, and so, save your money. Exception: your split 3s don't fare well against the 2. HIT.

♣ ***NEVER split two 4s or 5s*. HIT the 4s. DOUBLE DOWN on the 5s against a dealer's 2 through 7, and HIT against the dealer's 8, 9, 10 and Ace.**

Two 4s equals 8, which is not a bad total to hit. With a 10 you have 18. With an Ace you have 19. With a 2 you have 10, with a 3 you have 11 — good totals, because my research shows 11-point hands achieve totals of 19 or more than 50% of the time! The alternative — splitting those 4s — would be bad. You'd have two hands of 4; my research shows each of those new hands would bust 32% to 60% of the time, depending on the **flow of the cards** (we'll get into that, and other advanced topics, in Chapter 10)! Ouch! Now, with your pair of 5s, the total of 10 points is a great foundation upon which you will often build a strong total! That's often better than splitting and then hitting individual 5s, which often draw to a stiff. My studies show that those separated 5s would bust even more than the 4s! That's not a good thing to do. So, keep the 5s together, and play them like any hand of 10 points.

♥ **With two 6s, SPLIT them against the dealer's 3 through 7. HIT them against all other up cards.**

This hand totals 12. Not great. With a 10, you'd bust. Two hands of 6 are better — versus the dealer's weakest cards, that is. Plus, it lets you get more money on the table when the dealer is most likely to bust (although the dealer's 7 doesn't bust a lot, interestingly enough, my data shows that it draws to lower scores than the dealer's 6!).

♠ **With two 7s, SPLIT them against a dealer's 2 through 7. HIT them against the dealer's 8 or 9. SURRENDER them against the dealer's 10s or Ace. (If surrender is not allowed, then HIT.)**
Very similar to your pair of 6s. Two 7s equals 14. Not a great total. You might bust with 6 of the possible 13 hit cards. Two hands of 7 each offer more hope of achieving two winning hands. The dealer's 8 or 9 are too strong to split against, with your resultant split hands of 7 apiece, but you still have a better than even chance of pulling a card that won't bust your 14 (and might help) if you HIT. The dealer's 10 and Ace are so strong and your options so weak when compared to those up cards, that you'd do best to get half of your bet back. It's a losing situation. In fact, you will lose 50 hands out of 100 at the VERY LEAST facing the 10 and Ace with your pair of 7s, no matter what option you choose. Surrender is the least of all evils in this case.

♦ **SPLIT 8s, EXCEPT: SURRENDER against the dealer's 10 and Ace, if allowed. If not, SPLIT.**
Two 8s equals 16, *the worst possible total.* If you split them, you will have two hands of 8, which, are much more promising — 62% of the possible 13 cards you might now get (Ace, 2, 3, 9 and the 10s) would give each your new hands hopeful, if not winning, totals. One thing, though — your individual 8s don't stack up well against the dealer's strongest cards. See Chapter 5 for more details on why you should surrender your 8s against the 10 and Ace; if surrender is not allowed, you will then lose less by splitting your 8s than by hitting your 16. This is another way this book is unique. Most others say "Always split 8s!"

♣ **SPLIT Two 9s, UNLESS the dealer has a 7, 10 or an Ace, when you should STAND.**
Two 9s equals 18, which isn't bad at all. So, you DON'T split this against the dealer's up card of 7, because *Blackjack The SMART Way* research shows that the 7 most often busts or scores 17 points for the dealer — therefore, we've already beaten that, and don't want to split the 9s and potentially mess that up! You DON'T split 9s against

the dealer's 10 or Ace because my research shows the 10 and Ace usually reach higher totals than your 9 (plus both cards bust less!). You don't want to lose two hands! However, since the numbers from my studies indicate that your 9 draws to an 18 or higher the majority of times, you are on the right side of mathematical probability if you split against the other up cards — the dealer's 2 through 6 have weak results vs. the 9; the dealer's 8 draws to lower totals, on average, than your 9; and, when facing the strong dealer's 9, it's wise to split, because your two 9s (totaling 18) will usually be out-scored by the dealer's 9 and will not be enough to win. In splitting them, you will, well, you'll actually lower your odds of LOSING. This, unfortunately, is an unavoidable losing situation for you.

♦ **NEVER EVER SPLIT 10s. STAND.**
You've got a great point total here, 20. That 20 will win for you most of the time. You're likely to spoil that strong total by splitting. The 10s make up less than a third of the deck. The odds are 69% that you'll spoil EACH of those 10s with lower hit cards if you split them. Plus — if you do this move, you'll send the other players at your tables scurrying to other tables to get away from you, or YOU might have to run for cover!

♠ **ALWAYS SPLIT Aces** (see soft hands section, page 39). Two Aces equals two or 12 if you *don't* split them. Not great. But, of the 13 cards you might get as your hit cards, 8 of them (62%) would give each of those Aces a winning score. That mitigates the restriction you face here — that the dealer only gives you one card upon each split Ace.

A Practical Example

Now, let's see if you know how to read the Basic Strategy Charts, starting on page 50. Take a moment to review them, and then we'll do an example.

OK— let's say you were dealt the cards on the top of the next page, and the dealer's up card is a 7 (see top of next page):

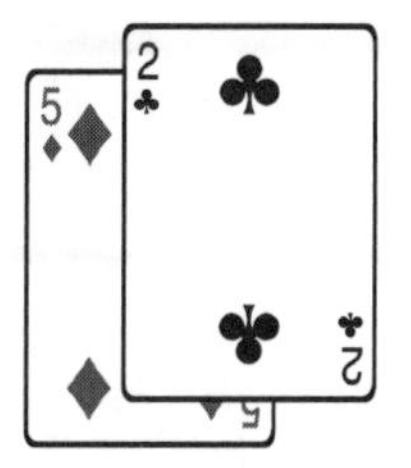

That's a poor total of 7. Go to CHART 1A (page 50), look up your 7 on the left column and move your finger over to the dealer's 7 column (the up cards are across the top). It says "H" for HIT... OK, but what if you hit and then get a three?:

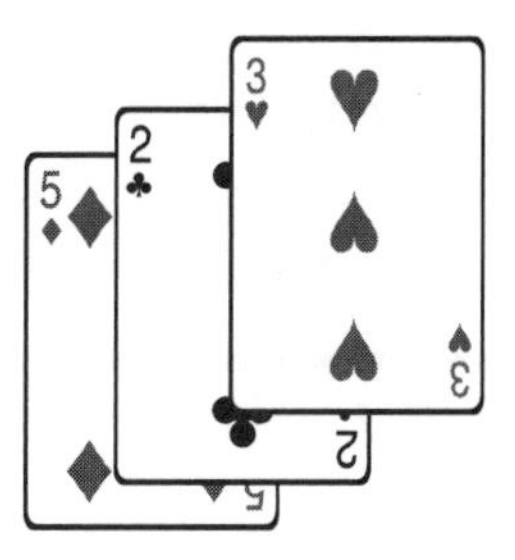

Now look at CHART 1B (page 51). You have a 10 against the dealer's 7. The chart says you HIT a 10 against the dealer's 7.

OK, so you HIT again, and, guess what? You get another 3!:

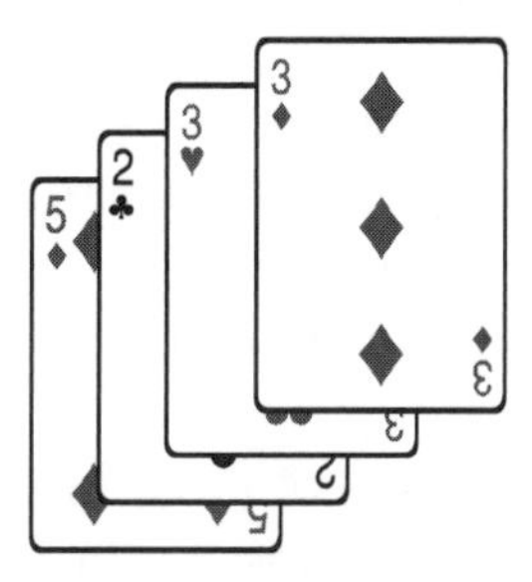

Uh oh! You've got a 13, and CHART 1B tells you to HIT a total of 13 against a 7.

So you HIT...and you get. . .

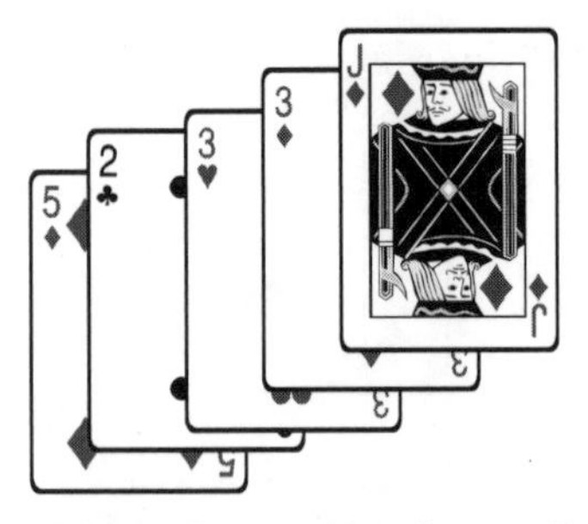

...a JACK, a 10-pointer! Oops! You busted! (Get used to it!)

The point I am trying to make here is -- you will bust on a certain number of hands every time you play. You will never win every hand — not nearly! So, do yourself a favor and keep your emotions in check when you do bust.

How To Place A Bet

OK, now let's discuss how you get into the action. (If there's an ongoing round being played, wait until it is completed.)

In front of your seat, drawn on the green felt top of the blackjack table, will be a small circle, square or other geometric shape designating your betting spot (see DIAGRAMS A & B, pages 55 and 56). Place your bet, in chips, in that spot, before the dealer starts to deal the next round. (You can purchase chips from the dealer between rounds.)

Here's how you stack your chips, if you have a wager composed of different denominations — you're supposed to stack your chips in reverse order to their monetary value, going from highest to lowest, with the highest chips on the bottom.

The dealer will then deal you two cards — your *hand*.

(You can usually place bets at more than one betting space to play more than one hand at a time, but many casinos require that each bet then be TWICE the table minimum. Really, though, beginners and intermediates should not even consider this. It's hard enough to decide how to handle one hand. There are a lot of things to keep track of and numbers to remember, and that easily gets forgotten if you start going back and forth between

hands to make appropriate decisions for the different circumstances that affect each hand. Plus — you tend to attract too much unwanted attention when you take more than one betting spot. You'll understand why you will want to avoid being scrutinized by casino personnel, when you read Chapter 11.)

The Dealer Commences Action

Now, here's how the play goes at a typical casino:

The dealer shuffles the cards when the dealer reaches the plastic reshuffle card (although at some casinos the dealer does this at his/her discretion!). When the cards are shuffled, a player is then handed the reshuffle card to "cut" the cards, and the card below that marker then becomes the top of the pile; the cards above the marker are moved to the bottom (you can refuse to cut the deck if you so choose, by the way). The dealer then usually puts the reshuffle card about 40% up from the bottom of the card pile and "burns" (discards) the top card, or, in some casinos, the dealer burns as many cards as there are players, WITHOUT showing you those cards. (It makes card tracking more difficult. Do not EVER play at casinos that burn more than one card!).

The dealer waits for all bets to be made — the players placing their bet of chips in their betting spot(s). Then, the dealer deals two cards to each player and themselves, one card at a time. The dealer's first card is turned up (either immediately or after the dealer has dealt everyone their first two cards), and the dealer's second card will be the "hole card," kept face down under the first card until it's the dealer's turn to play out his or her hand (see DIAGRAM A, page 55). (At a very few casinos, the dealer turns the *second* card up to become the up card; whatever the policy, it should be done in a standard fashion.) Players then take their turns, starting with the player to the left of the dealer.

After all players have played their hands, the dealer then turns the hole card over and takes more cards if necessary, until he or she reaches a total of 17 or more points OR busts (except, or course, in casinos where dealers must hit their soft 17s). Players that beat the dealer in points, or simply win because the dealer

busted and they did not, get paid in chips an amount equal to their bet, or 1.5 times their bet if they have a Blackjack.

If the dealer gets an up card of an Ace, they immediately ask players if they want Insurance. If you do, you place an amount of chips equal to half your bet within the horseshoe shaped Insurance area in front of your bet (see DIAGRAM A, page 55). If you have a Blackjack and would prefer even money, say "Even Money," and the dealer will pay you an amount equal to your bet. The dealer then slides their hole card over an electronic device which tells them whether they have a Blackjack or not. Typically, one light lights up if the answer is "no" and play continues. Two lights means "yes," and all players lose except for those who also had a Blackjack, who *push,* unless they took Even Money or Insurance.

By the way, the dealer at most casinos also checks 10s in this fashion, to make sure they don't have a Blackjack. They do NOT offer Insurance in that case, however.

A Word About Mistakes

OK, so now you know an intelligent and conservative way to play EVERY hand against every dealer up card, and you've been practicing with cards at home, and what do you find?

You always forget something! Perhaps you also make a few mistakes in the course of playing. Get used to this. I'm still kicking myself for not doubling with an 8 against the dealer's 5 the other night, *knowing* that 10s were coming. I indeed got a 10 and won, but I could have won twice as much if I had only acted on my correct determination and doubled down.

Every blackjack player goofs and makes wrong moves from time to time. Don't sweat it. You can survive making occasional minor card strategy mistakes. Like an Olympic skater, you can get get up from a fall on the ice once in awhile, and still go on to become a winner.

However, *you must NEVER make costly errors in handling your bets or your money.* In that regard, the following chapters will be even more important to you than this one.

Let Me Spare You Some Grief

Before we move on to a different topic, I need to address a common question. No, you should never adopt a strategy akin to the way the dealer plays. Some players insist on learning the hard way why it's not wise to play your cards using the same "strategy" as the dealer's, drawing a card on every hand until you reach a total of at least 17. DON'T try this foolish method!

The reason you will lose more than the dealer playing this way is this: you must play your hand BEFORE THE DEALER. Therefore, you must pull a card using this strategy whether or not the dealer is likely to bust (where you might win by standing on one of your stiffs). When you bust YOU lose your money. When the dealer busts, the dealer personally loses nothing.

Wouldn't it be wiser to learn to stand on some of your more dangerous, bustable hands in situations where the dealer is likely to give you a win by busting?

What You Should Do Now

OK, now it's important that you study the charts in this chapter, practicing over and over at home until you remember every situation you will run into at the casino. Then, once you've read this book in its entirety and are ready to play at a casino, *always review your charts and notes at least an hour before you actually play*, to get your strategy down COLD. It's *your* money.

Where Do We Go From Here?

This Basic Strategy that you just learned — which beginners and intermediates will use exclusively, and advanced players on occasion — is only the tip of the iceberg. You now must learn some very important principles that will make you a smart gambler, and protect your hard-earned money.

You are not ready to enter a casino yet.

CHART 1A: HOW TO PLAY HARD HANDS

	A	10	9	8	7	6	5	4	3	2
4-8	H	H	H	H	H	H	H	H	H	H
9	H	H	H	H	H	D	D	D	D	H
10	H	H	H	H	D	D	D	D	D	D
11	H	H	H	D	D	D	D	D	D	D
12	H	H	H	H	H	S	S	S	H	H
13	Sur/H*	H	H	H	H	S	S	S	S	H
14	Sur/H*	Sur/H*	H	H	H	S	S	S	S	S
15	Sur/H*	Sur/H*	Sur/H*	H	H	S	S	S	S	S
16	Sur/H*	Sur/H*	Sur/H*	H	H	S	S	S	S	S
17+	S	S	S	S	S	S	S	S	S	S
BJ	Even**	S	S	S	S	S	S	S	S	S

*Hit these combinations if surrender is not allowed.

**Take Insurance if Even Money is not allowed.

CHART 1B: HOW TO PLAY HARD HANDS AFTER TAKING ONE CARD

	A	10	9	8	7	6	5	4	3	2
4-8	H	H	H	H	H	H	H	H	H	H
9	H	H	H	H	H	H	H	H	H	H
10	H	H	H	H	H	H	H	H	H	H
11	H	H	H	H	H	H	H	H	H	H
12	H	H	H	H	H	S	S	S	H	H
13	H	H	H	H	H	S	S	S	S	H
14	H	H	H	H	H	S	S	S	S	S
15	H	H	H	H	H	S	S	S	S	S
16	H	H	H	H	H	S	S	S	S	S
17+	S	S	S	S	S	S	S	S	S	S

CHART 2: HOW TO PLAY SOFT HANDS (ACE COMBINATIONS)

	A	10	9	8	7	6	5	4	3	2
Ace-2 to Ace-5	H	H	H	H	H	**D**	**D**	**D**	H	H
Ace-6	H	H	H	H	H	**D**	**D**	**D**	**D**	H
Ace-7	S	H	H	S	S	**D**	**D**	**D**	**D**	S
Ace-8	S	S	S	S	S	S	S	S	S	S
Ace-9	S	S	S	S	S	S	S	S	S	S
BJ	**Even***	S	S	S	S	S	S	S	S	S
Ace-Ace	**Sp**	**Sp**	**Sp**	**Sp**	**Sp**	**Sp**	**Sp**	**Sp**	**Sp**	**Sp**

*Take Insurance if Even Money is not allowed.

CHART 3A: HOW TO PLAY PAIRS OF LIKE CARDS (If Post-Split Doubling & Splitting Are Allowed)

	A	10	9	8	7	6	5	4	3	2
Two 2s	H	H	H	H	Sp	Sp	Sp	Sp	Sp	Sp
Two 3s	H	H	H	H	Sp	Sp	Sp	Sp	Sp	H
Two 4s	H	H	H	H	H	H	H	H	H	H
Two 5s	H	H	H	H	D	D	D	D	D	D
Two 6s	H	H	H	H	Sp	Sp	Sp	Sp	Sp	H
Two 7s	Sur/H*	Sur/H*	H	H	Sp	Sp	Sp	Sp	Sp	Sp
Two 8s	Sur/Sp*	Sur/Sp*	Sp	Sp	Sp	Sp	Sp	Sp	Sp	Sp
Two 9s	S	S	Sp	Sp	S	Sp	Sp	Sp	Sp	Sp
Two 10s	S	S	S	S	S	S	S	S	S	S
Two Aces	Sp	Sp	Sp	Sp	Sp	Sp	Sp	Sp	Sp	Sp

*Surrender if allowed. If not, SPLIT.
**Surrender if allowed. If not, HIT.

CHART 3B: HOW TO PLAY PAIRS OF LIKE CARDS (If Post-Split Doubling & Splitting Are NOT Allowed)

	A	10	9	8	7	6	5	4	3	2
2-2	H	H	H	H	Sp	Sp	Sp	Sp	Sp	H
3-3	H	H	H	H	Sp	Sp	Sp	Sp	H	H
4-4	H	H	H	H	H	H	H	H	H	H
5-5	H	H	H	H	D	D	D	D	D	D
6-6	H	H	H	H	H	Sp	Sp	Sp	H	H
7-7	Sur/H**	Sur/H**	H	H	H	Sp	Sp	Sp	S	H
8-8	Sur/Sp*	Sur/Sp*	Sur/Sp-*	Sp	Sp	Sp	Sp	Sp	Sp	S
9-9	S	S	Sp	Sp	S	Sp	Sp	Sp	Sp	S
10-10	S	S	S	S	S	S	S	S	S	S
Ace-Ace	Sp	Sp	Sp	Sp	Sp	Sp	Sp	Sp	Sp	Sp

*Surrender if allowed. If not, SPLIT.
**Surrender if allowed. If not, HIT.

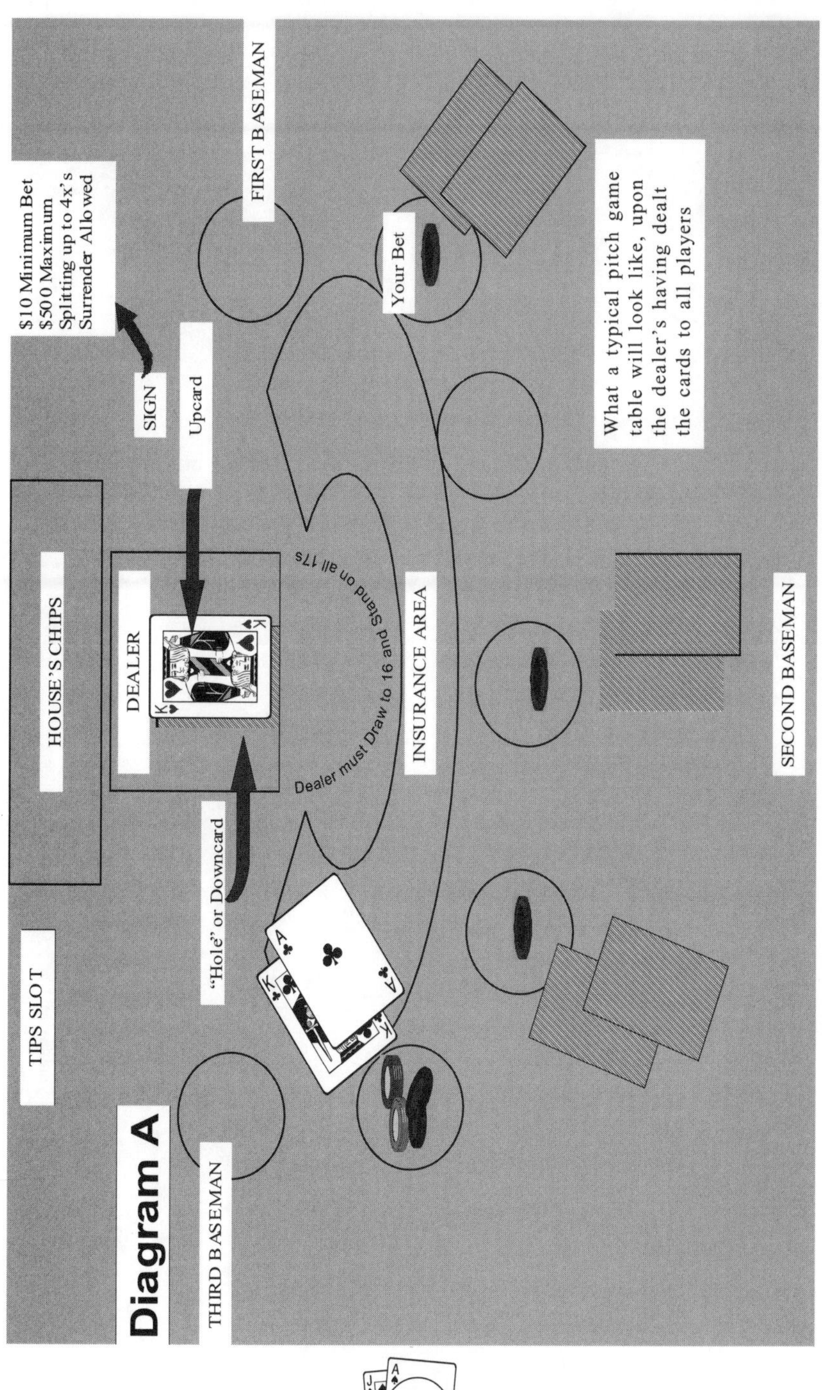
Diagram A
THIRD BASEMAN
TIPS SLOT
HOUSE'S CHIPS
DEALER
"Hole" or Downcard
Upcard
SIGN
$10 Minimum Bet
$500 Maximum
Splitting up to 4x's
Surrender Allowed
FIRST BASEMAN
Dealer must Draw to 16 and Stand on all 17s
INSURANCE AREA
Your Bet
SECOND BASEMAN
What a typical pitch game table will look like, upon the dealer's having dealt the cards to all players

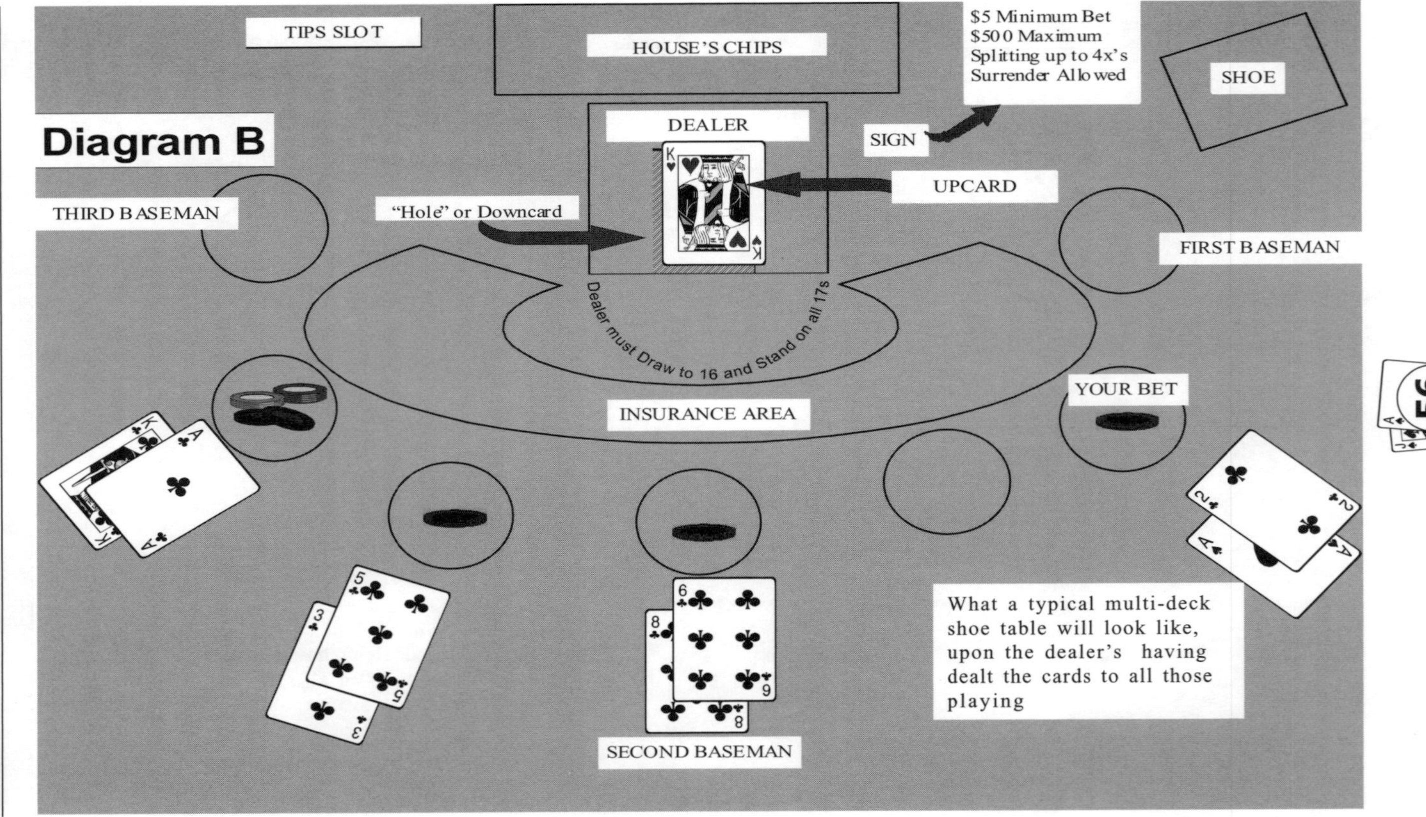

What a typical multi-deck shoe table will look like, upon the dealer's having dealt the cards to all those playing

3
THE WORLD
OF
THE CASINO
3

Let me take you into the world of the casino.

The atmosphere is one of dazzling lights, shiny mirrors and gaudy colors. It is visually overwhelming.

At some casinos, the smell of stale cigarette smoke clings to every pore of the place.

At all casinos there are mazes of alleys created by cash-register-like slot machines that greedily gobble coins and bills fed to them continually by bleary-eyed slots players.

And the noise! The slot machines emit clunking sounds on their gorging cycle, and then belch out coins with cymbal-like crashes on their disgorging cycle. As if that weren't annoying enough, they occasionally let loose with the clanging of bells to signal that a slots player has scored a jackpot.

You have to walk past all of this to get to the blackjack tables. Finally, in the distance, through the dark of the casino, you see lights shining upon the welcome green of the felt-topped black-jack tables, usually situated near the craps tables – where players tend to scream and shout, adding to the cacophony.

You now notice the blackjack players, sitting in semicircles, bent over their cards, many of them obviously...*unhappy.*

That's right. Most players are losers and that doesn't make anyone happy. Some even grumble how crummy the cards have been. Never mind. You don't have to let them drag you down. It does sober up the fun a bit, though, doesn't it? Let that be a reminder to you that *your money is on the line*.

It's Your Job To Pick A Good Casino

Not all casinos were created equal. Some casinos are huge, and contain many blackjack tables from which to choose, with different minimums, numbers of decks and rules (some tables, for instance, might not allow players to join the game until the shuffle). The average casino outside of Las Vegas, Reno, Tahoe and Atlantic City and one or two other stateside casino towns, however, are small to medium-sized and do NOT have many blackjack tables. The smaller the casino, the greater your limita-

tions will be when you are looking for a good table.

Pay Attention to the Atmosphere

At some casinos, the atmosphere is cheery and friendly. You see players winning and having a good time. The dealers enjoy joking around with the players and root for them.

Some casinos have bad vibes. As soon as you enter, the negative atmosphere awakens you to tangible reasons why you should probably turn right on your heels and leave.

For example, there's a casino in my home state that a lot of players avoid because the place is so dark you can barely see your cards. The place is painted black, the players always seem depressed. It's not a very nice place. Why would you want to play at a place like that, when you're looking to have some fun?

Also, some casinos seem to feed their dealers nasty juice. It's no fun to play when the dealer is humorless and negative, or, worse, is giving you a rough time – criticizing your moves, or rushing your play. If you get bad vibes when you enter a casino, DON'T play. Walk right out. Don't be embarrassed, and don't play just because you drove 20 miles to get there. *It's your money.*

Do They Show You The Cards?

I also prefer to go to casinos where they bring in new cards at specific hours, which they then spread out face up so you can see for yourself the decks are legitimate – that there are no missing or extra cards.

Don't Be Desperate!

So, be picky about the casino you go to! The game will be far more enjoyable if you choose a place where all the factors are how you like them. Believe me, it will pay off in the end! Part of the "trick" to upping your win rate is being discriminating about

where you play.

The Cardinal Rule Upon Entering a Casino

If, upon entering a casino that's new to you, the atmosphere seems nice, JUST look around. DON'T SIT DOWN YET! *BEFORE you sit down at a table, walk around the casino and get a feel for what its advantages are, and see if it has any disadvantages.*

I especially like the 1- or 2-deck games, so if a casino doesn't have either of those, I'm going to avoid it. That's important to me. More decks at the table and it becomes a different game.

Only two blackjack tables? You won't be able to change tables if the cards are cold. Not a very good place to play!

Many casinos have small plastic signs on the tables, next to the dealer's left hand. Read those carefully. The signs list some of the game rules particular to that casino. They enumerate some of what you are allowed to do (example: "Surrender Allowed"), and any restrictions you might face (such as "Doubling Only on 10s & 11s" or "No Re-splitting Aces").

In some regions, such as Las Vegas, it's harder to find casinos that display these customary signs. So, if you are at a casino without the signs, you must then ask the dealer specifically about any possible restrictions you will want to avoid. Your first question should be: "Is Surrender allowed?"

If a casino severely limits your ability to double down don't play there – that's one of your best ways of making money. If no re-splitting is allowed (that is, if, let's say, you split two 8s and you get another 8, but you cannot split that new pair of 8s), you'll have to alter the way you play — see CHART 3B, page 54. You probably don't want to do that. No Surrender? That's a major plus, and I always seek out casinos that allow it.

How To Pick A Good Casino

To summarize:

Shop around and find a casino where the conditions are as

favorable as they can be; one that:

- Has the game you want to play — the number of decks you prefer to play against; pitch vs. shoe games, for instance. I won't play against more than 4-decks, and prefer 1– or 2-deck games, where it's easier to keep track of the cards, and the **flow of the cards** is more predictable, less prone to wild swings. Don't compromise on this issue.
- Has an ample number of blackjack tables — the more the better. You then stand a better chance of finding a good table within that casino when your table is bad and you need to change tables. (Any less than 8 tables, and you might find your only option is to leave the casino after suffering minor losses at a bad table, and that's very inconvenient and makes for a difficult time of it. In fact, it tempts you to play at a less than optimum table, and that's bad.)
- Allows doubling down on any 2-card combination. Any restrictions here severely hurt your chances of coming away a winner, or winning what you should. Plus, if there are restrictions, they usually amount to a near banning of doubling!
- Allows doubling down after splitting. Without this, you would have to change your splitting strategy, and you really don't want to do that — it limits your gains. Plus, I don't recommend that you try changing your successful strategy to suit a restrictive, less-than-desirable casino.
- Lets you split at least up to 4 times. Anything less, and you'd need to re-think splitting those 8s, for example. Once again, you don't want to have to remember several different strategies when you can win more by sticking to your guns and finding a casino that's best for you.
- Allows re-splitting of Aces. Although a rare situation and not one of your "essentials," this lets you win more often when the opportunity arises.
- Allows Surrender. This is a powerful option that you should seek out. It lets you get more money on the table because you know you can always get half of it back if you are in a no-win situation with a high bet out. Plus — it spares you half your inevitable losses in obviously lop-sided losing hands.

Now, you should try to *avoid* casinos where:

- The dealer must hit their soft-17s. This will result in more losses to you.
- The dealers "burn" (place in the discard tray) more than one card after shuffling. One card burned doesn't make a huge difference to your ability to keep track of what cards have been played, but any more than that is cause to find a better casino.
- The dealer places the re-shuffle card such that you will see less than 50% of the cards before he or she must re-shuffle (this may vary from table to table, however — check and see). To benefit from the predictability of the game, you need to see as many cards as possible, so find a casino that shows you 60% or more of the cards before dealers must shuffle.
- You get too much negative scrutiny from casino employees, and they subject you to countermeasures or dirty tricks. Or, their heavy-handed breathing-down-your-neck style of observation makes you feel uncomfortable.

How To Pick A Good Table

Now, *knowing how to pick a good table is a very important thing to learn.*

Steer away from the tables where everyone's depressed and complaining, and find one where people seem at least somewhat happy, if not outright smiling and laughing and of good cheer. Those tend to be the better tables, where the luck of the cards has been pretty good. The more crowded the better. Think about it — no one leaves a good table!

But we also want to watch the action for awhile at any table we might consider joining, before we actually sit down to play.

If the dealer seems to be on an improbably good winning streak – winning even with his or her weakest up cards, constantly turning up high totals like 20s and 21s, not to mention an unusual number of Blackjacks – *avoid* that table at all costs!

These are tables where the players are either pretty glum, or outright disgusted, saying things like "not AGAIN!" as the dealer snappily collects the player's lost bets with a strange zeal. We want to avoid these tables.

Also, avoid tables where the dealers deal extremely fast or seem overly confident they're going to win every hand, always expecting to turn up a winning card when drawing their own cards, not even seeming to pause a split second before collecting player's bets.

Find a table where the dealer busts occasionally and loses not infrequently, at which at least one or two players seem to be winning. Watch at least a few hands to be sure. Look at how many chips the players have in front of them – if at least one has a large pile of chips in front of him, and others have medium-sized piles, that's probably a good sign (although, granted, you never know how many chips they started off with).

You can even ask one of the players at an opportune moment "How's this table doing?" If the answer is "Not bad," that means it's OK. If the answer, on the other hand, is "I've been losing here for six hours," move on. Not long ago, I sat down next to an acquaintance, ready to play, and I asked him how he was doing.

"This dealer always kills me!" he responded dejectedly. Yet, he then placed another bet, as I watched in amazement!

"Thanks for telling me!" I said with a grin, and promptly got up to look for a better table.

It's also wise to choose a table where there are no annoyanc that would distract you from concentrating on your game – a nasty player or dealer, or someone smoking if that bothers you

The "No Mid-Point Entry" Table

Some casinos offer tables with signs that say "NO MID- ENTRY." Wow! I *love* those tables. While you'll have to it's time for the dealer to shuffle to enter those games, i it. That way you avoid what I call the "**One-Hand Har Harriets**" and the "**Coupon Charlies and Charlene**

avoid the shills – the casino employees who pretend to be players (you'll learn about them in Chapter 11).

The **One-Hand Harrys and Harriets** bop from table to table, never knowing what they're doing, always seeming to come to your table in the middle of a winning streak, which they promptly mess up by interrupting the flow of the cards (in joining the game, adding a player) and by playing stupidly. They put down only enough money for one or two hands and then leave, having spoiled the action at your table.

The **Coupon Charlies and Charlenes** are similar, except they don't bop from table to table. They're typically slot machine players who just happened to get a coupon in the mail, who interrupt action by using their "$5 Match Play!" coupon to play one or two hands, which they play poorly and lose, and they then go off to play the slots, having destroyed any winning streak you were enjoying before they came to the table.

The funny thing about the NO MID-POINT ENTRY table is that the casinos invented it thinking it would be a benefit to them, and NOT the player! The theory was it would prevent card counters from watching on the sidelines, and then jumping into the action when the cards looked favorable. In actuality, it's much more of a blessing to the player. The more stable the **flow of the cards**, the better able you'll be to keep track of how the cards might break for you. Plus, your winning streaks won't be jeopardized by card fluctuations.

If you can find a NO MID-POINT ENTRY table, RUN to it!

Should You Ever Play The Dealer One-On-One?

NEVER, NEVER, NEVER play the dealer alone. I have *rarely* – repeat — *rarely* won when I attempted this.

For many reasons, you're likely to go down fast:

- You won't see many cards before it's your turn to play, and so you won't have the advantage of watching how the cards are breaking by watching fellow players play their hands first.

- The play is a lot quicker and so it's easier to get confused and lost.
- The dealer, if it's a pitch game, tends to deal you fewer cards before reshuffling, which will quickly end any possible winning streaks for you and make it difficult to get a feel for how the cards might break (each new shuffle creates its own set of unknowns).
- If you're on a down cycle, your pile of chips will go down so rapidly, you'll get confused as to whether you're in a normal down cycle or a real plunge.

Trust me – until you're an *expert* player, *don't even consider this.*

The Number of Players at the Table Matters

What I advise is that you play only at tables where there are at least two other players, preferably *three* or more.

The advantages are many:

The pace is more comfortable. If you're sitting in or toward the third baseman's seat as I advise (see Diagrams A and B, pages 55-56), you'll have more time to observe the cards and think about what move you might want to make.

You'll see a good amount of cards before making your decision, so you can make a more informed choice as to whether to risk taking more cards.

Plus – and this is MY theory – by sitting at a table with a good number of players, you are effectively lessening the casino's advantage in using more than one deck of cards.

Why does this seem to work? With three or four players at a table, they effectively *divide those decks between themselves*, so the cards become more predictable and even break better! It then seems as if the odds almost become that of the single-deck game.

And, once again, ***crowding*** *at a table tends to be a good sign* — if it's hard to find a seat there, it might be because the players have found a good thing and don't want to leave! *No one wants*

to leave a good table!

Empty tables, on the other hand, are often empty because the cards have gone on a very bad streak and have driven the players away.

Avoid Tables With Horrible Players!

I have discovered, by the way, that *the best way to beat the house most often is by bringing with you several friends who all play well*, or by sitting at a table with good players. That's when you'll see your most protracted winning streaks.

A bad player will ruin a table sooner or later. The normal flow of cards is disturbed and the winning cards that would tend to come your way somehow end up being diverted. When you've played often enough, you'll find this is true.

I've demonstrated this at my seminars. We'll play a hand, and everyone sees how well playing on the right side of the percentages works. Then, we'll replay the same cards, but, this time, we'll pretend one of the players is making stupid moves. More times than not, these mistakes play into the hands of the dealer. Try it for yourself.

There is considerable debate about this subject, but, trust me, most good players have recognized the validity of this syndrome.

So, if you see someone splitting 10s, or standing on a hand of 5, or any other crazy moves, pick up your chips and RUN to another table!

Avoid the Blackjack Variants

There are only two types of blackjack games you should consider playing – straight ahead blackjack, either dealt from a dealer's hand, or from a "shoe."

Stay away from all blackjack variants, usually identified by cutesy or strange names. By the time you figure out all the rules, your money will be gone. Then, on the way home, you'll realize that the variant game had rules that made it very difficult to win.

To "Pitch" or to "Shoe" — That's The Question

Some casinos have 1- or 2-deck "pitch games" where the dealers hold the decks in their left hand, "pitching" (tossing) cards to the players, who then hold the cards in one hand as they play (see Diagram A, page 55). The idea behind having you hold your cards is to thwart card counters, but you won't get into trouble if you show others' your cards or peek at the extra card you're given face-down under your chips when you double down.

There are disadvantages, admittedly. Pitch game tables often require higher minimum bets than the others. Not infrequently, you see less cards. Dealers many times will re-shuffle after dealing out only 40 to 50 percent of the cards, the amount depending on the policy of the casino. And card counting becomes difficult, if not impossible. By the time your hand comes up, many players' cards might be unseen, slipped face down under their chips, or held tightly in their hands, out of view. (For this major dilemma, read my second book, *Cutting Edge Blackjack*, which has a chapter with a breakthrough method to guesstimate those down-turned cards, and continue to use card counting at pitch game tables!)

In contrast to the pitch game tables, there are tables where there are multi-deck *shoes* – 4, 6 or 8 decks of cards typically in clear plastic open-top boxes – from which the dealers pull each card with their left hand, dealing them face up to the players (see Diagram B, page 56).

As I suggested before, there are advantages to playing at shoe game tables. You'll see more cards and more rounds before the cards are re-shuffled. Plus, the casinos tend to have their dealers put the re-shuffle card further back into the cards, so you usually see up to 70% of the cards. And more important -- card counting and **Card Observation** are easier, because all cards (except the dealer's hole card) are dealt face up.

I prefer the pitch games, however. The advantages outweigh the disadvantages — especially if you are advanced enough to use my method of counting cards at those tables, in my second book.

While finding 1-deck pitch games is difficult in most areas outside of Las Vegas, 2-deck pitch games seem more available. (Beware, though, even if you do find a 1-deck game. A 2-deck table where you see a substantial number of cards before the dealer re-shuffles is better than a 1-deck table, if – at the 1-deck table – you see that the dealer is shuffling up after much less than half the cards are dealt!)

It can never be emphasized enough – with fewer cards being used, it's easier to keep track of what cards have been played. Playing at a table with only 1 or 2 decks is a big plus. As you will find out in Chapter 8, at a pitch game table, you will know better which cards are due, and so you can make more astute decisions that will translate into bigger profits.

For example, a few weeks ago, playing at a 1-deck table, I noticed that three Aces were dealt in the first round! Wow! That told me a LOT! Number one, it indicated that doubling with a 10 might not be as profitable a move. There was only one Ace left. Number two, the dealer was then less likely to have a Blackjack in later rounds, or any Ace-enhanced totals. Perhaps it was time to inch up my bet a bit. Now...what would that have told me if the same thing had happened at a table with 8-decks? Nothing.

Another example: if you have seen eleven 10s in the first two rounds of action at a 1-deck table, you might NOT want to double down on your 11, even if the dealer has a weak card.

In contrast, what would that same scenario tell you at a 6-or 8-deck table? Not much.

At a 1-deck table, there are 16 10-point cards in play, and 4 Aces. At a 2-deck table, there are 32 10-point cards, and 8 Aces. With less of those cards in play, it's more obvious when things are askew. Because that gives you a better awareness of whether those crucial cards are either depleted or overdue, you can play a much better game.

With a 6-deck game, there are 96 10-point cards and 24 Aces. With an 8-deck shoe game, there are 128 10-point cards and 32 Aces! It's mind-boggling!

So, if you're in a situation where a 10 would bust your hand, will you ever be fairly sure you're NOT going to get one, when you're playing against 6 or 8 decks? Will you remember roughly how many Aces and 10s were played?

In the middle ground, there are the 4-deck shoe tables. I'm not adverse to playing at these tables if there are no 1- or 2-deck games. The action at 4-deck tables is not as extreme as the 6- and 8-deck shoe tables, and you can still play a good game. And there are advantages over the pitch game tables. As I mentioned before, the cards are dealt FACE UP, so card counting and **Card Observation** are easier to do (see Chapter 8).

Plus, interestingly enough, splitting and doubling opportunities arise more frequently. Not only that – with less frequent shuffling, your winning streaks sometimes last longer than the average pitch game win streak, so often interrupted by reshuffling.

What Minimum Bet Table Should You Play At?

Table minimums are posted on a small plastic sign, usually by the dealer's right hand.

Smaller casinos typically have lower minimums – most tables being in the $1, $3, $5 and $10 range, with an occasional $25 table.

In the larger casinos, minimums typically fluctuate, often being raised to their maximum levels on weekend nights. In Atlantic City, for example, it is not unusual to find that the cheapest table has a $25 minimum, especially on weekends. To some, this will pose no problem. I personally love the $25 tables, but most players cringe at the thought of playing there.

No, this book is especially aimed at the average player, to whom the thought of placing even a minimum of $5 or $10 on each bet initially might make them gulp for fresh air. For that reason, and also because of the vagaries of the game, I recommend that you always play the $5 tables, or, if they're full, the $10 tables.

Of course, you can also sit at lower minimum tables if they're offered (typically $1 or $3 minimums) and still play a $5 minimum

game, which is what I'd suggest you play. Too low a minimum bet and you'll never make any money and you'll never know when to quit because you'll never reach a satisfying conclusion. Too high a minimum ($15, $25, $50 and up) and you're courting a scare during a down cycle.

The $5 or $10 tables are perfect for the conservative method I'm teaching you, because, while you won't make a ton of money when you win, you should make a satisfying amount of money on your winning days, and your down cycles and occasional losing days will be manageable. Plus, you won't have to bring a ton of dough with you!

Does It Make A Difference In Which Seat You Sit?

Now, although you usually have a choice of sitting at one of seven seats at any table (although some tables, especially in Vegas, have just six seats), as I indicated before, you should try to sit in the third baseman's seat — the one immediately next to the dealer's right hand — or as near to it as you can get (see Diagram A, page 55). That gives you the advantage of seeing a lot of cards before you have to make your decision as to how to play your hand. And by the way, always ask the players there if it's OK to join them if you're entering the game mid-stream, before a fresh reshuffling of the cards. Some players resent newcomers jumping in at that point. Many don't, however.

If they ask you to wait for the next shuffle, decide whether you want to wait for that or not. If it's a good table, you probably would do well to cool your heels and use your waiting time constructively – let each hand be a mental quiz as to how you would want to play them.

How to Join the Action

When the dealer has swept the table of cards (or reshuffled the cards if you're waiting for that), you'll gently place your money on the table, in front of you, inside the Insurance circle,

near the dealer. The dealer will then grab a stack of chips to match the amount of cash you've given him or her, turn toward the floor manager (a casino boss who monitors the tables from a center section behind the dealers) and say to the floor manager "changing $100!," upon which the floor manager will look over and acknowledge the transaction. The dealer will then slide your chips across the table, until they're in front of you, and you're ready to play!

Oh, and if the dealer tries to give you green $25 chips, politely say "no, just red chips please." You won't be making many $25 bets. Mainly, you'll need those red $5 chips.

Plus, playing the green chips tends to draw unwelcome casino attention.

Strategic Stacking

Listen to me carefully, now – always keep your $5 chips divided into 5-chip, $25 stacks.

I call this *Strategic Stacking*. The stacking of your chips in this way allows you to quickly determine visually how far you're up or down.

It also alerts you to the rare instance where someone might have helped themselves to some of your chips.

I'm always amazed at the haphazard piles most players have in front of them. How do they know if they're up or down, or by how much?

Guard Your Chips!

Now, take my word for it -- it would be a good idea for you to place your chips on the table right in front of you , guarding them at all times. I always protect my chips now. I learned the hard way.

I have had chips stolen from me by sleight-of-hand artists on several occasions (over the course of many years). Each time was the same. By the time I noticed my carefully-stacked piles were diminished, there was no evidence to be had as to who had taken my chips, or how.

It is very likely the thefts were NOT done by players at my table, by the way. In fact, after seeing televised videotapes of casino thieves in action, I am almost certain I was victimized by "hit-and-run" passersby, who probably grabbed my chips when my attention was diverted, and then quickly walked away. Just be aware that this type of thing does goes on, on rare occasions.

Every Player's Doing Differently

By the way, you'll soon notice that, unless the dealer busts, it's rare that all players win or lose at the same time. Typically, some are doing well, others not so well. It has to do with the normal break of the cards, and/or players' varying playing abilities.

A Confusing Scene

Another word of warning – the casino environment can be a confusing one. Whereas, in big casino towns, such as Atlantic City and Las Vegas, dealers will sometimes help beginners by offering occasional advice (sometimes asking "Do you REALLY want to do that?" for instance), this is NOT usually true elsewhere. In fact, some casinos encourage dealers to mislead you.

At one casino, for example, a dealer tried to discourage a friend of mine from surrendering – a move that gives you a tremendous advantage, when used properly. By intimidating players in such a way, some casinos successfully discourage the less confident players from using a very smart option. You have to stick to your guns and what you know to be good strategy and laugh off such bullying.

The same dealer also objected to MY surrendering one hand by saying unkindly afterward "Everyone lost because you surrendered!" I laughed and snapped back: "Do YOU play Blackjack? Because I'd love to see how YOU play! It was smart to surrender the hand I had!" She shut up, which is what I was hoping for, but

we left the table anyway. Who needs guff like that from an ignoramous?

Everyone's A Know-It-All

Also confusing is the advice you tend to get from other players when they notice you are a beginner – and it's often presented in a rude way. SO, LISTEN UP : DO NOT VARY YOUR METHOD BECAUSE OF SUCH ADVICE. IT IS WRONG 99% OF THE TIME.

Understand – most players at casinos are LOSERS (how else are those monuments to grandeur bankrolled?). Big shot players may sound confident with their advice, but don't listen to anyone unless you observe them winning a respectable amount of money *most of the times you've seen them play* — not just in one sitting.

You will only *rarely* get good advice. But even then, don't forget – different players have different styles. DON'T PLAY MORE THAN ONE SYSTEM AT A TIME. IT'S CONFUSING AND IT WILL LEAD TO LOSSES. STICK TO YOUR GUNS AND STAY WITH WHAT YOU KNOW IS RIGHT FOR YOU.

Think about it: Do you really think good players would expose themselves to casino scrutiny by teaching you their secrets to beating the house, right in front of the dealer and casino bosses?? No! They'd keep their genius to themselves! Smart winners don't want to be noticed by the casino management, who might bar them from the casino or throw countermeasures at them to disrupt their game.

That's another reason why it should be obvious that the "loudmouths," the know-it-alls, are more often than not, just full of hot air.

Why Most People Who Go To Casinos Are Losers

OK. *Why* do most people who play blackjack go home losers?:

- Many never took the time to learn an effective strategy, and then practice it to perfection.
- Most play on hunches.

- Most don't understand how to manage their money – they'll put more money on the table when they're ***losing,*** hoping that their luck is due to get better; or, they'll go up and down in their bets without any semblance of a winning plan.
- Most don't know how to pick a good casino, or even that it is important.
- Most don't know how to pick a good table, or even that it is important.
- Most sit at one table and play until their money is gone. They are habitual losers.
- Most don't know WHEN TO LEAVE – either on the upside or downside – and wind up STAYING TOO LONG.
- Most are waiting for that mythical fortune to pile up, the huge winnings that you'll see only in a blue moon. If they DO win some money, they're not content to leave with it, and promptly throw it back.

Be Businesslike

Another thing – the temptation once you get going is to chat with other players or the dealer as you play. Resist this.

You need to concentrate! Be polite, but let people know with your body language that you don't want to be disturbed. Otherwise, you will lose track of how the cards are breaking, how you're doing at the table, and how the dealer's doing. You'll then make mistakes.

Mark my words. Ignore this warning at your own peril. Your money is on the line. Shhhh!!! Think!

You can talk to fellow players, if you feel the need to, while the dealer shuffles (although in general, it's best to maintain a low profile). Ignore this advice at your own peril! You will beat yourself up on the way home and all night if you make stupid moves because you weren't paying attention to the game.

Oh, and part of being businesslike means you DON'T DRINK when you play. I mentioned this before, but it bears repeating: This may seem like a leisure activity, but it can also feature the sting of monetary losses if you don't respect it.

Your Relationship With The Dealer

Fitting in, with your businesslike attitude, is the way you comport yourself at the table. You'd be smart to be outwardly cordial toward the dealer — primarily in body language. No need to make any enemies. You want the dealer on your side, if possible. But keep conversation to a minimum. Remember, your goal is always to keep as low a profile as possible, to avoid casino scrutiny. If you're rather quiet, and you don't get known by casino personnel because of anything you say (because you won't say much), you won't "red flag" yourself in any way.

DON'T Make The Dealer Your Friend

Now, be *cordial*; do NOT treat the dealer as your *friend*. That would require you to raise your profile, which you should avoid at all costs. But there's an even more important reason. One of my students (let's call him John) learned that one the hard way.

John related to me how he used to befriend all the dealers. He even tried making friends with the casino bosses.

Then, one day, bad news. The dealers John considered his friends could not allow him to play at their tables. Their bosses were concerned that they seemed too chummy. So now, John had generated unwanted scrutiny AND he was limited in the number of tables at which he could play!

But that wasn't the worst part. The casino bosses then began to suspect (wrongly) that John was *cheating* in cahoots with one of the dealers he had befriended. I can't get into details for privacy reasons, but, it got worse from there. Suffice it to say, don't go down this painful road!

Tipping, The *SMART* Way

It's interesting when it comes to tipping the dealer. Few players seem to know how or when to do this. Many tip the dealer no matter what. Some never tip the dealer.

While it's true that the dealer depends upon tips to make a living, that doesn't mean you should throw your hard-earned money the dealer's way for no reason. Would you tip a surly waitress? Please don't say yes!

First of all, it's CRAZY to tip a dealer when you're losing. There are various things a dealer can do to make your life easier. If you tip them when you're losing, what incentive do they have to help you out? Tipping is one tool you can use to can get certain advantages.

I'll never forget the dealer who, upon noticing the current shuffle had produced a very bad flow of cards for everyone at the table, promptly told us cheerfully: "I'll shuffle up after this hand!"

She was letting us know she was going to help us out by trying to rearrange the cards into a better sequence. She had not dealt out the cards down to the shuffle marker. In fact, she had only dealt two or three hands. She was just helping us out.

I promptly tipped her the first hand of the newly shuffled cards. That let her know: Thanks for being nice. Plus, it gave her an incentive to continue being nice.

Dealers can *really* shuffle the cards, or they can give it "window dressing" while actually leaving a bad string of cards largely intact. Tip the ones who *really* shuffle the cards when the cards are bad. The pretenders are working against you.

Dealers also deserve tips when they see you're in the middle of a winning streak, and they DON'T shuffle up too soon, or every time you put out a large bet.

If, on the other hand, it looks like they're trying to spoil your game, and they're working hard to defeat you, to win back your winnings for the house, DON'T even THINK of tipping them! There ARE dealers who seem to be rooting for the casino to win, and doing everything they can – and there many things they CAN do in this regard – to beat you.

Some dealers root for you and make the game fun. Fine, tip them when you're ahead. (But, still, don't tip them while you're losing.)

But, DO NOT tip the nasty dealers and the Quick-Ricks who

throw the cards at you and speed up the game ridiculously!! You're not giving them any incentive to be friendly and make things pleasant! Would you throw a dog a bone if he had just bitten you?

How to Tip

Now, there are two ways of tipping. You can either give them a dollar, a $2.50 or $5 chip in between rounds, or you can place a bet for them in front of your betting spot, to ride along with the fate of your hand. Smart players do it the latter way, because, then, you get the dealer on your side, to root for you, and, perhaps, to even help you out somehow.

You're still not ready to enter a casino.

THE "TRICKY 2s" & THE "SILENT 7s"

Beware the Big Bad Wolf in Sheep's Clothing: *The Tricky 2*

One of the most amusing times I ever had at a casino involved a trip to a large Atlantic City casino. I sat down in the second baseman's seat (smack in the middle of the table, directly opposite the dealer) at a packed table. The gentleman next to me was apparently a tourist from a foreign country, and had stacks and stacks of big chips in front of him – he was a high roller. However, although he apparently felt superior to those around him, it quickly became apparent that he did not understand the nuances of the game. He was very haughty and was quick to criticize the play of others.

The dealer had an up card of 2 and, having watched the play of cards carefully, it was obvious to me that low cards were due. I had a 13, and elected to "hit," that is, ask the dealer for another card. Right away, the man next to me flew into a rage.

"No, no no! You don't hit a 13 against a 2! You don't know how to play! You should go to another table!" He was as insulting and inappropriate as he was wrong.

In fact, many experts would agree with my play, but that was not the point. I smiled, as I noticed my hit card was a 7, for a superior total of 20. Turning to the man calmly, I said in a friendly voice:

"OK, my friend. I'll tell you what! I'll make a bet with you that my way of playing is the correct way. I'll give you $5 every time I lose playing my way against the dealer's 2, if you agree to pay ME $5 every time my strategy wins. Or, make the bet $10, or, $25! I don't care, because I'm gonna win that bet."

The odds were in my favor. Figure it out for yourself: 8 of the possible 13 cards improve that hand of 13 — Ace through 8, for a percentage of 62%. A significant majority of the time, my move was correct, and that's how you play — by the percentages. Add to this equation that my system told me that low cards were due, NOT cards that would bust my hand. Plus — *the DEALER's chance of getting a winning total with his 2 up card was significant*. I was aware of what I call the **Tricky 2s** and this man was not.

"No, I no do that!" he said angrily. (Yet, HIS playing style cost him that hand.)

Miraculously, the dealer then seemed to come up with an inordinate amount of 2s as up cards in the next 5 minutes! I won every time, playing my way. The man next to me lost every time because of his faulty reasoning. All of a sudden, after losing against yet another 2, he went ballistic. He started shouting in a foreign language what I figure were not niceties, and then grabbed his pile of chips to leave.

"Please, sir, let me color you in," pleaded the dealer (dealers must exchange players' stacks of red $5 chips, for green $25 chips, so the table doesn't become depleted of the more commonly played red chips).

"No! I no give to you!" the man shouted in his loudest voice, everyone now turning around to look at him and wonder what set him off. Of course, I knew what got him so angry — he'd been proven wrong! — and I was softly laughing at the scene.

The man wasn't a big winner, by the way. He just brought a lot of money to the table. If he were a winner then, perhaps, his superior attitude might have been understandable on some level. Instead, it just ticked me off.

The point I'm making here is twofold – watch out for the ***Tricky 2s****, and, of course, stick to your own strategy and don't let a "know-it-all" bully you into playing a strategy that will cause you to lose your money.*

The truth of the matter, which you rarely read NOR hear about, is that – ***at BEST*** *–* ***the dealer busts only about ONE-THIRD of the time when his or her up card is a 2****. Many books and dealers will tell you to STAND on anything above an 11 or 12 against a dealer's 2, implying that the dealer is likely to bust. Very wrong. That 2 is practically non-existent. The dealer can pull up to a total of 19 points (including the hole card) and win!*

Do you realize how many card combinations produce totals of 15 through 19 to make the dealer's up card of 2 a winner? HUN-DREDS! Especially in a multi-deck game!

In fact, what I'm telling you is hinted at, buried in one of the many charts Julian Braun of IBM produced during his revolutionary computer studies of the 1960s. It theorizes that *the dealer's 2 is to the dealer's advantage if the card count is moderately to very negative* (I'll teach you about counting in Chapter 8, but it basically means that *if 10s have been depleted, the dealer's 2 is strong)*. My research has proven, however, that it is *always* the dealer's card.

Let's explore this. The 10-point cards account for only 4 of 13 cards. So, 9/13s (69%) of the time, the dealer will have cards that total LESS. If the hole card is a 9, the dealer has 11 points, with a 62% probability of drawing a 6 or greater, giving the house a winning score of 17 or more. If, instead, the hole card is an 8, the dealer now has a total of 10 and has a 62% chance of getting a 7, 8, 9, 10 or Ace, obtaining a winning total. If, instead, the dealer's hole card is a 7, and now has a total of 9, he can draw ANY card and not bust; AND 54% of the cards the dealer might get (Ace, 8, 9, 10, J, Q, K) provide a winning total. Even if the dealer's hole card IS a 10, then ***9*** of 13 cards would improve that score! (The popular myth that the dealer's hole and hit card will likely be 10s, busting the dealer, is right just 9.5% of the time!)

What I am suggesting is that the dealer's 2 is NOT your friend. It should be played like a dealer's strong card. The 2 most often gives the dealer strong results. The research results I will share with you in my second book, *Cutting Edge Blackjack*, will dramatically bear this out. (In this book, however, I do not want to overload you with too much math.)

Your Basic Strategy Charts (in Chapter 2) take the strength of the dealer's 2 into account. As an advanced player, later on, you will learn how to use this information even more to your advantage. You will learn that sometimes it's wise to pull a card against the dealer's 2, if you have totals up to and including a 15 or 16 — when you have learned how to predict when the low cards are overdue. *When low cards are definitely coming, go for it!*

Just understand – *the dealer will only occasionally bust if he or she has a 2 up card; the dealer will more often than not score a strong winning total of 18 or more*. So, if you *know* the dealer won't likely bust, YOU must pull to a winning total.

And that's the closely guarded secret that the casinos don't want you to know about the dealer's **Tricky 2s**. I'll talk about this further in Chapter 10, on Advanced Strategy.

Take Advantage of the Dealer's "Silent 7"

Now let's talk about the myth of the dealer's 7, said to be a dealer-friendly card. Is it really? Or is it a sheep in a wolf's clothing?

Shortly after writing the First Edition of this book, I was leafing through Lawrence Revere's excellent book *Playing Blackjack as a Business*, and I became excited when I stumbled across this line:

> "Notice that if the deck is very negative [when, in his counting system, Aces and 10-pointers have been depleted], ***the best card the dealer can have for the player is a 7."***

(I put part of the sentence in italics and bolded it for your consideration. The bracketed explanation is mine.)

NO ONE ELSE I'VE READ HAS TAKEN NOTE OF WHAT I CALL THE **SILENT 7** BUT HERE, REFERRING TO JULIAN BRAUN'S COMPUTER STUDIES CHARTS, MR. REVERE HINTS AT IT, IN PASSING. He apparently did not recognize what he was "on to," because he did not integrate that insight into his strategy!

What we want to do is not just say "That's interesting!," but, instead, take a closer look at the dealer's 7, and then *adjust our thinking and strategy, when facing it.*

One interesting thing about Mr. Revere's chart (page 132 of his book) is that — although he uses a far different counting method than you will learn in Chapter 8 — it reveals to us that when the count is moderately negative (when low cards are overdue), *the 7 is the* ***only*** *dealer up card aside from the 6 that provides the player with a winning advantage. In that situation, the 7 is likely to make the dealer bust or help the player win, and, more to the point,* ***it's even more likely to cause the dealer to lose than the dealer's 6!!!***

In fact, the dealer's 7 always lets you to win more than you will lose. (This has been proven in dramatic detail in the data I will reveal to you in *Cutting Edge Blackjack.*)

Suffice it to say, the popular myth that the dealer's 7 is a bad card for you is absolutely WRONG.

Interestingly enough, when the count was positive — when 10s were overdue — Revere's computer studies showed that the

dealer's up card of 7 was even more advantageous to the player than when the count was negative, meaning, the player tends to win even more against it in that situation.

Well, in fact, I had proven my theory to my satisfaction years ago, without the aid of a computer. Here's how I reasoned it out and proved my theory regarding the **Silent 7**:

When the dealer has a 7, let's examine what that really means. The dealer's hole card could be any one of the four 10-point cards, and give the dealer a total of 17 points. Or, the dealer could have an Ace in the hole, with a total of 18 points. Fine. But that's only 5 hole cards out of a possible 13. Not exactly a majority of times.

Yes, it is true that 3 more of the 13 possible hole cards (the 2, 3, or 4) would combine with the dealer's 7 without resulting in a dangerous stiff hand total. But I believe that way of thinking is misleading. As you will see, that does NOT tell the whole story.

Because, if the dealer's hole card *is* a 2, 3, or 4, what are the odds, then, that those cards will produce a winning hand?:

If it's a 2, giving the dealer a total of 9, 7 of 13 possible hit cards (54%) would provide the house with a winning hand. However, of those cards, 2 would result in a total of 17 and 18, which are low winning totals. More to the point — only 5 of the 13 possible cards (the Ace and the 10-pointers) , or 38%, would give the 7-2 combination a strong winning point total.

OK, now if the hole card is a 3, giving the dealer a total of 10, 8 of 13 cards (62%) would provide the house with a winning hand — but only 6 of those cards (less than 50%) would give the dealer a strong winning total.

And if the hole card is a 4, giving the dealer a total of 11, 8 of 13 cards (62%) would provide the house with a winning hand. But only 6 (less than 50%) would give the dealer a strong winning total.

So, let's see what we've shown here:

With 5 of 13 hole cards — 38% — the house has a total of between 17 and 18 points — low on the winning scale of things. If your hand, facing that 7, was higher than 18, YOU'D win those

hands. Well, since 18 is not amongst the 3, stronger winning totals — 19, 20 and 21, you'd stand a good chance of beating it, if not tying it. OK.

And, the 3 other hole cards we've examined (the 2, 3, or 4) would either pull to a weak winning score, or put the dealer in danger of busting, more than not.

Those are the GOOD hole cards for the dealer. What about the possible hole cards we haven't looked at — the 5, 6, 7, 8 and 9? These 5 cards would combine with the up card of 7 to give the dealer *stiffs* — dangerous, bustable hard totals of 12 through 16.

Does this "picture" really give the dealer the edge with a 7 up card? I think NOT!

So, then should you *stand* on a 13, 14, 15 or 16 against a dealer's 7? Sometimes, *yes* — if, as an advanced player, you are pretty sure the dealer's hole card is NOT a 10 or an Ace, and, simultaneously, the card you'd likely draw would bust your hand. Yes, you often should play the dealer's 7 differently than traditionally recommended!

You will really be able to take advantage of this information, when you've mastered some of the more advanced concepts that I am about to teach you.

Suffice it to say, I think I have proven beyond a reasonable doubt that the dealer's 7, more often than not, acts like a ***player's*** card. I call it the Silent 7 because the 7 *silently* masquerades as something it is not. It's a sheep in wolf's clothing, and this is the first book I know of to reveal this.

So, with this understanding, let's update our list of *which dealer up cards favor us*:

We will now call these dealer up cards OUR CARDS, the PLAYER'S CARDS:

And we will now call these dealer up cards, the DEALER'S CARDS:

With your understanding of which cards are truly in your favor and which ones are NOT will come an ability to make smart, profitable moves. You'll see how to put this knowledge to good use, and find out about the dealer's 8 in Chapter 10, on Advanced Strategy, and, in the following chapter, in which you will learn when it is smart to double and split, and when it is NOT.

You are still not ready to enter a casino.

5
DANGERS
IN
DOUBLING
&
SPLITTING
5

There will be times when the odds are especially in your favor that you will wish you had put a bigger bet on the line, to make more money in a likely winning situation. Fortunately, there are times when you're allowed to do so — but, it is important that you realize that it is NOT when you have your very best hands.

You can put more chips on the table after your bet's been placed and your turn arrives, in just two restricted circumstances.

You can do so:

❶ If you agree to take just one more card — that is referred to as ***doubling down***, or, simply, ***doubling.***
❷ If you have a pair of same-point cards and you agree to separate those cards into two new hands — that's called ***splitting***. The new hands would be played out independently, just as you would play any other hands, with one exception — your pairs of Aces. The dealer will only place one card upon each of your split Aces.

In both of these cases, you may put additional chips into play,

but only an amount equal to or less than your original wager. (And, by the way, although you are often allowed to double with LESS than the amount of chips you placed as your original bet, that doesn't make much sense to me. I believe that if it makes mathematical sense to double, then you should DOUBLE your bet. Also — one more thing. Be aware that some casinos restrict your ability to double down, with rules such as "Doubling On Totals of 10 & 11 Only." Don't play there!)

Unfortunately, many players have been lured by pervasive and misguided thinking, into doubling and splitting in some losing situations where it's really unwise. In this chapter, I hope to steer you clear of these common mistakes.

Contrary To Popular Thinking...

Doubling down can be a great tool with which to make a maximum amount of money. But, it would only be wise when:

❶ You will most likely draw to a winning total and beat the dealer, with the addition of just one good card.
❷ The dealer is very likely to bust and your hand won't bust with the addition of one more card.
❸ Or, you have just split a pair of like cards at a desirable time, and now have a new hand that fits the criterion in either of the two bulleted items above.

However — I want to warn you that doubling down can sometimes be the casino's best friend!

"No kidding!" you say. "No one taught me that!"

Perhaps it's because, interestingly enough, many blackjack books and videos have been written by former or current casino employees, who often urge players to double down and split recklessly. They give beginners just enough information to be dangerous to themselves. These writers are typically NOT blackjack experts or players, and yet their "Basic Strategy Charts" — full of errors — have become the standard of the industry, mis-

leading legions of novice players.

Think about it. Would it be a big stretch of the imagination to suggest that casinos might actually WANT you to double down or split in situations that might not be smart? You'd give to them TWICE the amount you'd normally lose to them in a losing situation!

Along those lines — isn't it curious that the *dealer* will often URGE you to double down, or split? Those are the times that you should ask yourself: "Are they really doing me a favor by telling me this?"

If a dealer truly gave you great advice that resulted in your walking a way a big winner, that dealer wouldn't last long at that casino, would he? He'd be fired in no time! (And casino bosses would have no trouble spotting this helpful fellow; there'd be LEGIONS of players FLOCKING to this dealer's table, for the privilege of hearing his words of wisdom, words that had turned many of his minions into millionaires! Come on! Get real!)

Just keep in mind that when you double down, what's the agreement you make with the casino? *They* allow you to double the amount of money you have as your bet, if *you* agree to take JUST ONE MORE CARD. That's a drawback few players take seriously enough. And, with splitting, the potential drawback is that you must put *twice* the amount of money on the table you had initially.

Now, these are good options sometimes, but other times they are definitely NOT.

When Is It NOT Smart to Double Down?

In spite of what many books tell you to do, there are many times that traditionally recommended doubling down moves pose too much of a danger.

For example, let's say you have an 11 when the dealer has an Ace (see illustration on the top of the next page):

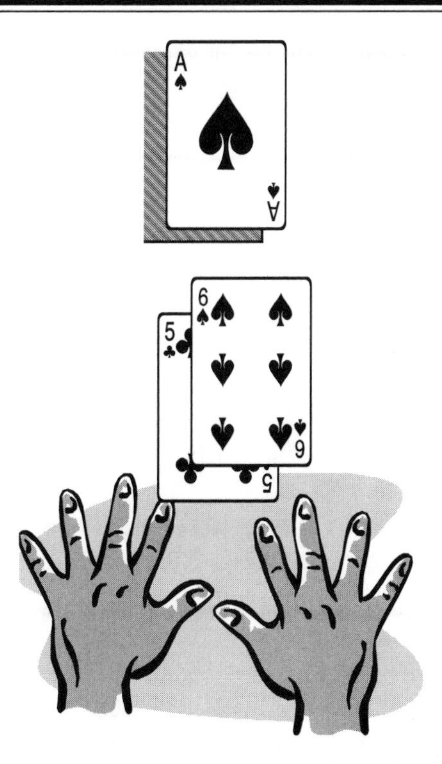

Many players have been taught that they should double down here. I'll give you just one example, but this advice has been given in many books, and you can check for yourself. For instance, in *Scarne On Cards* by eminent writer John Scarne (page 161), he writes: "Always double down on a count of 11 no matter what the value of the dealer's up card is." You will see soon why that might not be a good move.

The 50-50 Rule

Now, first of all, you should know what I call **The 50-50 Rule:**

> *When you and the dealer have the "same" cards* — for example, if the dealer's up card is an Ace (for a possible 11 points) and your hand totals 11 points — *you will only win roughly 50% of the time.*

It's a matter of simple probability. Two equal hands tend to achieve equal results, or so it seems — but things are not always equal.

Things Are NOT Equal

The dealer has an unfair advantage when you double — you are limited to taking just one more hit card, unlike the dealer. And, if you draw an Ace, 2, 3, 4, or 5 as your one hit card, you're hanging in the wind with a non-winning score against one of the dealer's best cards. In fact, even if you draw a 6 or 7, you'll be unlikely to beat the dealer's Ace. In other words, MOST OF YOUR HIT CARDS WON'T HELP YOU.

So — unless you can count cards (it's easy! — I will teach you how in Chapter 8) and the count is EXCEPTIONALLY good, why would you want to double here and stand a good chance of losing TWICE the amount of YOUR bet in this situation, now that you realize your odds are significantly *less* than 50% of winning?

NO — YOU ONLY WANT TO DOUBLE DOWN WHEN YOU HAVE A CLEAR WINNING EDGE ON THE DEALER!

The dealer's Ace is far too strong a card to double against, with your hand of 11 points, unless, you've become an advanced player, and can predict pretty well when the 10s are likely to come (you'll learn how in Chapter 8). Even then, you might be taking on more risk than you should.

Other Traditionally Recommended Foolish Moves

OK. How about when the dealer has up cards of 9 or 10 points (the dealer's two other strongest cards) and your hand totals 11? Many books say *always* double on your 11. Yet, my studies have shown that, *ONLY 5 OF 13 POSSIBLE HIT CARDS WOULD HELP YOU HERE — only a 9 or the 10-pointers would combine with your 11 to give you a CHANCE of beating the high scores the dealer's 9 and 10 tend to achieve. Only 38% of your possible hit cards might lead to a win; 62% would probably hurt you!*

I think you'll agree that the odds of pulling a winning card here are NOT overwhelming! WHY do it, especially if, in doubling, YOU RISK LOSING TWICE THE AMOUNT OF YOUR BET? HIT your 11, and you'll be able to take a second card if the first is too low to be any good. You'll have a much better chance of winning.

Another Example of Questionable Traditional "Wisdom"

OK — now let's say you have a hand of 10 points versus the dealer's 9. Many pundits say DOUBLE. Let's examine that.

My latest studies (whose results are unveiled in detail in *Cutting Edge Blackjack*) show that you would need to get a 10 or an Ace on your hand of 10 points if you want to beat the score the dealer's 9 draws to most — 19 or higher.

That means, if you choose to double down on your 10 against the dealer's 9, you'd be putting twice your original bet in jeopardy in a situation where only 5 of the 13 possible hit cards would give you a likely win. You'd have roughly a 38% chance of winning — if all things were equal, which they are NOT, as you've seen.

Sure, a 9 might give you a push, but a possible push is no reason to risk more of your money.

Why *double* when HITTING that 10 gives you a better chance of winning WITHOUT risking more money against a strong dealer up card?

Why The Dealer's 8 Requires Caution

OK — now let's say you've got a score of 10 against the dealer's 8 (see the illustration on top of the next page). This is another situation where the traditional advice is that you should DOUBLE. But my studies indicate here that you'd need to draw a 9, one of the four 10s, or an Ace to beat the dealer's 8, which, more than not, draws to an 18 or greater. You'd have, at best, approximately a 46% chance of winning, limited to one hit card.

Don't forget the amount of times when you will draw a stiff and you will lose when the dealer simultaneously draws to a winning total. That will occur more than 20% of the time!

This is clearly a losing situation; why, then, would you want to put TWICE YOUR ORIGINAL BET at risk? NO! HIT this hand and you will then win more hands than you will lose, with less downside risk. The restriction of getting just one hit card in doubling down here is too big a limitation.

Need I Say More?

These examples regarding doubling give you a demonstration of the thinking that led to some of the unorthodox strategies in *Blackjack The SMART Way*. Many more such moves are discussed in a later chapter, on Advanced Strategy (Chapter 10). They hopefully gave you many valuable insights about the perils of doubling down.

For now, let's move on to the dangers inherent in splitting.

When is Splitting A Smart Move?

Now, splitting is similar to doubling in that some pundits have taught the majority of blackjack players to split where it makes little sense. In fact, once you're ready for Advanced Strategy, you will see that you will be doing LESS splitting as an advanced player than as a *Blackjack The SMART Way* Basic Strategy player! With the additional information you'll learn in later chapters, you'll realize that many of the traditionally recommended splitting moves are too risky to consider — depending on the card count (or, in other words, the **flow of the cards**), about which I will teach you soon.

Let's look at when splitting makes sense. It should usually be done only in a situation where it's mathematically very probable that you will win, but there's one exception. Splitting your hand of two like cards into two new hands is smart when:

❶ The dealer is very likely to bust, and you want to get more money on the table, because you'll then probably win with both of those new hands.

❷ The dealer is likely to draw to a weak winning score at best, and your hand is a dangerous stiff that, if split, would create two strong hands that would probably beat the dealer, or, at worst, give you a push.

❸ You're in a losing situation, whether you split or not, but, with splitting, you stand a chance of at least breaking even, OR losing LESS than you would otherwise. (This reason will account for only a small minority of splitting moves.)

HOWEVER — there are times when splitting is NOT smart. For instance, the dealer's up cards of 2, 3 and 4 demand some respect when the number of high cards played significantly outnumber the number of low cards played. You'll also want to get a bit more cautious with the up cards of 5 and 6 in that situation!

You will need to learn some more advanced concepts before we can discuss this in detail. We'll return to this topic again in the Advanced Strategy chapter (Chapter 10).

There are some examples we can look at now, though.

When is Splitting NOT A Smart Move?

Consider the situation below:

This is a situation in which many might think it is smart to split that pair of 6s, but my studies have indicated just the opposite. There are many reasons, actually, but let's just explore one aspect that makes it all clear.

OK, put your extra money down, and split those 6s. So, you have two hands that begin with the total of 6. (See the illustration on the top of the next page).

Now, we certainly don't want to get a hit card that gives us a stiff (a hand that totals 12, 13, 14, 15 or 16), do we? Then, we'd have the possibility of busting with the next card.

And yet, one of the peculiarities of the 6 (and all of the cards have their own peculiarities), is that it has a terrible chemistry with MOST of the possible hit cards you might get. Any of the cards below (62% of the possible hit cards) would combine with your 6s, to make your hand a stiff:

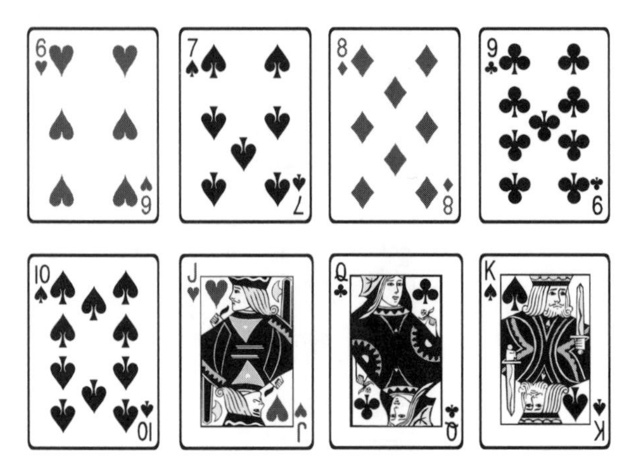

Now, combine THIS with the knowledge you gained in the last chapter about the dealer's Tricky 2. That 2 causes the dealer to draw to winning totals more than not.

Do you really want to put more money on the table, to wind up with TWO hands that look like probable losers?

I don't think so!

Oh, Holy Cow!

One of the sacred cows of the blackjack pundits is their vehement insistence that you always should split your 8s. You get the impression that to suggest otherwise is to be labelled a heretic.

Well, let's you and I explore this question. Let's look at when the dealer's up card is an Ace. (See example, on the top of the next page.)

The dealer's Ace is a formidable beast, it is. It busts less than 15% of the time! Your 8 will bust 25% of the time. Already you are unequal footing.

Understanding what the numbers are telling you — you will most certainly LOSE 25% of your hands, from the get-go. You cannot stand on your stiffs against the dealer's Ace. So, whether or not the dealer busts is immaterial. (And you know that some of the times that the dealer's Ace busts will undoubtedly be when you bust, too, thus robbing you of some of the benefits of the dealer's already paltry bust figure with the Ace.)

Now, if you split your 8s instead of surrendering, as I suggest, you will then have TWICE as much money against the dealer's Ace as you would have had normally. You will be playing two hands for every Ace you see. So, if I see 100 Aces and surrender, I'll lose 50 units, let's say, if I make steady, $1 bets. If you split and see 100 Aces, and are making the same steady $1 bets (just for argument's sake), you will lose 50 units from the get-go, because your 25% bust rate now applies to 200 split hands! You'll immediately lose as much as I will in surrendering.

OK. So, after you lose those 50 hands when your 8s bust, in the remaining 150 hands you'll have against those 100 Aces we talked about above, you'll then have to win 100 of them JUST TO BREAK EVEN!!! Now, what do you think your chances are of winning 2 out of every 3 hands you face against the dealer's Ace? Next to nil. Think about it!

You will lose more by splitting those 8s than by surrendering them in this situation.

How About Splitting 8's Against The 9 or 10?

Now, the dealer's 10 is no less strong than the dealer's Ace, and the dealer's 9 is nearly as powerful an adversary.

Until you are an advanced player, the best course of action with your pair of 8's would be to surrender them against the 9 and the 10, for the same reasons enumerated above.

The dealer's up cards of 9 and 10 only bust slightly more than the dealer's Ace, for instance, and both draw to strong winning totals, like the Ace. You cannot, therefore, afford to bust 25% of the time, with TWICE as much money on the table, playing TWICE as many hands, when, as you saw above, it would then mean that you would need to beat the dealer's 9 or 10 in 66% of the remaining hands JUST TO BREAK EVEN!

Now, the one mitigating factor here is, when the dealer's hole card is not a 9 or 10, you would have a lot better odds of winning by splitting your 8s. To take advantage of this exception, however, you will need to understand advanced concepts and develop advanced skills.

Suffice it to say, when you absorb the material in later chapters of this book, and become an advanced player, there will be times when you might then consider making this move, in limited situations, as you will see in Chapter 10, on Advanced Strategy.

This Method Is Designed To Conserve YOUR Money

In fact, once you're ready to learn Advanced Strategy, I will teach you that there *are* limited circumstances when you might want to consider doing a few of the doubling moves I suggested in this chapter that you should NOT do, as a Basic Strategy player.

However — even advanced players must pay attention to the concepts presented in this chapter. Because those players will not infrequently still need to play according to Basic Strategy at times. When? When they're playing their first hand immediately following the shuffle, for example, when it might not be clear what cards will be coming next. Or, when they join a table in mid-action, and they don't know what cards have been played.

Most importantly — I want you to learn to play *conservatively*, so your gains become higher, your overall winning rate increases, and your down cycles are fewer and smaller.

My intention in this chapter wasn't to catalog the many ways *Blackjack The SMART Way* is unique, but to give you just a few examples that should convince you that this is the way you want to go. There will be many more examples of SMART doubling and splitting in Chapter 10.

My purpose here was to take some time to discuss some of my more controversial recommendations in greater depth. Plus, I wanted to give you some insights and guideposts regarding the mathematical concepts underlying the *Blackjack The SMART Way* system, with which you can do your own thinking, on the spot, at the casino, to make profitable moves.

Next, let's take a look at the all-important world of bet-making.

You are still not ready to enter a casino.

6
THE NEED FOR BRAKES
9

I debated long and hard whether or not to include this story in my book, fearing that some might misconstrue it and conclude that my strategy was to blame. Nope, my one big scare was caused by foolishly IGNORING my own advice.

It happened a decade ago, before I had completed and perfected the strategy you see in this book. I was still an intermediate player, testing out my nascent theories and concepts.

It was the night I took a friend of mine, Maggie, to her first casino. I had taught her my new method, and had promised to bring her to Atlantic City. (Maggie was in her 70s at the time!)

After a 4-hour drive, we arrived at the casino, and found a good table. Maggie was obviously a beginner, but everyone, including the dealers, took kindly to her. They helped her every chance they could. She was confused about how to give hand signals, so I occasionally had to contradict her hand signals and the dealer graciously accepted my directions. Maggie was ecstatic as saw she was winning. We had great fun.

It didn't take more than 2 hours before Maggie had won about $200, and she couldn't have been happier! I was up well over $400, and Maggie was eager to take her winnings home with her, so we stopped at this point. We had been "comped" free dinners by the casino (I was still seeking comps back then, not yet wise to the negative aspects of casino scrutiny), and so we took a break to enjoy one of the fine restaurants there, and then we took a walk on the Boardwalk.

That's when I made a greedy mistake. Knowing full well I should have left with my winnings, as I now teach you to do, I suggested to Maggie that we play on.

Maggie was the smarter one. She said happily that she didn't want to play anymore – she wanted to take her winnings home. But, she said, she would gladly watch me play.

Oh boy. For the next 3 or so hours, I ran into terrible hands at a string of miserable tables. I was still relatively new to the game, and I made some big mistakes – disregarding my system, raising my bet dramatically, desperately hoping my luck would change. Big mistake! I went down over $1,000. Yep. Over

$1,000. It was a lot of money to me.

I had brought $1,500 in cash with me to the casino. I needed that much to stay in the game, for at most Atlantic City casinos, the table minimum went up to $25 or more at most tables on a Saturday night.

Anyway, here I was, with an elderly friend, 4 hours from home, at midnight on a Saturday night, down a lot of money, and mentally fatigued not only from normal play, but also from the emotions that had been gripping me for the past 3 hours.

I decided that, if Maggie agreed to stay, I would not stray from my system, and I would make one final – levelheaded – attempt to make up my losses. Maggie, who'd been having a great time watching everyone play, graciously agreed. I then moved from table to table, going down even further initially. I was down to about $300, when, at about 2 am, I found an active table, where the players seemed happy and celebratory, one fellow having a huge stack of green chips in front of him. I sat down to his left. (This was one of those casino behemoths, with LOTS of blackjack tables, which is a blackjack players dream! I was confident that I'd find one good table, eventually.)

The next two hours were unbelievable. I exhausted my wits in keeping track of the cards, this time keeping my bets strictly according to my system, and I quickly began to recoup my losses. Hundreds of dollars in chips began to come my way, and, by night's end, I was actually AHEAD by about $50. Of course, if I had been SMART, I would have brought home 9 times that amount, and gotten home at a more reasonable hour.

This was certainly an object lesson for me, and it led to some important innovations and changes in the early development of my system. Here's some of what I learned:

Number one, QUIT while you're ahead. Number two, don't chase losses with bigger bets. Number three, you CAN lose a lot of money if you play stupidly. And, finally, the higher the minimum bet you play, the higher your losses can become if your system doesn't have the requisite "brakes."

Now, a few readers who play the high stakes tables might

wonder why the fuss over a $1,200 down cycle, which, at the $25 minimum bet tables I played at, is equivalent to 48 Units (a Unit is equal to your minimum bet, as you will learn in the next chapter). First of all, the loss was caused by a mistake – I foolishly abandoned my more conservative betting system in a rash panic, partly due to my playing inexperience at the time. So, I want to warn others who might be tempted to do the same NOT to. Also, if you let your one-day losses mount to more than your average one-day gain, you are looking for trouble. Losses add up just as surely as gains do. No; 48 Units is way too high a loss. These days, I keep my losses on my very occasional losing days down to roughly 6 to 10 Units. This is how you become and stay a winner.

By the way, it's interesting to note that – had I STARTED OUT the night by playing at the last table I played at – I would have walked away with more than $1,200 in winnings!

One reason I tell you this story is because that night turned out to be a pivotal, watershed event, a necessary experience in the evolution of the *Blackjack The SMART Way* system. It was at that point that I realized I needed to formulate a smart system of "brake-points," to put the brakes on when it made sense to stop playing and go home – whether I was winning or losing.

I then created fail-safe measures, to elimate the possibility of wild downside swings; reduce overall risk; ensure that winnings were brought home and were not ever thrown back; and, make my system smarter and more conservative. You will find these innovations scattered throughout this book; they are now an integral part of my system, which has come a long, long way since that fateful night in Atlantic City. Years of research and seasoning at the tables have made it the unique and unusually successful system you see in these pages, a system that has now been used by countless readers to great success.

Incidentally – Maggie never returned to Atlantic City. I now live 2,000 miles from her and cannot take her there, and she, now in her 80s, has unfortunately lost her mobility. But she still proudly brags to anyone who's interested, that she once played blackjack in Atlantic City, and came away a $200 winner. Such are the joys of blackjack.

7
MONEY
MANAGEMENT
-- Featuring --
The 3-Level,
Notch-Up, Notch-Down
Bet Management System
7
109

OK, folks. Can you guess what I call "A Player's Biggest Disadvantage In Placing Bets?"

YOU MUST PLACE YOUR BETS *BEFORE* YOU SEE YOUR CARDS AND THE DEALER'S UP CARD. You never know if your upcoming hand will be good (and, therefore, worthy of a higher bet), and you never know if the dealer's hand will be strong (and, therefore, a time when you should place the same or lower bet).

That's one reason it's usually not very smart to bet a fortune on any one hand. Of course, even if you COULD bet AFTER seeing your cards and the dealer's up card, you still would probably not want to bet a fortune because *you never have total certainty you'll win even with a strong hand.* There are no situations in which you have a 100% chance of winning – not nearly. Most favorable-looking hands have a pretty high chance of losing – in the 35-40% range, at least.

Popping The Balloon of Yet Another Cherished Myth

This may seem obvious upon mentioning it, but it apparently is not. There are a lot of people – usually old-school diehard card counters — who believe, without knowing what cards they'll get next, that if the COUNT is very "positive" (meaning 10s are overdue), they should raise their bet dramatically. *Without knowing what cards you're going to get?*

Let me ask you this — What good is a count of +10, for instance, if the dealer then deals you a 10 and a 6, with the dealer getting an up card of a 10 (AND a probable hole card of 10)? The DEALER is just as likely as you to get those overdue 10s! You really want a big bet on that one?

It really ticks off some card counting aficionados when I point this out. But, think about it. Why increase your bet astronomically in a situation where the dealer is likely to pull to a strong winning total?

If anything, you should want to have more money down when the dealer's likely to get a weak hand, with a weak up card, if you wanted to subscribe to the "get the maximum bet down now!"

crowd. But you don't want to join that bunch. One big loss and you'll see why.

One thing that makes *Blackjack The SMART Way* such a strong system is that it has you use a conservative betting system that is devoid of knee-jerk card count reactions.

How 'Bout Keeping Your Bet The Same, Each Time?

OK, you say, what if I keep my bet to one amount, the minimum! Will that bring me gains and minimize losses? Nope. A lot of people seem to think so, but that won't work! Instead, it will minimize your gains and guarantee a large number of losing days.

Those seminal computer studies done by Roger Baldwin, Wilbur Cantey, Herbert Maisel, James McDermott, and Julian Braun in the 1960s proved that any winnings with that method would be absolutely minimal, at best.

So, how do you get around this inherent difficulty?

You will use a money management system that is most likely to get more money on the table when your cards are good, and diminish your outlay when your cards are bad.

The Simple 1-2-3-1 Method: Thinking In Units

The first bet management system I'm going to teach you is for beginners who want to keep things simple at first.

Now, you've got to think in terms of ***Units*** when betting. What's a Unit? The lowest bet you want to place, in the course of one session at the casino. For argument's sake, and because it's such a popular low stakes minimum for most players, we'll use the $5 chip as our 1 Unit bet in this chapter.

We'll talk in terms of Units for several reasons. Number one, it makes it easier to teach players of all levels and betting inclinations – whether you like the $5 tables, or the $100 tables, or whatever, you will all be able to follow what I'm about to teach you.

I also do this partly because it makes things easy for you to

remember, if you choose to play at a wide variety of betting minimum tables. And, finally, it's also because you don't want to think in terms of money when betting. If you think in monetary terms, your emotions will take over and you'll make mistakes by worrying and becoming overcautious.

Thinking of our bets in terms of Units (especially if we make 1 Unit = 1 chip: in other words, one $5 chip, $25 chip, whatever) will also make it easier for you to keep track of where you're at in the system, visually. If, for instance, you momentarily lose track of how many hands you've won, you can simply look at your bet, see how many Units there are, and you can probably think your way back to where you were in your betting system.

OK, so, for our purposes, we'll define ***1 Unit*** as being *the lowest Basic (minimum) Bet you'll ever place. At a $5 table, it's very simple — 1 Unit will equal 1 red $5 chip*, as you see below:

Good. Now, keep your bet at 1 Unit until you win a hand. Then, place the chip you've won on top of your previous bet, "notching up" your bet for the next hand to *2 UNITS*, as you see below (at the table, you would stack these, one on top of the other):

OK. If you *lose* your next hand, go back to a 1 Unit bet. However, if you WIN, place one of the two chips you've won on top of your previous bet (taking the other winning chip for your "stash"), making your bet now 3 units, as seen on the top of the next page:

You're now playing with the house's money.

No matter what happens next, win or lose, you will then return to your minimum, 1 Unit bet, and start the cycle all over again.

That's because winning streaks don't last forever and you may not be ready to move on to my more sophisticated betting system that's excellent, but requires more thinking than the simple 1-2-3-1 beginner's method.

For those who are ready to graduate from the basic 1-2-3-1 method and are eager to learn my field-tested system, get ready! (I'm really excited about what I'm about to show you!)

The Best Table for You

First, you have to make sure you have enough cash with you when you go to the casino. *I always suggest that you take 40 times the minimum bet you're going to make.*

It's funny – when I tell students that "you have to bring with you 40 times the amount of your minimum bet in cash to the casino, to stay in the game," they often respond, "that's a lot of money to lose!" To which I respond, "I don't go to the casino to lose. I expect win most of the time, which I do." Plus – there are brakes in my system, as you will learn, that will prevent you from losing very much on an occasional losing day.

The reason for the guideline of bringing roughly 40 times your minimum bet is that there are down cycles you will encounter. And, during one of those down cycles, you might have a great hand, where you'll want to split your hand of two like cards, split again, and then again, and then later want to double upon several of those new hands.

If you don't bring enough money, you might find that you've run out of chips and can't make those desirable moves. You

might then leave a loser, when you might have scored a big gain had you brought enough cash to stay in the game.

Another reason to bring an amount of cash equal to 40 times your minimum bet is that – if you don't – you might then get into the dangerous habit of running to a money machine for more cash, which I hope you NEVER do. That would cause you to get confused about how much money you've played and lost, and get into a syndrome of throwing money away on days where you might do better to cut your losses and leave.

The lowest I've generally gotten in a down cycle in recent years has been 16 Units. That's the lowest. And most times, I bounce back up. So bear that in mind, as a guideline, and also to reassure you that down cycles of that nature are not necessarily insurmountable. Any more than 16 Units, though, and you'll have to analyze carefully whether you really should continue playing, or put on the brakes and cut your losses.

So, to summarize: The 40-times-your-minimum-bet rule has three functions:

❶ It will insure that you have enough money to survive the normal down cycles and stay in the game, with the hope of bouncing back.
❷ It will be your absolute loss limit beyond which you should never go. So, if those chips are gone, LEAVE. (In fact, I will teach you how to keep your losses on any losing day to about half your stash, at the very most.)
❸ It will prevent you from getting into the destructive habit of going to the money machine to get more money.

You MUST have a way in which to cut losses on bad days, so that, by year's end, you will come out way ahead.

Incidentally, don't give the dealer all the money at once. Place five $20 bills on the table when you first arrive (never give them a $100 bill; you'll draw too much attention). The great majority of times, that will be sufficient. I want you to have to reach into your pocket for the rest of your cash if needed, because that will serve as a reminder to you to take a moment and

think about whether you should continue playing much longer.

The Concept Of The "Basic Bet"

OK. Now it's time!

I will now teach you a bet management system that I am very proud of. It is conservative in that it greatly minimizes your downside risk, and yet maximizes your gains. It is very easy to apply and it's been tested and proven successful time after time.

I have named it the **3-Level, Notch-Up, Notch-Down Bet Management System**. (Incidentally a Las Vegas gambler told me he applied this method successfully to baccarat, too!)

In this system, we will think in terms of the **BASIC BET**, which I define as *the lowest minimum bet you will want to put out on the table*. Now, this Basic Bet will *vary*, depending on what **LEVEL** you're on: **0, 1, 2, or 3**.

You want more money on the table only during times when the cards are going your way. So, you will steadily go up or down, in betting Levels, from 0 to 1, to 2, to 3, increasing the value of your **Basic Bet** to catch the wave of a winning streak, or lowering its value to avoid the brunt of a losing streak.

Once at a new Level, you will "notch up" your bet, one Unit at a time, if a winning streak develops, or "notch down" your bet back to your **Basic Bet** upon the start of a losing streak.

This is how you make the **3-Level, Notch-Up, Notch-Down Bet Management System** work for you. When the cards are good, you want to capitalize on it. So, you raise your Basic Bet to a higher base level. When the cards are bad, you reduce your **Basic Bet** to a lower base level.

You Have Maximum Flexibility

This is a very flexible method, designed to respond to the changing **personality of the cards** over time, during any one casino visit.

Let emphasize this here: THIS IS HOW YOU MAKE YOUR

MONEY. YOU MUST LEARN THIS METHOD AND STICK TO IT.

If you change systems or make up your own method as you play, YOU WILL ALWAYS LOSE MONEY. It's the *consistency* of your application of this money management and betting system (as well as the wisdom behind it) that will produce winnings for you.

Always Start At 1 Unit

OK. Here's how it works.

If you've just sat down at a new table, or the cards have just been shuffled, your **Basic Bet** should start at scratch, which will be your 1 Unit bet. That's the value of your **Basic Bet** in Level 1.

Since we've decided in this chapter that $5 will be your lowest minimum bet, and since you're only using the red, $5 chips with which to play, it's even easier to remember the value of your lowest Basic Bet. Your lowest **Basic Bet** will always be ONE CHIP:

$5 = 1 UNIT
= Your Lowest Basic Bet

So, 1 UNIT will kind of be "home base." You will return to this level, which we'll call **Basic Bet**, LEVEL 1, when things are not going your way, as outlined below:

ALWAYS RETURN TO BASIC BET LEVEL 1 (1 UNIT) WHEN:

- *You first arrive at a table.* You don't know yet how the cards are breaking.
- *The cards have just been shuffled.* You don't know yet how the new order will break.
- *The cards are bad.* You want to minimize losses when winning hands are scarce.
- *A new player joins the table before a new shuffle.* This

interrupts the flow of cards, creating uncertainty as to how the cards will now behave for you.

- *A player leaves the table.* This interrupts the flow of cards, creating uncertainty as to how the cards will now behave.
- *A player sits out a hand* (doesn't place a bet, simulating the loss of a player). This interrupts the flow of cards, creating uncertanty as to how the cards will now behave for you.
- *A player takes an extra betting spot* (simulating the arrival of an extra player). This interrupts the flow of cards, creating uncertainty as to how the cards will now behave.

To implement this is easy. At a $5 minimum table, you'd just plunk down your $5 chip in your betting spot under the above conditions.

The beauty of the **3-Level, Notch-Up, Notch-Down Bet Management System** is that it brings you down to a much lower level during bad times than you will be during good times, therefore weighing the odds much more in your favor.

Think about it. Players often get confused when they weigh the odds of anyone coming away a winner at blackjack. They concentrate solely on the number of hands they are likely to win. They forget how important an influence a good bet management system can have on your outcome.

If you get your bet up to a high level (relative to your minimum bet) when the cards are good for you, and reduce your bet severely when the cards are bad for you, you will then come away a winner even if you win only 50% of the hands!

When Should You Raise Your Bet?

OK, now, how do you accomplish this?

It's a bit confusing for some at first. But, really, it's simple. Your bet – first and foremost – will be based on what Level you're on. The higher the Level, the higher the bet. The better the cards, the higher the Level you're going to want to be at. Now, within each Level, you will raise your bet in increments, too, to take advantage of a good flow of cards.

Within each Level, you're going to raise your bet each time you win, notching-up by 1-Unit increases. This is illustrated below.

In the example below, "A" equals our **Basic Bet**, at Level 1 (of course, you'd pile these chips on top of each other in your betting spot during a game; they're shown side-by-side below only for the purpose of illustrating the system):

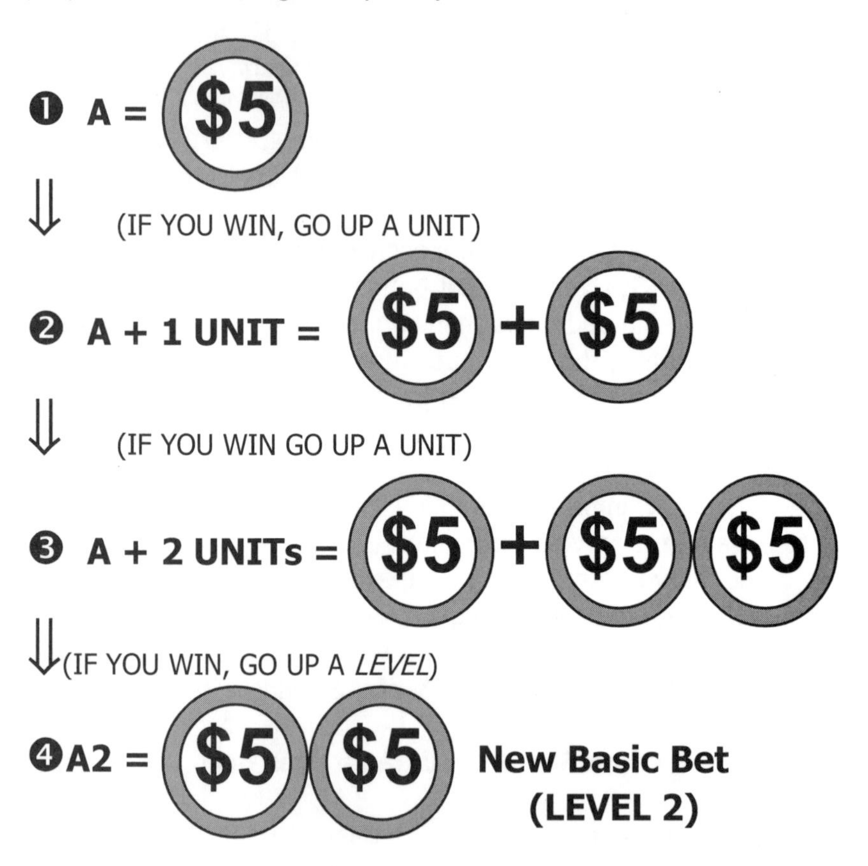

At the end of the example above, "A2" is your NEW, higher, Basic Bet. You are now at a higher Level (Level 2), with a higher starting point, because things are going well. By the way, *if you lose a hand before reaching Step 4, you would go back to betting*

*your **Basic Bet** of 1-UNIT.*

If you decide even before you get to Step 4 that it's obvious you're sitting at a good table, you should raise your **Basic Bet** to 2 Units (two $5 chips), and move up to LEVEL 2, Step 1. Perhaps the dealer's been busting more than usual, after getting a higher than average number of weak up cards. The point is, once you master this system, you can jump up or jump down a Level, with proper discretion.

How To Decide When to Raise Your Basic Bet

When and how you raise your Basic Bet depends upon how the cards are breaking. You must determine this for yourself. Are the cards:

- ♥ **Great:** (during play, you're winning a great majority of hands and you're going way up in chips) – go to Level 3.
- ♥ **Good:** (you're moving ahead steadily but not too quickly) – go to Level 2.
- ♥ **Neutral:** (you have the same number of chips you came with, the cards are neither decisively in your favor nor the dealer's) — stay at Level 1.
- ♥ **Bad:** (you're going down in chips, or staying down a bit) – stay at Level 1.
- ♥ **Horrible:** (you're declining rapidly) – stay at Level 0.

When you first arrive at a table, or after a shuffle, consider the cards "neutral," until the **personality of the cards** reveals itself.

The THREE LEVELS of Basic Bets:

Level 1

Your lowest betting level is Level 1. You're going to want to start here if you've just moved to a new table, the cards have just been shuffled, or if the cards are neutral (you're neither losing nor winning).

The key part of the **3-Level, Notch-Up, Notch-Down Bet Management System** is the use of this minimal level to reduce your risk. If, during uncertain times or bad flows of cards, you go down to Level 1, but keep your betting level at Levels 2 or 3 during good times, you will accomplish three things:

❶ You will minimize your exposure to losses on a rare losing day.
❷ You will minimize the attrition caused by losing hands on a winning day.
❸ You will increase your odds of winning – although you expect to win about 50% of the time, you are making sure that most of those wins will be with higher bets than the bets made during losing streaks. Your gains, with winning hands, will be double or more, on average, than your losses, with losing hands.

OK. So you will have 3 betting Levels, and, within those levels, 3 progressive Steps. Here's how Level 1 works:

- **Step 1: Your Basic Bet = 1 Unit:**

Keep your bet at 1-UNIT unless and until you win a hand.

This will, in a sense, be Level 0. It will, in and of itself, tip you off to a horrible table. Why? If you have never been able to go beyond this step, if you have never had more than one chip in your betting spot during your stay at a table, this chip is telling you that you have not yet won a hand.

Keep careful track of how many hands in a row that you must place 1 Unit bets. Lose 6 hands in a row, and it's time to move to a different table.

If, however, you win a hand, you move up to Step 2, placing the chip you've won on top of your Step 1 bet:

- **<u>Step 2: Basic Bet + 1 Unit</u>:**

If you lose the next hand or push, return to **Step 1**. *Otherwise, if you win the next hand,* take one of the chips you've won and stack it with your bankroll of chips. You've now broken even, and you're playing with the house's money. Put the other chip you won on top of your bet, so your bet for the next hand is now 3 UNITS:

- **<u>Step 3: Basic Bet + 2 Units</u>:**

If you lose the next hand or push, return to Step 1. Otherwise, *if you win the next hand, YOU'RE APPARENTLY AT A GOOD TABLE.*

Take all of the chips you've just won and stack them on your bankroll of chips. Take one of the 3 chips or Units off your bet.

You are now "notching up" to Level 2, Step 1. Your **Basic Bet** is now 2 Units.

In notching-up your **Basic Bet** to a higher level, you are getting more money on the table in what you now believe to be a "good" situation.

Level 2: When The Cards Are Good

This is the level you'll want get to as soon as possible. As long as

a table gives you a good amount of wins, you want to keep your bets above your minimum, defensive level, Level 1.

Here's how to bet when the cards are good:

- **Step 1: Your Basic Bet = 2 Units:**

Your **Basic Bet** is now 2 Units. Keep it there if you lose or push. If you lose twice in a row, go back to **Level 1, Step 1** (and go back to playing with a 1-Unit **Basic Bet**). *If, instead, you win,* put one of the chips you've won on your bankroll stacks, and place the other on top of your **Basic Bet**, now making your bet 3 UNITS:

- **Step 2: Basic Bet + 1 Unit:**

If you lose the next hand or push, return to **Step 1** of this Level. Otherwise, *if you win the next hand,* take two of the chips you've won and secure them on your bankroll stack, and place the other chip on top of your bet, which now becomes 4 UNITS:

- **Step 3: Basic Bet + 2 Units:**

If you lose the next hand or push, return to **Step 1** of this LEVEL. Otherwise, *if you win the next hand,* it's obvious you're onto a "great" flow of cards, so SKIP TO **Level 3**, **Step 1**.

Level 3: When the Cards Are Great

Boy, you really want to have maximum bets down on the table when things are going great! However, don't get overheated! We'll raise our **Basic Bet** to 3 Units here, and that's the maximum **Basic Bet** I recommend that you play. If you have to double, split or a wondrous combination of both, you'll have a lot of money on the table on one bet.

Here's how to bet when the cards are great:

- <u>**Step 1: Your Basic Bet = 3 Units:**</u>

Your **Basic Bet** is now 3 Units. *If you lose one hand or push*, keep your bet the same. *If you lose two hands in a row*, go back to **Level 2, Step 1**. *If you WIN*, stash 2 of the winning chips and use the other chip to raise your bet by 1 Unit:

- <u>**Step 2: Basic Bet + 1 Unit:**</u>

If you lose the next hand or push, return to **Step 1** of this Level. *If you lose two hands in a row, return to **Step 1** of **Level 2**.* Otherwise, *if you win the next hand*, add 3 of the winning chips to your bankroll stack and use the other chip to raise your bet by 1 Unit:

- **Step 3: Basic Bet + 2 Unit Level:**

If you lose the next hand or push, return to **Step 1** of this Level. *If you lose two hands in a row, return to Step 1 of Level 2.* Otherwise, *if you win the next hand,* put all of the chips you've won on your "stash" and keep your bet the same (**Basic Bet** + 2 Units) until you lose; then, go back to **Step 1** of this Level.

Boy this is REALLY an unusually great table!!! It'd be rare if you got this far, but I've seen it happen. Meantime, you can cycle through Steps 1 and 2 of Level 3 whether or not you get to Step 3, so long as you don't encounter two losses in a row.

Take a moment here to reflect on what I have had you do. Look at Step 3 above. You are up to a $25 bet. I am essentially getting you to play at a higher minimum bet level than you might normally feel comfortable with, by notching your bets up in a conservative fashion.

In addition, notice, also, that you are reaping a high percentage of your profits from any winning hand, once you get up to Levels 2 and 3. You are stashing a majority of your winning chips. This, too, increases your odds of coming out ahead.

OK. So, you've now seen how high your bets will get, in the best of situations. Now, to SOME of you, the betting spread (the range, from low to high) might not seem to be enough. But – consider two things.

Number one, if you faced your maximum betting situation – where you split your cards 4 times, and doubled on every one of those hands – your bet, with this system, at a $5 table, at Level 3, Step 3, would have your total bet up to $200. I think many of you

in that situation will have a split second reaction of "omigod!" before you (hopefully) calm down and play the hand out as you should. That's one reason why the average player should not place any higher than $25 bets.

Number two, the quickest way to being barred from a casino is to increase your bets too dramatically. You don't want to win the battle and lose the war. This betting system will prevent you from drawing too much heat.

The wonderful thing about the **3-Level, Notch-Up, Notch-Down Bet Management System** is that, while it's conservative, it gets your bet up to a healthy level, for maximum profits. Plus, the proof is in the pudding – it works *great!*

Don't Panic And Avoid Good Moves

NOW, ALTHOUGH I TALK ABOUT PLAYING CONSERVATIVELY, LET ME MAKE THIS CLEAR – THAT DOES NOT MEAN YOU SHOULD PLAY SCARED. DON'T GET SCARED AND TURN DOWN OPPORTUNITIES TO DOUBLE DOWN OR SPLIT, NO MATTER WHAT YOU HAVE ON THE TABLE, SO LONG AS THE TABLE IS GOOD OR GREAT. THAT'S HOW YOU MAKE DRAMATIC GAINS!

OK. So, what happens when the cards are neutral, bad or horrible?

When the Cards are Neutral or Bad

In the normal flow of things, you will run into some moderately crummy cards, and your bankroll or winnings might begin to go down. Go back to **Level 1** and follow its steps.

Level 0: When the Cards are Horrible

If you run into a sudden "buzzsaw," losing hand after hand, *you should think in terms of finding a better table.*

In the meantime, if you've decided to play another hand or two, here's what you should do (see next page):

Steps 1, 2 & 3: Your Basic Bet = 1 UNIT AT ALL TIMES

ALWAYS keep your bet at the 1-Unit level with horrible cards. Do **NOT** raise your bet at any time. Get your feet ready to move your body to another table. (See pages 123 and 125 for my **6-Unit Cheat-Proof Rule**.)

How to Adjust the Method for a Crowded Pitch Game

The **3-Level, Notch-Up, Notch-Down Bet Management System** needs some adjustment at 1- and 2-deck tables, especially crowded ones, where you only get 2 to 4 hands before the dealer reshuffles. Obviously, you're not going to get to progress through very many notch-up steps before the next shuffle.

So, here's what you'll have to do:

❶ If the cards are breaking well and the **personality of the cards** doesn't change much from shuffle to shuffle, follow the steps of **Level 2**, for a "good" table.
❷ If the cards have been dynamite, and you've noticed the character doesn't change much with each shuffle, go up to **Level 3**, but quickly notch down to **Level 2**, or even **Level 1**, if you experience two or more consecutive losses.

When You Should LEAVE a Casino

At some point, you need to put on the brakes and leave the casino.

Here are the primary reasons you should stop playing and head for the door (see top of the next page):

- You've won a good deal of chips (at least 20 times your minimum, 1-Unit bet), and the card flow has changed for the worse. You've lost three hands in a row, or three out of the last 4 hands.
- You're up more than 10 Units, but, after two hours of choppy play, you're tired and you're not on a winning streak.
- You've finally returned to neutral after a long struggle back from a down cycle.
- **You've lost 6 Units within a dozen or less hands of sitting at a table**. I call this my **6-Unit Cheat-Proof Rule.**
- You've lost roughly 20 Units, you've been at the casino for an hour or two, winning streaks are hard to come by and it isn't likely things will change for the better. This is my **20-Unit Down-And-OUT-Rule**.
- After a winning streak, a pit boss suddenly takes an "interest" in you and directs the dealer to inflict countermeasures against you. *Especially pay attention to this!!!*

The point is, ***winning cycles don't grow on trees***. You're only likely to see one or two major winning cycles during an average trip to the casino (if you limit the time you spend there as I advise). If you've passed gains of 10 times your minimum bet, don't leave without taking home your winnings. Remember the **First Principle of Winning at Blackjack**: be happy with your gains, no matter how meager they might be.

Your one winning cycle of the day might be one long steady climb that suddenly changes, turning into a steady loss of hands, at which point you should leave.

Or, suddenly – in no time (perhaps within 15 minutes of entering the casino) — you've got a winning stack of chips anywhere from 20 times your minimum bet, to, perhaps, 40 times or even more on an extraordinary occasion. *Then* you run into several losses within 4 or 5 hands. THAT's when you leave.

Or, you've been unable to go on any protracted winning streak, you're even, or a bit down after two hours of play, and the cards just won't break in your favor. You leave.

You get the idea.

Knowing when to leave is the most important thing I will teach you. It will greatly contribute to making you a winner. (And watch how surprised everyone seems to be when you walk out a winner!)

How To Know When to Take Your Winnings Home

The hardest thing to do is to leave when you're ahead. You keep thinking you're going to win even more. That's when greed starts to kick in and you're about to make some costly mistakes.

The other night, going up more than $100 after only 15 minutes or so at a $5 table, I knew it was time to go, and I forced myself to walk away. But part of me wanted to keep playing. I love the game, and HAVING to leave after only 15 minutes of fun seemed almost unfair. A new dealer had come in, I'd lost the first three hands, and the small casino didn't have another pitch game table open, where I prefer to play. Their shoe games contained too many decks – 6 – for me to want to play there. I left.

You must get used to that fact – the winnings sometimes come right away. If you don't know enough to leave, you'll throw your winnings back and get very depressed as your chips go into a swoon and you realize how stupidly you've been playing. A smart player refuses to play foolishly.

Stack Your Chips My Way!!!

In always stacking my chips with the **Strategic Stacking** method – in 5-chip, $25 piles – as I have advised you to do, I always know what I have. I will set aside my gains in 5-chip stacks in an area to my left that symbolically indicates to me that these chips are "saved." As I win more and more, I add stacks of chips to the area I've reserved for my "saved" winnings. I tell myself, OK, if I start to go down, this is what I will bring home – I will leave before I get down to these chips.

You should start doing this when you reach 10 UNITS of winnings ($50 at our $5 table). You go up to $65, let's say, but come back down to that winnings level of $50 — LEAVE.

If you surpass 15 UNITS in winnings ($75), raise your mental marker to that level, and make sure you go home with at LEAST that amount in winnings.

Keep raising your mental marker every 5 to 10 additional UNITS in winnings and you'll have a system of checks and balances going for you, so you'll always leave a winner.

Don't forget – this is not a game that will make you rich at the $5 minimum bet level. So, don't get greedy like most players and expect to make a lottery-sized fortune at any one sitting — *10 to 40 UNITS is your most likely "take" on any winning occasion.*

Conversely, don't let your LOSSES ever exceed your typical one-day "take." That way, your winning days will outnumber your losing days, and your losses will not overtake your winnings.

While, in testing this book, I did on one occasion fall to $125 (25 times my 1-unit bet), that was on an occasion I discovered that the dealer was cheating and I promptly left the casino, never to return there. Losing when the dealer is cheating is a foregone conclusion. I will help you spot and avoid these rare rogue dealers in a later chapter.

Leaving if your losses mount to roughly 20 units, is a good rule to use, to keep a losing day to a minimum. Some days you might want to leave BEFORE you get that low, if you've played a couple of hours, and your losses, whatever they are, seem insurmountable. Or, as I said above, you might want to leave if you've gone down 6 units within a dozen or less hands upon arriving at the casino, and you're not sure if you can EVER win there – I don't call that my **6-Unit Cheat-Proof Rule** *for no reason!*

I once went to a small casino I'd been to only once before. On my prior visit I'd gotten the impression that no one could win there. But I thought, since I had some time to kill, and since I had become pretty good at spotting dirty tricks, I might as well conduct a research project for this book.

I took out only $30 (normally I give the dealer $100, but I was wary of this casino), and sat down at the only table that was

open. (There were only two tables open!) There was just one other player, whom I am now convinced was a casino employee pretending to be a player – a *shill*. The dealer was returning the cards to the shoe, apparently having shuffled them before I arrived, and she appeared ready to deal the cards as soon as I got to her table.

In sitting down, I disobeyed two of my rules. I didn't wait and watch how the cards were breaking. And I sat at a table with too few players (you shouldn't play at a table unless there are at *least* 2 other players there, to maximize the favorable break of the cards). I could have saved myself some money. I will never make those mistakes again!

I don't remember exactly how many hands were played. No more than a dozen or so. This dealer got TWO Blackjacks within the first FOUR hands, and, miraculously, kept pulling scores of 20 and 21. I noticed there seemed to be a torrent of 10s, mixed with an occasional lower card, and then a torrent of low cards began. I only had one or two good hands (two 10s each time), but I won only one of those hands! In fact, I think I won only 2 hands the entire (brief) time. *The dealer never busted.*

In hindsight, because the dealer frequently won by just one point, and the cards seemed to follow a pattern of having been set up beforehand (they "smelled"), I believe what I was facing was a **cooler deck**. That's a set of cards pre-arranged by the dealer to beat a certain arrangement of players (in this case, it was an apparent trap for the straggling lone player who might walk into this dead casino).

I've gotten to the point where I can smell when something's wrong, and so I got up after going down 5 chips in less than 5 minutes, as I have advised you to do. After I brought my sixth chip to the cashier (who seemed surprised and annoyed that I did not BET my last chip), I walked out, and I will never play at that casino again.

I left, very pleased at how well my **6-Unit Cheat-Proof Rule** had worked. If you can keep your losses way down on a bad day,

you're going to do great.

What You Might Expect to *Lose* Without This System

I recently encountered an attractive young woman who moved to a table where I was playing. After awhile, I asked her how she was doing. "I'm down 2 *thousand* dollars," she responded dejectedly. I didn't know what to say at that point and never did say anything more to her than "oh my," or something like that. She didn't seem like the sort of person who could afford to lose that kind of money. That's what happens when you don't learn to play properly.

Don't Panic and Act Out of Desperation

It's the low cycles that cause the most problems for players and lead many to dig a hole too deep for themselves. They don't have or stick to a good system, and then they play from desperation when they see losses mount. They don't know when to leave. They don't recognize when a losing streak is a temporary and normal part of the game that will give way to a winning cycle with persistence, and when it's NOT and it's time to leave.

So, when they start to go down, they panic and irrationally throw large bets on the table, thinking "next bet, my luck will change, next bet my luck will change."

The Dangerous Small Martingale System

That's akin to what's called the Small Martingale System, where players try to recover their losses by putting down bets that exceed the amount that they've lost.

Let's do the math on this one so you never attempt to do this:

OK, you lose a $5 bet. So, thinking you're very smart, you put down $10 on the next bet.

You think "My luck's gonna change, so by increasing my bet to $10, I'll make up my $5 loss and win $5 more!" But, you wind up

losing that hand. So, with the same philosophy in mind, you put down a $20 bet. Oops! You lose that bet, too.

OK, so you think: "my luck's really due to change now!" and you put down a $40 bet, which, upon losing, leads to an $80 bet.

Your heart starts to pound. That's a lot of dough to you. That hand, you draw two 8s and want to split. Now you have $160 on one bet, and you draw another 8. Split again? You have to! A 16 is no good, and you believe that splitting 8s here is a good move.

Now you have $240 on one hand, and you draw a 3 on the first 8. Double? You realize that it's the right move, and so, in a sense, you have to!

Now you have $320 on the table. On one hand. Lose this, and you might run up against a $500 maximum bet limit, on your next hand. CAN'T HAPPEN? I've SEEN it happen!

You get the idea. *You get into dangerous territory very fast with this method and, believe me, the losses can mount very, very rapidly*. DON'T EVER TRY THIS. Especially in today's modern casino environment.

NEVER, NEVER, NEVER bet more money than the minimum table bet when the table is horrible. *NEVER, NEVER, NEVER play out of desperation, or allow losses to grow so large they frighten you.* Sometimes the cards just refuse to break well for you, no matter what table you sit at, and you have to know when to call it quits.

One of the purposes of this book is to teach you how to avoid such pitfalls and play a safe, conservative game that minimizes your exposure to losses.

The Myth of The High Roller

I was in Las Vegas recently when I saw one of those notorious high rollers attempt the Small-Martingale scheme at one of the Strip's most posh casinos.

He was at a $100 minium table, playing the dealer one-on-one. He placed a $200 bet, and the dealer drew a face card as his

up card. The dealer won the round, and the player upped his bet to $300. The player must have been thinking: "I'm due for a win. I'll win back the $200 I lost, and make $100 on top of that with the next hand!"

The dealer once again drew a face card as his up card, and the man lost that hand, too.

His next bet was $1,000. He must have been thinking: "OK, now I'm REALLY due for a win. I'll win back the $500 I lost, and win $500 on top of that!"

The dealer drew an Ace as his up card. You guessed it. The man lost this round, too.

Now, high rollers have this mystique about them. People often assume they're the better players, which isn't always true. People also often assume that these guys can afford to risk incurring huge losses. Often, that isn't true, either.

Well, after this guy lost the $1,000 bet, he looked as if someone had hit him in the gut and knocked the wind out of him. The dealer picked up on it, and actually stopped dealing for a second, attempting to make small talk. He must have felt sorry for the guy on some level.

This player, through his faulty betting system, was playing blackjack like it was a game of roulette, a game of chance, instead of a game of probabilities.

The lessons are clear:

If your bet management system is overly aggressive and based on hunches rather than sound thinking, it doesn't matter what card strategy or system you're using – you're going to wind up a big loser.

Plus – don't become overawed by the big shots. Their style is not to be emulated. Unless, of course, you're a millionaire, and $1,000 means nothing to you.

Also – pay attention to what the dealers are getting as up cards and what scores they reach. These could be red flags, as you will see later, in Chapter 9, on the X Factor. This high roller was oblivious to obvious warning signals you should become aware of.

The story you just read is true, and could happen to you. Don't repeat this man's mistakes!

Life Imitates Art

If you saw Robert de Niro play a casino boss in the wonderful movie "Casino," you might remember the end where he refers to kids playing in some Las Vegas kiddy place, while their Moms and Dads "drop their house payment in the casino."

It's no joke. One of the most common mistakes players make is that they do not know when to stop.

In fact, de Niro comments earlier in the movie that his job, as a casino boss, is "to keep the players playing."

"The more they play, the more they lose," he intones.

Yep. That validates what I've told you about limiting the time you play; taking home your winnings; limiting your losses; and, knowing when to leave.

You are still not ready to enter a casino.

CARD COUNTING & CARD OBSERVATION

To card count or not to card count? That is the question. And, if you *do* card count, what does it tell you? Can you really base your betting management on what it indicates?

I'll answer these questions shortly, but, first, let me make it clear that you do not *need* card counting to be become a regular winner. When you are ready, however, you might want to use card counting to make some of the trickier card decisions you'll face.

Keeping Track Of The Cards

As you found out in Chapter 1, one of the three primary factors that make blackjack a winnable game is its predictability. It's very similar in that regard to the game of Bridge, where, by keeping track of every visible card played, players try to predict how well they will do.

If you're playing a 1-deck game, for example, and you've seen three Aces in one round, you know there's just one Ace left. Or, perhaps you've seen ten 10s in one round. Then, only 6 remain. That can be powerful information.

The difference, in the game of blackjack, is that you don't have to memorize every card's suit, nor do you usually need to remember most cards' specific values. You don't need to remember, for example that the 2 of *spades* was played. You'll generally be more interested in determining what the relative proportion of high and low cards is — amongst the cards that have been dealt, and the cards that remain.

One way or another, however, you'll want to become adept at keeping track of the cards.

If card counting seems daunting to you, I will offer you an alternative way of accomplishing the same task, later in this chapter. That's my **Card Observation** method.

Many of the players who have studied with me have said they feel more comfortable using **Card Observation**. It's easier than card counting, and works great.

And, by the way, if you choose to be a card counter, you

should still use **Card Observation** too, for the added information it provides.

The Limitations Of Card Counting

Card counting is just one of a half dozen tools that will help you make card strategy decisions in card situations that require a choice of 2 or 3 possible moves. It's a good thing to have in your arsenal but – here's another place I differ with some others — I believe that *it is NOT a great tool to use to decide how to bet.* I will explain this later on.

In fact, I'd like to debunk the myth of card counting as "god," in this day and age of multi-deck games and casino countermeasures. To me, it's not even in the top eight most important tools I will teach you in *Blackjack The SMART Way*, in making you a winner, which are:

❶ My method of picking a good casino. If you're in a bad casino, card counting can't undo the damage.

❷ The *Blackjack The SMART Way* method of picking a good table. If you are at a bad table, card counting can't make you a winner.

❸ My rules with regard to knowing when to leave both a table and a casino. The card count doesn't speak to this at all.

❹ The **X Factor** (explained in the following chapter).

❺ **Card Observation**, which you will soon learn. The card count will mislead you at times — for example, it can be "neutral" in situations where the important 10-point cards are actually depleted; **Card Observation** won't let you miss that fact. **Card Observation** also tends to be better at predicting what the crucial dealer hole card might be.

❻ *Blackjack The SMART Way's* perspective on which up cards are in your favor. If you play these wrong, it doesn't matter what the card count is.

❼ **The 3-Level, Notch-Up, Notch-Down** betting system, along with its companion money management method

(Chapter 7). This is much more instrumental, actually, in helping you to surmount the odds and become a winner.

❽ A complete understanding of the mathematical foundation underlying the game, which enables you to get a grip on the odds of your winning a particular move, and calculate them, on the fly. Many times, it's the probabilities of the various choices that you're facing that will rule your decision.

In my second book, *Cutting Edge Blackjack*, we'll add other concepts that are also more important than card counting, such as **The Circle of 13** (also found, in part, on my audio book *Preparing YOU To WIN*), the **Tell Numbers**, and much more. But that's for when you're ready to deal with lots of numbers.

Card counting is a useful tool, but it is NOT the dominant tool you should rely upon to manage your card or betting strategies.

Card Counting Can Actually Spoil Your Game

Another warning — be careful before you attempt card counting at the casino. It can be confusing and misleading, not to mention distracting, for beginners or even intermediate players. This practice is really only for advanced players.

If you try to card count before you're ready to, you will undoubtedly find that while you might be able to keep a good count, you are no longer able to keep track of the game as well, which I believe is more important! Considerations such as how the dealer's doing and how you're doing are much more important to how you play the game (that'll be covered in the next chapter, about the **X Factor**).

Like everything else in this book, you must practice card counting at home until it's second nature to you. You'll know when you feel capable of pulling it off at the casino. It's especially important that you get to the point that you can do this seamlessly, without tipping off the casino that you're doing it – they don't like card counters!

That Being Said...

In spite of all this, card counting can be the icing on the cake – helping you with an occasional hand. So, once your skills are honed and you are verging on becoming an advanced player, you will then be ready to tackle this practice.

I certainly don't mean to throw out this aid. I just want you to put it in its proper perspective.

The Basic Premise of Card Counting

Now, here's how card counting works. Those who are uninitiated are often unduly afraid of attempting to learn this, because they think it involves memorizing every card that was played — their point values and suits. No, card counting is an approximate method that attempts to predict in general what cards are likely to come next – high or low. That's what you're most concerned about: will you get a high card or an Ace when you need one, or a low card when you don't (or vice versa)?

The basic premise is that, once the cards are shuffled, the high and low cards generally balance each other out. Yes, there are 13 cards, but, in my system, we're NOT going to include Aces in the main count – Aces can either be high or low cards. So, from our perspective, the 6 high cards that remain – the 8, 9 and four 10-pointers – indeed balance out the 6 low cards we're concerned about — the 2, 3, 4, 5, 6 and 7. We're breaking down the cards into balanced halves that will be meaningful.

The phenomenon that makes card counting telling is that, once the cards are in play, this balance often gives way to situations where either high or low cards have been played in greater numbers than their counterpart. (Not always – sometimes the cards, or, in this case, the "count," will return to a more balanced, or neutral situation.)

If you can quantify that frequent imbalance in terms of a numerical value, then it can be useful. Then, you'll know whether

more high cards have been played than low cards or vice versa, relatively speaking, and to what extent the symmetry is off. Whatever has been depleted is less likely to come next.

OK! Let's see an example of how this works.

Let's pretend for a moment that, instead of 52 cards made up of 4 sets of 13 different cards, we have just 10 cards in our game, and here's what they are (see the illustration below):

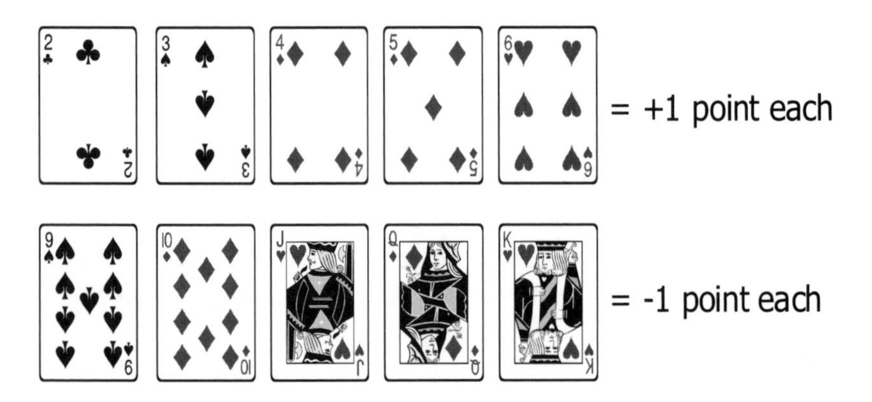

As you can see above, in our make-believe game, 2s through 6s comprise our five low cards, and 9s and 10s are our five high cards.

Also as indicated above, we will arbitrarily assign each of our low cards, a value of **+1**. To balance these out, we will then assign each of the high cards an opposite equal value of **–1**.

Since you have five each of the low and high cards, they balance each other out in *number*, AND in arbitrarily assigned *points*. Adding the points assigned to the five low cards, they total **+5**, using our counting system. Adding the points assigned to the five high cards, they total **-5**.

OK, let's start our game, which will follow the rules of casino blackjack.

Now, let's say you're playing alone against the dealer, and these were the cards that were dealt (see the top of the next page):

DEALER

YOU

OK, so there are four cards, all of which, being high, carry a **–1** point value; so the card count is now:

$$4 \text{ times } -1 = -4$$

What does this tell you?

That *low cards are most likely to be coming,* because a disproportionate number of high cards were played, resulting in a high negative count.

You can be especially certain here, because our little game contains only 10 cards. With 52 or more cards, the same principles apply with regard to your ability to predict what's coming next, based on the card count, but your certainty level will be lower than presented in this example.

In the good old days, when all blackjack games consisted of 1 deck and all the cards were dealt, card counting's certainty level would get especially good toward the bottom of the deck, and smart players made a killing off this factor. Hence, the development of countermeasures such as re-shuffling well before all cards are dealt, and multi-deck games. It's still a worthwhile tool, however. Stick with me here.

One more example.

Let's say, instead, that the following cards were dealt in the first round:

DEALER

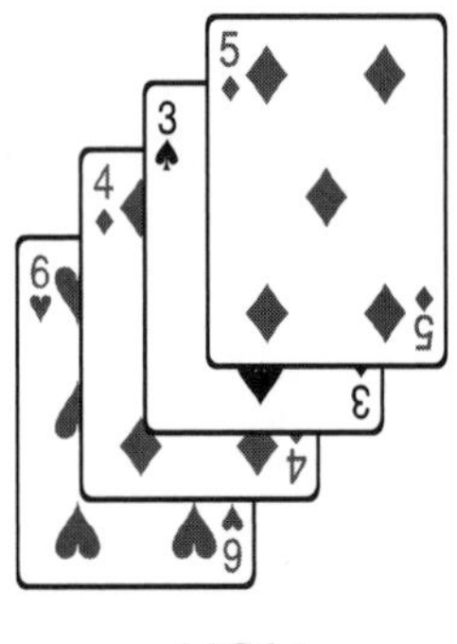

YOU

In this case, your hand consists of four low cards, for a total of **+4**, and the dealer's hand has two high cards, for a total of **–2**, making the count:

$$+4 \text{ plus } -2 = +2$$

That tells you a higher proportion of high cards than low cards are due. Why? The "**+**" indicates that more LOW cards were played out than high cards in the game so far, and the number, "**2**" tells you by how much. So, the cards remaining are now rich in high cards. Inspecting the cards we have left, you will find this

is true. There are 3 high cards to one low card. Your prediction is right.

However – it's still a mystery as to *when* that *low* card will be dealt, or the torrent of high cards. You only know that, if you draw a card right now it would most *LIKELY* be a high card (from a *probability* standpoint).

And *that's* how card counting works. I think you can see how you would find it useful in making card strategy decisions.

But What Makes Low Cards +1?

One reason why low cards are assigned a positive point value is that card counters consider it a good thing when low cards are played out, making the remaining undealt cards richer in high cards. It's a positive situation, because high cards are what the player wants – especially 10s. They combine to form hands that add up to great scores, and they are often needed as hit cards when doubling or splitting. It's also a positive situation when low cards are played out because low cards especially benefit the dealer. The dealer will bust far less when their hit cards are of smaller point values.

High cards are assigned a *negative* point value, because card counters consider it a negative thing when high cards are depleted. In that case, it becomes harder to successfully double or split in certain situations, limiting your money-making opportunities. It's also a negative situation because, with less high cards, the dealer will bust less.

Once again, *card counting gets more reliable the deeper you get into the cards*. Keep that in mind. Another reminder: you should assume the count to be neutral (zero) when cards are first dealt after a shuffle. *When the cards are neutral, be sure to follow Basic Strategy.*

Pick A Method, Any Method

Card counting was invented decades ago. Everyone who has

come up with their own system since the concept's inception is simply attempting to fine tune that brilliant idea. My system is no different. I've added what I consider subtle improvements to come up with a counting method I believe is most effective.

The system I developed was inspired by one recommended by Dr. Edward Thorp, the MIT math professor and author of one the first successful blackjack methods, in the early 1960s.

The All-Inclusive Counting System

To be useful to us, our card counting system needs to keep track of all of the cards. That's the beauty of my **All-Inclusive Counting System** – it tells us a lot more information than a system that leaves out one or more cards. And it breaks the low and high cards into halves that make a lot of sense when we're considering whether to double down, split or hit our hand.

OK – here's how it works. It's easy.

You will assign a point value of **+1** or **–1** to all of the cards *except* the Aces. You must count the Aces separately. You should know at any time how many you've seen, and how many remain unplayed. For example, with a 2-deck pitch game, if 4 Aces have been played, you know there are 4 left. We'll talk about Aces more in a moment.

You'll *add* a **+1** to our count every time you see a 2- through 7-point card. You'll *subtract* a point every time you see an 8- through a 10-pointer. (Note: totals might go into negative numbers, such as "**-1**," "**-2**," etc.)

You will then take whatever ***total*** *you arrive at, and use it, based on how high its numerical value is, to analyze: 1) how well you can predict whether low or high cards are coming (the higher the number, the greater the imbalance between the high and low cards, and the more accurate your card count becomes as a predictor); and, 2) how, therefore, you want to play your cards*. You'll see how this works, in Chapter 10.

(FYI – The card count total you arrive at through the method I've described above is known as a *running count*. In the First Edition of *Blackjack The SMART Way,* I had you dividing the running count by the number of decks that remained, to use that

number, which is known as *the true count*. However, players reported getting confused – after dividing the running count properly to get the true count, they started counting using the true count, instead of reverting back to the running count. So, I am not recommending anymore that you attempt to use the true count. It's not necessary. The only thing you have to remember, then, in keeping a running count, is that it's more "valid" the more cards that have played. In other words, a +6 running count will not mean as much at the start of a 4-deck game as it will once you get toward the end of the cards that remain unplayed. Then, the concentration of high cards will be higher relative to the number of unplayed cards, and your count will become that much more significant and reliable.)

OK? So here's how the *Blackjack The SMART Way* **All-Inclusive Counting System** divides the cards, with their valuations:

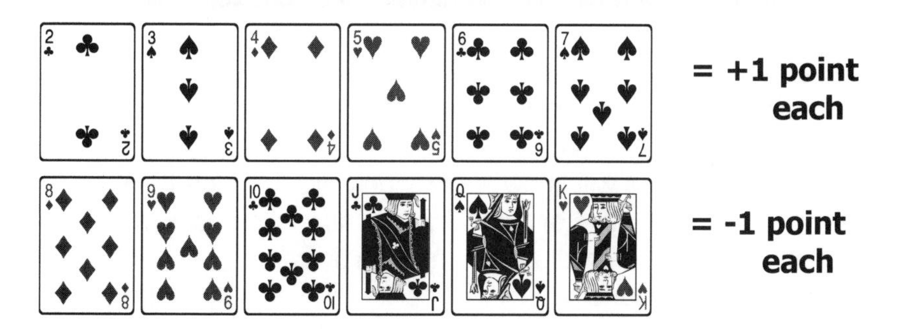

Notice how the six lower cards are balanced out by the six higher cards. Because the Aces can behave as either high or low cards (therefore fitting in neither category), you will be counting those separately. They're important to keep track of, however, because of their near-equal importance to both the dealer's hand and yours.

Why Divide The Cards In This Way?

I like my **All-Inclusive Counting System** most, of all of

what are generally called the plus-minus systems, because it separates the cards into what I believe are very logical camps. It puts cards that tend to behave similarly together.

If you need a high card, a 7 won't probably help you. Nor will the 7 be a very strong card for the dealer as a hole card, in combination with most up cards. It acts like a weak card, and so it makes sense to make the division there, and group the 7 with the low, weak scoring cards.

Plus – this division makes the count that much more useful:

If you want to double down, any of the cards I've put into the "high cards" category will help you in most doubling situations. Conversely, if 7s or lower value cards are due, you would know it is probably NOT a good time to double down.

If you want to split your cards, you often need to know if the dealer is likely to bust. Well, any two of the cards amongst my set of high cards would bust the dealer's 5 or 6 (except for the unlikely appearance of two 8s – one as the hole card, one as the hit card). Plus, since these high cards are rich in 10s (66% of them are 10s), this grouping is also likely to cause the dealer's 2s through 4s to bust. Conversely, if the low cards (as I've defined them) are due, you will know it's probably NOT a good time to split some of your pairs of like cards, because the dealer will probably not bust with those dealer-friendly cards.

If you must decide whether or not to draw an extra card to your hand, this grouping of the low and high cards will be especially helpful when your hand totals 14 or less. You'd know you could safely hit your hand, if the low cards, as I define them, are due.

Admittedly, this division of the cards won't help you as much when you have a hands that total 15 or 16. But, no grouping will solve all problems all of the time.

Yet, even with your 15, only one of my designated low cards would bust you — the 7. So, my system would still be a good guide. It would tell you that if the high cards are depleted, you'd have an 83% chance of getting a good card, within the group of low cards that are due. That's a pretty strong indicator. And, if

you know Aces are also overdue, you'd have an 86% chance of making the right move with the **All-Inclusive System**.

With your 16, only two of the low cards would hurt you, so you'd still have a 67% probability of getting a good card from amongst that bunch, if you knew that low cards grouped my way were due. And, if your independent count of the Aces showed you the Aces might start of appear as well, then the **All-Inclusive Counting System** low cards would give you a 71% probability of drawing to a winning score. That's not bad.

My System Is Also Revealing About The Dealer's Hand

Now let's say the count is strongly positive when the dealer gets his or her hole card.

With the dealer's strongest up cards of 9 through an Ace, you will know with that count that you are in trouble. Any one of the high cards in the **All-Inclusive Counting System** will combine with those to give the dealer a winning score. The dealer will then likely have a winning score of 17 on up.

With up cards of 7 or 8, that's another matter. Then, you'll know that the dealer at BEST will have a 17 or 18, but possibly less (unless Aces are overdue). You'll know, then, that you have a shot at winning.

(And, as we saw above, my card counting system works well when the dealer has the weakest up cards, too.)

What About The Aces?

Aces have no assigned point value. As I suggested above, you should count them – "1 Ace, 2 Aces, 3 Aces," etc. — separately. Now, Aces amount to just 1 of 13 cards, or less than 8% of the bunch. At any one time, that's not a likely card to get.

However, there are reasons why you would get a handle on the relative depletion or surplus of Aces in the remaining cards, and for two diametrically opposed purposes. Since the Ace is an especially powerful card for the dealer, you want to keep track of

the likelihood of the dealer getting one. Unlike others, I believe it is generally in your favor when Aces are depleted. The dealer's Blackjack is equivalent to the dealer's trump — most everyone loses in that situation. Plus, the Ace, as the dealer's up card, is so strong that it is in the player's interest to see LESS of them!

On the other hand, there are times when you might want to know if an Ace is coming your way. Aces can be great hit cards – say if you're doubling down on a 9 or 10 – and that's why you keep a separate count of how many are left (and when you saw the last one), to give you an idea of the probability of getting one.

So, BEFORE a round begins, you should be encouraged if Aces are depleted. When it's your turn, however, knowing if there's a surplus of Aces might lead you to double where you otherwise would not. The dual nature of the Ace, therefore, poses a conundrum of sorts, but I feel I've placed it in its proper perspective, above.

So, as you can see, Aces are kind of off in their own category. While the high cards as I've designated them benefit the player (especially in doubling and splitting) and the low cards as I've defined them benefit the dealer (in drawing to a winning total, and avoiding busting), the Aces provide a benefit to BOTH the player and the dealer. That's because of their dual nature (from the standpoint of their point value), their potential for forming all-powerful Blackjacks, etc.

The Ace is, however, (unlike the 10s) one of 13 cards. No system can isolate one card, and tell you with certainty when that particular card will come with the next hit card. But, you can "guesstimate" the probability of getting one, based on how many Aces were played, and how long it's been since you've seen an Ace.

The Neutral Count

By the way, there's another, subsidiary reason why counting Aces separately makes good sense. I believe that a card counting system works best when the cards on both sides are equal in

number, thus balancing out to a neutral total count of zero. Our system has six cards in each logical "camp," and so this achieves that goal.

This way, when the count is zero, you then know there are an equal number of high and low cards left. That's important information. It tells you three things:

➊ That you can't predict necessarily which type of card, high or low, will come next.
➋ That you should play according to Basic Strategy, unless **Card Observation** tells you, in spite of the card count, that the 10-point cards are either depleted or overdue (since there are other cards in with the 10s, this situation is possible).
➌ How the dealer up cards are likely to behave (you'll learn about this in the chapter on Advanced Strategy) – in a neutral count, with the cards divided as they are with the *Blackjack The SMART Way* **All-Inclusive Counting System**, you will know that some of the up cards will be more "player friendly," for instance.

What Your Count Tells You

Let's look a little more at how card counting works:

Again, if the point total is positive, it means that more LOW CARDS have been played than HIGH CARDS. If the point total is negative, if means that more HIGH CARDS have been played than LOW CARDS. Your point total will NOT tell you very much at the **+1** or **–1** level, or even the **+2** or **–2** level, but the higher it gets, the more valid it is in predicting what cards are due to come.

That is not to say that, if the count is very positive, stray low cards will not appear in the bunch to come. They will. The reverse is true, too. If the total is very negative, stray high cards will appear in the flood of low cards to come, making card counting an inexact science.

And that's all the information from card counting will tell you – the relative likeliness of what's to come.

Why You'd Be Smart To Play The Pitch Tables

Of course, the count is more valid right off the bat with a 1- or 2-deck games, which feature fewer cards than at the 4-, 6- and 8-deck tables. It goes back to our example above, which contained only 8 cards.

The problem at 1- and 2- deck tables, though, is that the cards are dealt face down, then held in players' hands, and then frequently slipped under players' chips face down, so you can't see many of them when your turn arrives.

How to count there? When you are ready for more advanced concepts, read *Cutting Edge Blackjack* to learn my new, breakthrough method on how to count cards at pitch game tables! (Until then, you'll have to count the cards as they are picked up after a round, using a number that's unfortunately not very valid by the time the dealer's hole card is dealt, or your hit card.)

What Dr. Thorp Had Recommended

In contrast with my **All-Inclusive Counting System**, one system recommended in Edward Thorp's seminal book, *Beat The Dealer,* first printed in 1962, has you counting 2s through 6s as "**+1**" and 10s and Aces as "**-1**." That leaves out the 7s, 8s, and 9s. To me, that's not a complete enough picture. If you're trying to decide whether to hit a 14 against a dealer's 2, for example, an 8 or 9 would bust you just as quickly as a 10. Plus – a 7 would help you, but it's not being tracked. It is easier for beginners to master, but, whether or not it contains enough information to be effective is debatable.

In my humble opinion, I also disagree with including Aces in the point count, because their impact and desirability is very different from the 10s and other high cards. For example, a 10 could provide a winning score when splitting Aces. Drawing an Ace after splitting Aces, though, might provide almost certain disaster, because, in that case, it would add just one point to your total (and many casinos won't let you re-split those Aces). The same problem exists if you have a total of 11, and that's the hard total with which you double the most. The Ace is not the universal good card you want when you're considering double down or splitting that the high cards, with fixed point totals, tend to be.

(I don't mean to single out Dr. Thorp's otherwise excellent book more than any others, except for the reason that so many authors have imitated his thinking, in the books that followed his in the four decades hence.)

No – count the Aces separately, because it helps you in situations I already enumerated earlier.

The Spark For My System

Interestingly enough, on page 84 of *Beat the Dealer*, Dr. Thorp says, when testing his system at a casino, he suddenly VARIED it. You'd really have to be paying close attention to notice this change in thought. He doesn't explain it, nor does he go back and alter what he recommends YOU do with that information. He mentions it in just one sentence:

> "I was using the *variation of the point count* where 2, 3, 4, 5, 6, **7** are +1, 8 is 0, and **9**, 10, A are –1, when they fall."

(I added the Italics and bolded characters above, to bring out my point.)

In essence, he was *abandoning* the system he had recommended earlier, in favor of something he felt gave him more useful information. Here, he includes the 7 and 9, as I suggest you do. But he leaves out the 8, which puzzles me. Why? He also continued to lump the Aces in with the high cards. In any event, this was the sentence that inspired me to come up with the method I now recommend.

In practice, Dr. Thorp's system is much more complicated than I've indicated. He would have you keeping track of exactly how many cards have been played, and then have you divide the count by the number of cards left. You would then use the resulting

fractions as your point counts, and, boy, God bless you if you can do that! I know I can't. That's the case of a genius devising a system only another genius can follow.

Another of Many Alternatives

I'm sure there are many other good card counting systems. The thing is: do they give you the information you want to know? The only other one I will tell you about was the one I used when I first started card counting – a variation of Dr. Thorp's plus-minus system, contained in Edwin Silberstang's book, *The Winners Guide To Casino Gambling.*

In that system, you count 3s through 6s as +1, and 10s as –1. Although incomplete, this is an easy system for beginners. It doesn't give you a complete picture, but it just might work well for you in extreme point count situations.

If You Play A Shoe Game, Be Brilliant

Here's one great way to apply what you've just learned:

There will be times, I know, when you will wind up playing a 4- or 6-deck shoe game (please try NOT to play 8-deck shoe games!).

If you do, try using your skills in a way that I've never noticed anyone else recommending:

1) Get the card count at the moment the dealer's hole card is dealt!
2) Then, use it to figure out what the hole card is likely to be.

To me, the count at the moment the dealer deals his or her hole card is even more important than what the count is when your turn comes up! If you think of it, this is the best way to use card counting!

For example, let's say it's the fourth round following the

shuffle, and the count is –6 when the hole card is dealt. Don't you think it's a good guess the hole card is NOT a 10 in that case? *Pay careful attention to this!!!*

Now, the count likely will be different by the time your turn arrives. THAT count will give you even more information about how to play your cards, now that you know so much about the dealer's. For instance – if the dealer's up card is an 8, you should think twice about hitting your 15 or 16, shouldn't you?

Multi-Deck Headaches

One word of advice: card counting should preferably be done at tables of 4-decks or less. The information it gives you takes a long time to become valid if you're playing against more than 2 decks.

(Think about it: there will come a time when you're ready to play using a true count, where you've got to divide your point total by the number of decks that remain unplayed. So what would a running count of +**4** mean at 6- or 8-deck shoe games? At a 1-deck table, the running count would be the same as the true count. At an 8-deck table, that count of +4 – significant at a 1-deck table, would now be a true count of +1/2!)

Also, because the count becomes more instructional the higher the proportion of played out cards becomes (the more cards you've seen, the better able you are to predict what's left), that's another reason to stick to 1- or 2-deck games, if they're available. This information becomes apparent MUCH sooner than at other tables.

Why NOT To Tie Bets To Count

As I pointed out earlier, some pundits will tell you that, when the count is at least moderately positive – high cards are, in theory, due to come – you should make a significantly bigger bet on the next round. Some will even encourage you to wager the MAXIMUM BET ALLOWED BY THE CASINO.

I'm here to argue that this is very foolish indeed.

Number one, if high cards are due, isn't the dealer is just as likely to get those cards as you, and get a high, winning score? To my mind, that is NOT the time you want more money down!

Number two, the count that you obtain AFTER a round is done does NOT pertain to your next hand. If you were sitting in the first baseman's seat, it might be fairly good at telling you what your first card might be (although card counters warn you not to sit there). It would also say something very general about what the other players and the dealer might get as their first cards. Beyond that, I think you'll agree, the post-round count those pundits want you to use to make your bet would get a bit "old" and inaccurate. I don't know of a count that continues to be terribly relevant 8 or more cards down the road, do you?

Early on in my blackjack playing days I followed these schemes, raising my bet when the count was moderately to very positive, only to lose it when the dealer pulled a strong combination. The added risk was not justified by the results; the implication of the card count seemed like flawed reasoning to me; and, it led to higher losses than I would have had normally, that I then had to make up later. At the very least, it was NOT a conservative way to play.

So, what do we learn from all of this? Should we instead reverse what we were taught by the pundits, and increase our bet when the count is *negative*, when we know that *low cards* are due (with the hope that the dealer will then have a weak up card)? The problem with *that* is, if you double down when low cards are coming, you're less likely to get the 10 or other high cards that might "make" your hand.

No, I think you can see now you'd do best to divorce your card count from your betting management system. Card counting is much more useful as a predictor of what's to come, in the way of the dealer's hole card, or in fine tuning your choice of possible moves, than it is in predicting whether you're going to win the next hand or not.

In *Cutting Edge Blackjack*, I will provide the research data to

back up my assertions above, which more advanced players will want to study. Suffice it to say, the evidence is overwhelming.

And There Are Other Reasons...

I hasten to add that, in the years when I was starting out, I found that, of the many books on blackjack that are out there, there were a few superb books from which there was something to learn. *But the cult of the card-counting-based bet management strategy* always puzzled me. Why did they unfailingly suggest placing huge bets – hundreds, if not thousands of dollars – on one hand?

Number one, the average player cannot afford to bet this amount of money. I feel it's irresponsible in some regard to urge beginners and intermediates to play that way. It leads them to believe there's a great deal of certainty in pursuing what is, in my opinion, a reckless course. Number 2, I believe that it's foolish to risk a fortune on <u>one</u> turn of the cards, when the odds are never close to 100% that you will win that one hand.

I mean, is that really wise? Especially since, with the average favorable hand, your odds of winning will only be in the range of 50 – 60%. At BEST! What about the 40 - 50% of times when that hand loses? Can you afford the loss?

And, finally, increasing your bet significantly when you think you have an edge will only alert the casino bosses that you're a card counter. It's the quickest path to being barred from playing. The days when you could do that and get away with it are long since gone.

Leave The Big Bets To High Rollers

One more point – don't forget: if you are foolish enough to place what for you might be a huge bet on one hand, you might often find that you'll actually need to put much more on the table before your turn is through! You might get a pair of like cards that might sense to split into two hands. Then, you might get

another like card on one or both of those new hands; so, you might want to split those new hands, resulting in your now playing FOUR hands. You now have FOUR TIMES your huge bet on the table. And then, perhaps you might want to double down on at least one of your hands, if not ALL of them! You would then have EIGHT TIMES your huge bet on the table.

Remember – you made that large bet based on the count from the prior round of cards. It's not unlikely, based upon my research data, that your current hand did not live up to your expectations, which you based on what I consider faulty reasoning (if you went with the pundits' advice on making large bets in positive counts).

Some authors talk of winning these risky kinds of bets. You don't hear often of the times they don't. It can be catastrophic for you.

Read Between The Lines

It's interesting to note that one otherwise brilliant author, one of those who talks of making huge bets when his card count indicates 10s and Aces are overdue, admits that he did not put HIS money on the line when he tested out his theories at various casinos. He went to Vegas with friends who were millionaires, to bankroll his game! That way, he could survive the losses his system was incurring, and could then afford to return to play another day.

Few of us have such a luxury. Whereas he tossed off losses of about $10,000 with a shrug, you are unlikely to do the same.

Let's not lose our heads – blackjack, for most players, is *not* a way to get rich.

Sure, if a $1,000 bet means nothing to you, then you make $10,000 to $40,000 or more in one sitting – using the *Blackjack The SMART Way* system. That's doable. But, understand — blackjack's typical "yield" is only large if your bets are large.

Please, leave the big bets to the players with money to burn. Don't mortgage the house to get blackjack money. Play only with

surplus cash, and make bets that are reasonable for you. You will have some losing days, and you must be able to survive them.

Card Counting Is NOT A Precise Predictor

Please realize that card counting is an APPROXIMATION of what's to come — especially in this day and age of multiple decks and partially distributed decks. Why do some people believe it's a science? And you need to see a fair amount of cards before the statistical probabilities really start to become usable.

No player can tell you with certainty *exactly* what card is coming next under today's casino practices. Nor can they predict what your next hand will be before it's dealt. Nor can they predict what the *dealer's* next hand will be – that might be even more important! And yet, isn't that what's being implied?

No matter what the count of the cards is at any time at any table, some players will be doing well, others not so well – so what is it REALLY telling us? How well we might do – the probability of our winning the next hand – is NOT, in my humble opinion, what the card count tells us.

So, if that's true, do you really want to take the bulk of your "stash" and put it all on one hand? C'mon! That's the best way to LOSE a lot of money FAST, become depressed and then get desperate.

At the very least, those risky betting systems are not for the average player. Blackjack, in my opinion, should be kept a form of entertainment for the typical player, and be played conservatively.

An Easy Alternative To Counting: Introducing... Card Observation

If all of this is too much for you, you might do just as well using my **Card Observation** method.

You can often get just as much information from this method as from the more strenuous exercise of counting – sometimes

more. It's really amazing what it tells you about the dealer's hole card and your hit card. Plus – unlike card counting – you can use it to good effect when joining a table between shuffles.

OK, let's do an example. Let's say you have an 11 against the dealer's 8. You want to double down, but you notice that, of the five players who drew extra cards ahead of your turn, four were dealt 10s, and one got a 9. It appears unlikely that you'll now get the 10 you need, nor, perhaps, even a 9. You might wisely then choose to HIT your hand instead. We'll look at some more examples in just a moment.

You'll find that playing by **Card Observation** is not terribly different than card counting. What is has in common is that it measures the relative balance of high and low cards amongst the cards that have been played. It also has as its basis the laws of probability, which enables the player to get a handle on the cards' predictability.

The main difference is that card counting gives you a more complete overview of ALL the cards that have been played, whereas **Card Observation** gives you a more immediate picture of the most recent flow of cards.

Here's How To Do It

OK – here's how to make **Card Observation** work for you. It's a two-part process.

The first thing you'll want to do is guesstimate what the dealer's hole card might be (it is admittedly *guess*-timation, but so is card counting). For this, you have an often-revealing set of indicators – the second set of cards the players are dealt! These cards lead directly up to the dealer's hole card! (See **Illustration 8-1**, on the following page.)

Now, if you've done as I've advised and are sitting in the third baseman's seat or close to it, you will also have as hole-card indicators any hit cards that the players sitting to your right have taken. Those cards have come directly AFTER the dealer's hole card was dealt. So, you'll study these cards for what they might tell you.

Illustration 8-1

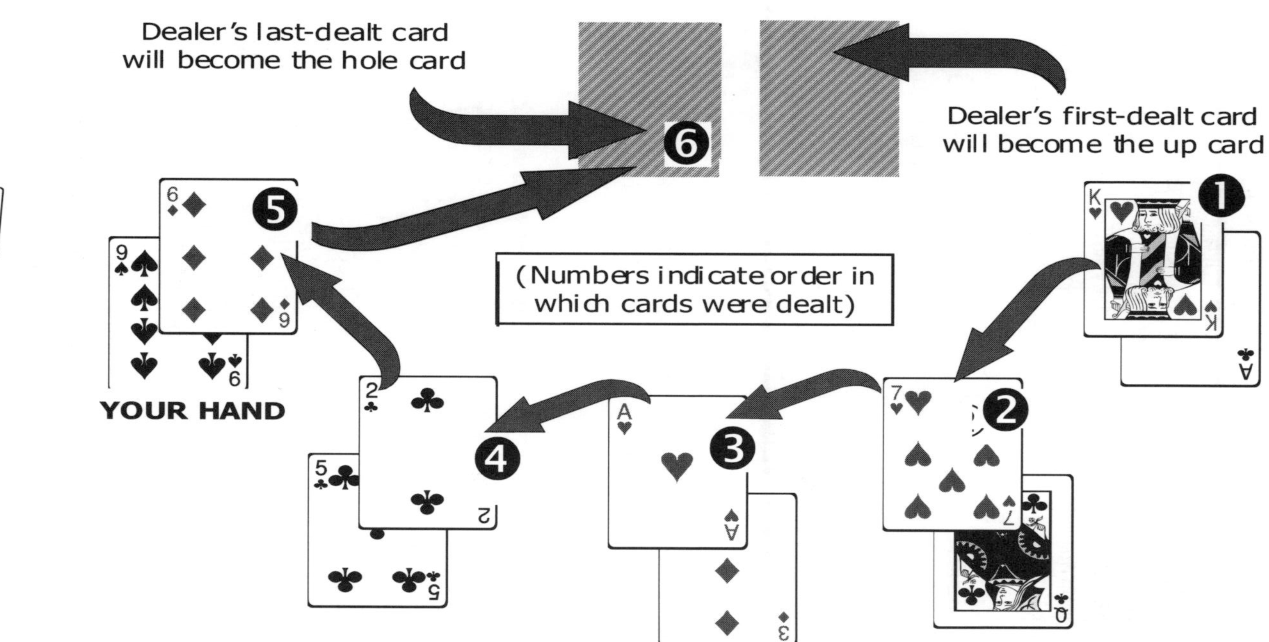

The second thing you'll want to attempt to predict, if you need to take an extra card to improve your hand, is what hit card you will get. That necessitates studying the 10 or so cards that were dealt immediately before your turn arrives.

(If you're at a table where there are only two other players playing, and they don't take hit cards, there might be fewer than 10 cards exposed for your analysis. You can still learn important information from those cards, but, obviously, the more cards, the better. That's another reason to consider playing at a table with more than 2 other players.)

Believe it or not, if you observe carefully and ask the right questions, you will often be able to ferret out the answers you need to know in order to make your best move. Let's see how this works.

Card Observation Involves Asking The Right Questions

OK – you now know what cards you need to analyze to figure out what the dealer's hole card might be, as well as your hit card. What does that tell you? A *lot*, if you know what questions to ask:

1. ***How many of the cards that you are observing are 10s? (Plus — what is the total number of cards?) So...in what proportion have they appeared?*** You'll need the numbers in the first two of these three questions to figure out roughly the percentage of 10s that comprise the cards on the table. Because 4 of the 13 cards in each suit are 10-pointers, comprising 31% of each deck, probability dictates that these cards should show up during the course of play in roughly this proportion. If there were 13 cards on the table that you were analyzing for hole or hit card information, you'd therefore expect approximately four of them to be 10s. If, instead, there are only 10 cards on the table, you would now know that there should be approximately three 10s (because you know that the 10s would then comprise 30% of the cards you're considering, which is roughly what their proportions

should be). OK, so, if the cards you're analyzing contain less 10s than you'd expect, then the card whose value you're trying to predict (the dealer's hole card or your hit card) might very well be a 10. If the 10s, however, are present in their proper proportion, or in greater than normal proportions, then it's likely the card whose value you're trying to predict will NOT be a 10.

2. ***How many of the cards are Aces? (And how long has it been since you've seen an Ace?)*** If an Ace is due, factor it in with the information you have on the 10s. If both are overdue when the hole card was dealt, and if both would combine with the dealer's up card to make a winning total, you must adjust your strategy to assume the dealer indeed has a strong hand. Keep in mind that the normal proportion of Aces amongst the cards is 1 in 13: 1/13 = 7.69%, less than 8%. That's not much. So, if there is an Ace amongst the cards dealt in the current round, it's highly unlikely the hole card, or your hit card would be another Ace.
3. ***How many of the cards you're analyzing are not 10s or Aces? In what proportions have they appeared?*** The 2s, 3s, 4s, 5s, 6s, 7s, 8s and 9s – like the 10s and Aces – should also appear in their normal proportions. Like the Aces, each of these cards has less than an 8% probability of appearing. That is: if you see two or more of one these cards amongst the 10 or so cards you're analyzing, then it's unlikely the card you're wondering about is one of those cards. However, if any one of these cards does NOT appear in the 10 or so cards you're studying, then you know that you have to consider those cards as possibilities when guesstimating the value of the card you're investigating.
4. ***What is the relative proportion of low cards to high cards?*** Sometimes, instead of looking at individual cards, it is more telling to reflect on generalities. Just as with card counting – it's the same principle – if a lot of low cards precede a card you are investigating, then that card is likely to be the opposite, a HIGH card, because high cards would then be overdue. And vice versa. If an overabundance of high cards precedes the card you're interested in figuring out, then that

card is likely to be the opposite, a low card, because low cards are overdue.

5. ***What does the Flow of the Cards tell you?*** The **Flow of the Cards** is my term for the order in which the cards you're analyzing were dealt. Oftentimes, that is a good indicator. For example, if you see four 10s in a row leading up to the hole card, it's unlikely that card is a 10. However, if the four 10s in a row were the *first* cards dealt to the 7 players at your table, and the cards following those consisted of low cards, an Ace and a 9, well, then the hole card might very well be a 10.

Here's One Area Where A Shoe Game Is Better

Of course, determining what strategic cards might be, through **Card Observation**, is easier with a shoe game. That's because the players' second dealt cards, which lead to the dealer's hole card, are dealt *face up*, unlike in pitch games, where they're dealt face down. Plus, any hit cards taken by players ahead of you (which are important indicators because they immediately follow the dealer's hole card), are also dealt face up – unlike some of the players' cards in pitch games (such as the extra cards dealers place face down under players' chips when they double down). This is one advantage to playing shoe games.

As with card counting, however, you'd do best to use **Card Observation** at tables with no more than 4 decks of cards. With 6 or 8 decks, the cards go through radical fluctuations and become very unpredictable.

(**Card Observation**, by the way, can be done at 1- & 2-deck pitch game tables — it's just not quite as precise. First, you should try to see all of the cards that were played in the prior round. Then, you should try to glimpse as many player cards as possible during the current round. You can do this by subtly peeking at the cards being held by neighboring players, or by politely asking your fellow players to show you what they have. Many times they won't mind doing so, if you extend the same favor to them. You might not be able to tell which of the players' two cards were the second-dealt cards that led up to the dealer

hole card, but you will often find useful information. For example, if you're holding a 13 at third base against the dealer's 2 and you have seen NO 10s, or 9s for that matter, amongst players' cards by the time it's your turn, you'd probably be smart to stand. When you're ready to tackle a skill that's on a more advanced level, once again, I will give you my breakthrough method of accounting for the face-down cards at pitch game tables, in *Cutting Edge Blackjack*.)

Determining The Hole Card

OK, let's go to some examples of actual hands played out in one of my research projects.

First, look at **Illustration 8-2**, on the following page, and see for yourself how the second cards dealt to the players (numbered 1 through 5) lead up to the dealer's hole card (numbered 6). Also, examine the cards and see what you notice, before I tell you how to apply **Card Observation** here. Take a moment right now, to do so.

Five Players Makes For A Good Number

Now, with five players, you always have 12 cards on the table after everyone's initial two cards were dealt. That's a pretty easy number to work with. We know, for example, therefore, that there should be no more than four 10s amongst those cards, because 10s account for a little less than 31% of the deck. (And even that would be high, because if four 10s indeed do appear, they would account for 33% of the cards on the table being 4 of 12 cards present.) All of the rest of the cards should appear just once, because they each make up one of the possible 13 cards in each suit.

Fine. Let's go through the **Card Observation Questions**, and see what you can learn.

How many 10s are there, and in what proportion? Five out of the 11 cards whose values are visible to you! That's nearly 50%

Illustration 8-2

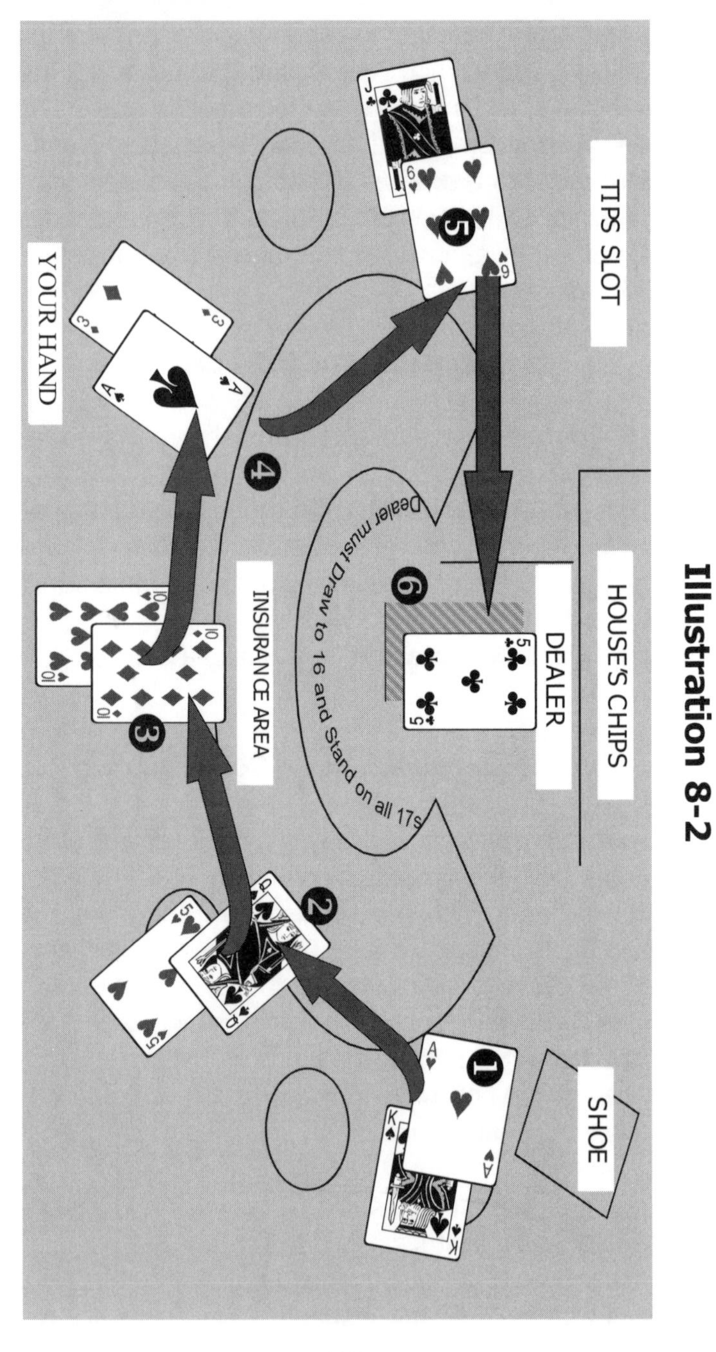

of the cards you can see, and two more than the laws of probability would say you should expect (you should expect 11 x 4/13 = 3 10-pointers)! You know now that it's unlikely – not impossible, but unlikely – therefore, that the hole card is a 10.

Are there any Aces? Yes! Two! That's one more than you'd expect. You can write Aces off the list in guessing what the hole card might be! It's very unlikely – not impossible, but highly improbable – that you'd find a third Ace on the table, according to the laws of probability.

What about the rest of the cards? Anything unusual? There are TWO 5s – they are over-represented (you'd expect just one per 13). There are NO 2s, 4s, 7s, 8s, or 9s; they are under-represented. So, the hole card is unlikely to be a 5. However, it might be any one of the cards NOT accounted for on the table.

What can you gather from **Card Observation Question 4** about the generalities you observe? Well, there is one more of the high cards than there are low cards (remember: you don't count the Aces in either camp). So, according to that standard, which mirrors the thinking that goes into card counting, the odds lean a little in favor of the hole card being a low one.

And, finally, **Card Observation Question 5** asks you: what does the **Flow of the Cards** tell you? Remarkable. *You've seen TWO Aces and two 10s amongst the five cards that were dealt immediately before the hole card!* It doesn't appear the hole card would be a 10 or an Ace!

Well, as it turns out, you're right! The hole card in this particular card trial was in fact...a 3. Since your main concern is predicting whether the hole card will be a 10 first and foremost, and then, whether it is going to be a high or a low card, I think you'd agree that **Card Observation** served you pretty well here.

Your questions on the relative proportion of 10s and Aces produced especially useful and revealing answers, such that you did not expect the hole card to be a 10 or an Ace. Your question on generalities was also correct in predicting the hole card was a low one. And the **Flow of the Cards** question was likewise very telling.

The one question that was NOT immensely revealing was ***Card Observation Question 3*** *– the one regarding the non-10s and non-Aces. That was inconclusive. So, remember: that question will often be the least important or helpful one of the five* ***Card Observation Questions****. You'd do best to rely most heavily on the others. Use Question 3 as the "icing on the cake," but don't expect it to give you too precise an answer. You're covering too many cards with that question.*

Now, let's get back to the example in **Illustration 8-2**, on page 164. You have already figured out what the hole card would be, but let's not get ahead of ourselves.

Let's say you are the player sitting just to the left of second base, with the Ace-3, and it's your turn. Let's pretend you haven't yet seen the hole card and the players to your right took no hit cards. What would you do, given what **Card Observation** has told you?

This particular example is a bit tricky. As you will see in Chapter 10, on Advanced Strategy – when low cards are due (which is equivalent in card counting to saying "when there is a negative count"), you have to be a bit more careful against the dealer's weak cards. However, in this case, the balance of low to high cards is not off by very much. So, we're not in dangerous territory.

Careful, now – the only card that's under-represented which would give you a winning score if you double now would be the 7. But, then again, the dealer's 5 is one of the very best up cards for the player, and so you would still be smart to double in this situation.

Well, as it turns out, that player's extra card, after doubling down, was indeed a 7! Not unexpected, given what **Card Observation** told you about the relative probabilities of what cards might come after the third baseman's 6.

Impressed yet? You should be!

Good job! Let's see what you make of the next example.

Insurance?

Another way **Card Observation** can be very useful is when you must decide whether or not to take Insurance, when facing the dealer's Ace. As an advanced player, there will be times you would want to take that option, whether you have a Blackjack or not. And one reason to take Insurance is if **Card Observation** tells you the hole card is likely to be a 10.

Let's look at **Illustration 8-3** on the following page, and see how this works. This is another example taken directly from the thousands and thousands of hands I've run in research trials.

The dealer has an Ace as the up card, and she asks the question all the players dread hearing: "Insurance?" It tends to make you nervous – no matter how many years you've been playing blackjack. It's a warning that the dealer might have a Blackjack, and anyone who doesn't take Insurance anxiously awaits the results of the dealer's checking the hole card, even though advanced players know that taking Insurance is NOT usually a smart move – since 10s account for less than 31% of the cards, you will LOSE your Insurance bet about 69% of the time!

OK, in this case, let's examine whether you should take the dealer up on her offer of "Insurance?" Once again, **Card Observation** begins with asking yourself the five **Card Observation Questions** as you look over the cards on the table.

Look closely at the table as represented in **Illustration 8-3**. In this example, you're playing with three other players, so there are 10 cards on the table, one the hole card, out of sight, after the first two cards are dealt to everyone.

Question 1: What about the 10s? There are three 10-point cards, which is in line with what you would expect. Remember, the 10s make up 31% of the cards, so 3/10 = 30%, which is exactly right. So, your first **Card Observation Question's** answer seems to tell you the hole card is probably not a 10.

Question 2: What about Aces? Since the dealer's up card is an Ace, it's very unlikely the hole card would be one, too. Plus, according to the laws of probability, only one Ace usually appears

Illustration 8-3

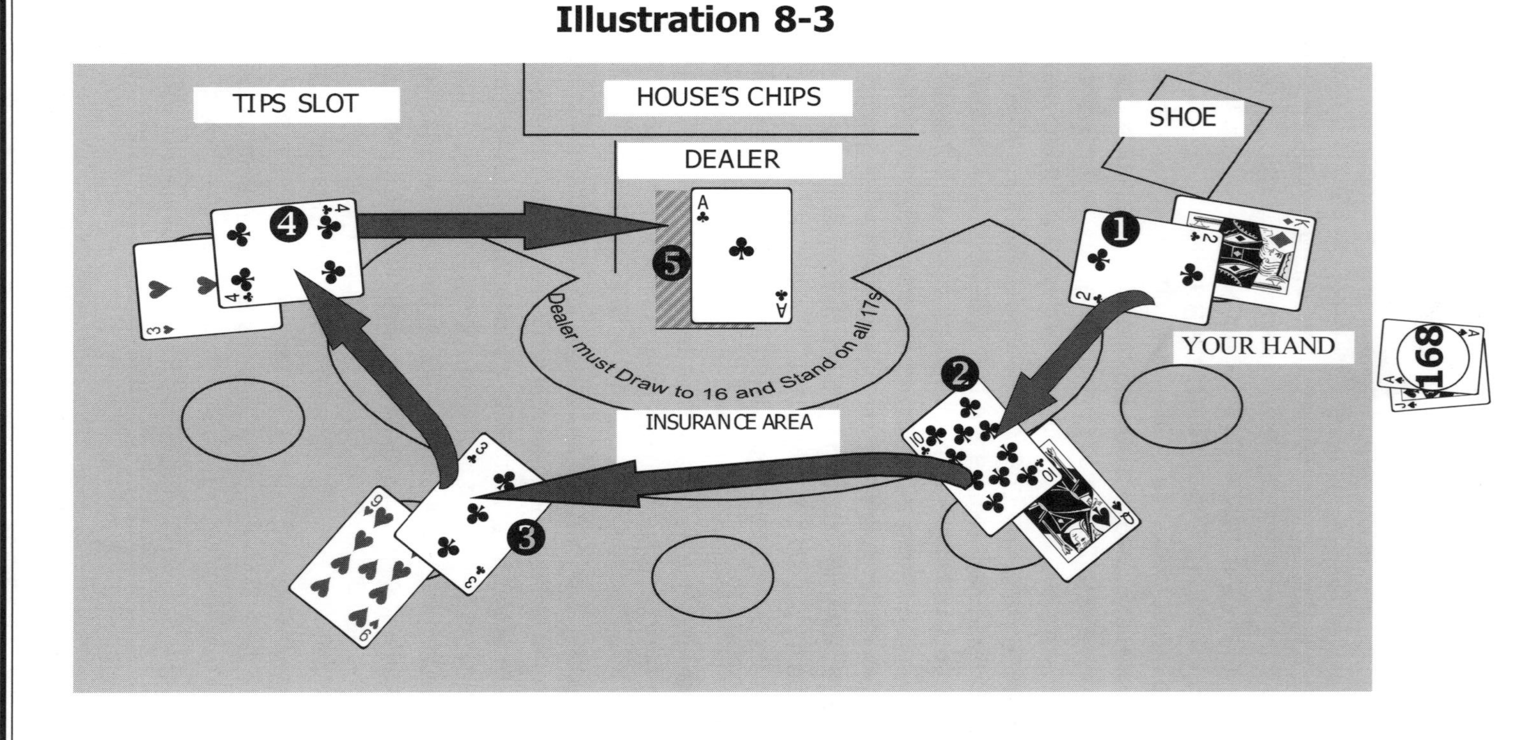

in 13 cards, and here there is one Ace in 9 cards – a higher concentration than normal. No, the hole card is not an Ace, in all probability.

Question 3: What about the other cards? There's one 2, two 3s, one 4 and one 9. With 3s being over-represented, it's unlikely the hole card is a 3. Nor is it probable that it's a 2, 4 or 9. Perhaps it's a card that hasn't shown itself – a 5, 6, 7, or 8, most of which are low cards.

The answers you've gotten so far are good for you! The hole card is unlikely to be a 9 or 10, so the dealer's score will probably not be 20, nor will the dealer likely have a Blackjack. No need for Insurance.

Question 4: What about generalities – the proportion of low to high cards? They're roughly balanced. NO leaning here.

Question 5: What about the **Flow of the Cards**? The higher cards seem to have come to an end with the 10 of clubs. There appears to be an imbalance in the flow here than benefits you – the low cards seem to be starting to come in a flood. Of the last five cards dealt, 4 were low cards. By itself, that news might be worrisome, but you know that the high cards have already appeared in greater numbers than would be expected (they accounted for 4 of 9 visible cards – nearly 50%!), and so it makes sense that low cards might be due.

No, you would not want to take Insurance here. You'd only be throwing that bet away.

And, once again the educated guesses we made through **Card Observation** were correct. In this card run, the hole card turned out to be a 5.

Card Observation For The Hit Card

One more thing. Let's say you're the first baseman. Let's use **Card Observation** to answer one more question: should you be afraid to bust here, with your hand of 12?

Based upon what **Card Observation** tells me, I don't think so. Why?

Your hit card would be the 11th card this round. As you saw, four of the nine visible cards were high cards. Question 3 showed you that two of the three cards that have not yet turned up on the table are low cards (the 6s and 7s) and might soon appear.

It's unlikely you would get the only card that would bust your hand – another 10.

In fact, the hit card that the first baseman was dealt in this card run was...a 6, one of the cards that Question 3 indicated was on its way!

Interestingly enough, the next card to be dealt, the third player's hit card, turned out to be an 8! That was another one of the cards that Question 3 told you was likely to show up soon.

So, **Card Observation** once again proved its merit, and pretty impressively, I might add!

Another Effective Way To Use It

I often speak of the **personality of the cards**, and the **Flow of the Cards**.

This is one area where **Card Observation** excels, which card counting doesn't begin to address. At the heart of it, **Card Observation** is an analysis of the cards, to detect revealing clues.

At my blackjack seminars, I bring players up to a simulated blackjack table, and show them, among other things, how powerful **Card Observation** is, how it works.

At my most recent seminar, the seminar-goers were amazed to see how I used **Card Observation** to pick out important patterns and trends within the cards, that lasted from shuffle to shuffle – the **personality of the cards**, as demonstrated in the **Flow of the Cards** – that led to a certain predictability.

For example, I pointed out that three Aces appeared in close succession. I then predicted that they would remain that way for quite some time, through several shuffles, at least. And they did. Knowing when Aces will appear is powerful information, indeed.

The same pertained to four 3s during the same demonstration.

And more important – there was a sizeable group of 10-pointers that appeared in a flood from shuffle to shuffle. You should have seen the looks on the faces of those watching these patterns unfold, and repeat again, as revealed through **Card Observation**.

Sometimes, It DOESN'T Work

Granted, **Card Observation** is not an exact science. There will be a minority of times where your predictions will not follow the laws of probabilities. But, then again, if truth be told, the same can be said about card counting, and I don't see players rejecting that practice because of its limitations.

Card Observation is a viable skill you can develop, that will lead to big payoffs at the blackjack table. It is, like card counting, great in deciding how to handle card situations where an advanced player has to choose between two or three possible ways to go.

It is not to be confused with the hunches upon which many players base their decisions. The **Card Observation Questions** speak directly to the underlying mathematical principles that make the game of blackjack winnable.

A Word to the Wise

Now, DON'T attempt card counting or **Card Observation** at the casino until you've practiced this at home to the point where you pull off these practices with finesse. If you try tracking the cards at the casino before you are really ready for it, your brain is going to overload, your game will suffer, you will probably look visibly agitated, AND you might tip off the dealer or casino bosses that you're a card counter, or a player with a system, and you might get barred. *I want to emphasize that this is NOT easy to do in practice. It is, however, well worth your investment of time.*

You are still not ready to enter a casino.

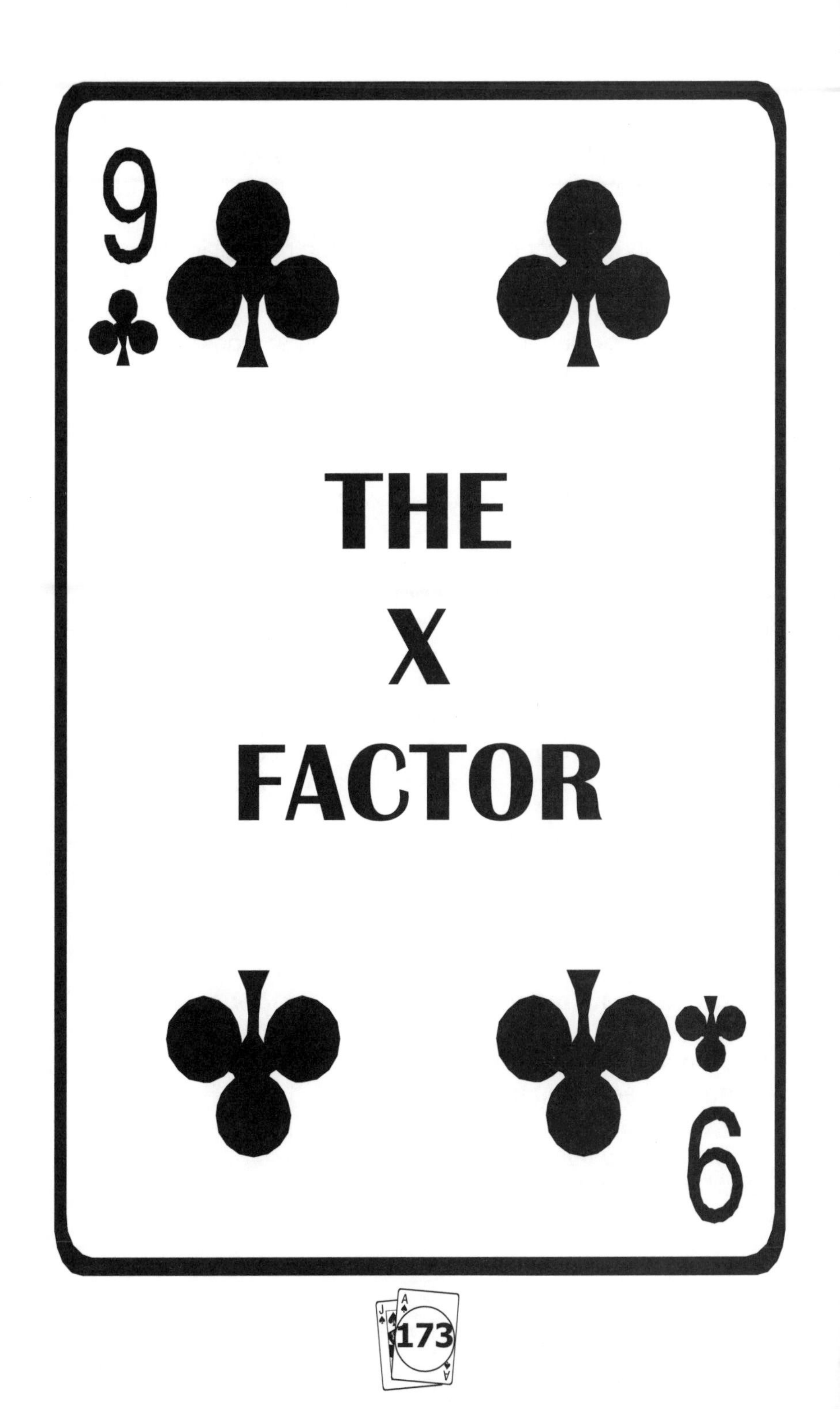
9
THE
X
FACTOR
6

You will not find the **X Factor** in any other book on blackjack. It is another of the unique features of the *Blackjack The SMART Way* system. And yet, I believe it is one of the essential concepts you must come to grips with if you want to maximize your gains and get consistent about winning.

Your ability to apply the **X Factor** to the particular game situation you are facing will be instrumental in determining how much money you will win or lose.

The **X Factor** pertains only to the action at a particular table. It gives you important information with which you can make more informed decisions about:

- ♣ How to play your cards.
- ♣ How to manage your money.
- ♣ How to know when to leave the table.

It gives you a constant measure of how good the table is for YOU in particular (NOT how good the table is for everyone, or the guy in the black hat who has two large piles of $25 chips – just you).

I mean, who cares if the point count is upwards +10 if the dealer beats you every hand? That can and does happen! That's one of the reasons why I've jettisoned card counting in making major decisions.

Plus — who cares if the dealer is busting a lot, if you bust before the dealer? Who cares if everyone at the table is doing great, if YOU are doing poorly?

The **X Factor** keeps you focused on indicators that matter most to your game.

I define the **X Factor** as *how well you are doing versus the dealer.*

It can also be expressed as *the* ***personality of the cards***. No one else seems to talk about this!

This is what will tell you how to manage your money.

This will also point out when you're at one of those rare but deadly crooked tables!

The Personality of the Cards

Yes, it's interesting, but even a random break of cards becomes familiar in terms of the number of hands you tend to win or lose. You will come to recognize that, with the introduction of new cards, the first shuffle produces a stack of cards of a certain personality. Over time, with successive shuffles, that personality will change; usually, in subtle terms.

The better you get at perceiving what that personality is, the sooner you will become a sophisticated player who wins more than basic strategists can win.

You'll come to recognize when the cards' personality is: in your favor; mildly against your favor; or, a terrible buzzsaw (when you'd want to leave that table). You will also get a feel for when the cards are "breaking funny" – when something is amiss. In addition, you will come to notice the repeating patterns peculiar to the cards at your table; the cards that stay in close association with one another, for example, no matter how many shuffles (note: this is based on original research and is NOT an endorsement of the card clumping theory, as I will explain later; I do NOT agree with that school of thought).

It will probably take some time before you learn to integrate the **X Factor** into your consciousness to the point where it becomes second nature to you. It might just be the most difficult of the new concepts I am presenting to you, to get a handle on. But it will also become one of the most rewarding.

For now, I am going to spell out how you can get in touch with the **X Factor** in concrete ways – through a series of questions must continuously ask yourself.

How The X Factor Works

To determine what the **X Factor** is telling you, you must always keep track (roughly) of how many hands the dealer wins, and how many you win.

And, below, you'll find some of the **X Factor Questions** you

should constantly be asking yourself as you watch the game unfold. Don't drive yourself crazy asking all of these questions all of the time. Familiarize yourself with what I am teaching you here, so simple observation will trigger one or more of these questions in your mind as you're playing:

- **Do the cards have a persistent personality** – good or bad – which repeats from shuffle to shuffle? They usually do. First of all, *are the cards generally good or bad for you?* Second, *what repeating patterns provide you with useful information*? For example: Do four 8s return, time and time again, close together? Or, perhaps the 3 face cards from a particular suit?
- **How many hands have you won this round**? Approximately what percent? 70%? 50%? 5%? The answer to this question is very telling! (You'd be surprised how few people keep track of this!!)
- Have you had any **winning streaks**? If so, how long did they last on average (how many hands)?
- Have you had any **losing streaks**? If so, how long did they last (how many hands)?
- **How often have you busted**?
- **How often have you drawn *great scores*** (totals of 19, 20, 21)?
- How are you doing with regard to **your chips**? Up? Down? Neutral?
- How often have you gotten a **Blackjack**?
- **How often have you split, or doubled down *unsuccessfully* – gotten very poor hit cards and totals and then *lost*?**
- How long was **the dealer's longest winning streak**?
- How long was **the dealer's longest *losing streak***?
- **How often does the dealer *bust***? (With weak *and* strong up cards.)
- *If the dealer busts, how often is it that you have already*

busted too?

- **How often does the dealer score a great total with a weak up card** (especially, 4 through 6)?
- **How often does the dealer get a Blackjack?** And, how often does the dealer get a Blackjack with an up card of *10?*
- **How often is the dealer's up card an Ace?**
- **How often does the dealer get great scores of 20 and 21*?***
- *How often does the dealer get weak up cards* (especially 4s, 5, and 6s)?
- **How often does the dealer get strong up cards — especially 9s through Aces?**
- How often **have cards come out in groups**, such as Aces; 10s; and low cards?
- How many players seem to be doing well? (Is everyone doing well? Or, are you the only one doing well? Or, is no one doing well?)

What The Answers Tell Us

Why do we want to know the answers to these **X Factor Questions**, and what do they add up to?

First, let's answer questions that pertain to the cards, then you, then the dealer, then last and least important, the other players at the table, and you will see!.

Once you start recognizing the **personality of the cards**, you'll see that the **X Factor** is a very good indicator, especially with regard to how to manage your bets, and knowing when to leave a table (as you'll see soon).

For instance, perhaps you've grown confident that, even past a shuffle, the cards are player-friendly. Then, you'll be playing at Level 2 or 3, with your **3-Unit Notch-Up, Notch-Down Bet Management System** (see Chapter 7). Or, hey, something is wrong; these cards are nasty! The dealer gets up cards of 10s and Aces, and nothing but, and then arrives at scores of 20 or 21! Go to Level 0 or leave!

The **personality of the cards** also refers to repeating card patterns, as mentioned earlier. If, as I advise, you are playing at a 1- or 2-deck table, you will especially be able to take advantage of this information. You will then have a better idea of how to play your cards when you spot one of the repeating, closely associated cards make an appearance after the next shuffle.

For example, if one of the repeating patterns involves a group of 3 Aces, you might be tipped off to a strong dealer hand, if the first re-appearance of these repeating Aces comes with the dealing of just *one* of them, with the players' first two cards. That observation would then lead you to the realization that the dealer's hole card might possibly be one of the other repeating Aces.

The **personality of the cards** is the hardest aspect of the **X Factor** to teach – at least in a book. At my seminars, in table-top demonstrations, it's rather easy. I can then point out that, "see how those four 3's keep coming back together, shuffle after shuffle?" and so on, and the seminar-goers are then instantly impressed as they see all of the patterns we notice re-emerge later on. (Actually, for those who are ready, I will go into this in detail in my second book, *Cutting Edge Blackjack*.)

Your ability to implement this powerful concept is based on your skills of observation. You'll want to work to improve this skill. This comes naturally to me, being a former reporter. It's the same skill a reporter uses when arriving at the scene of a story – the reporter asks him- or herself: what details can I notice that are telling?

Measuring How YOU Are Doing

So, let's talk more about the **X Factor Questions** that pertain directly to you – your hands, in particular, vis a vis the dealer's.

The approximate number of times you win, in number and percent, is the most important number of all the numbers you must ascertain during any stay at a blackjack table. This should give you a feel for how good the table is. We will call this your

table winning percentage.

At a good table, your **table winning percentage** should be in the general range of 50% of the number of hands played, or more (not counting pushes). If you're down around 10-20% or LESS, something is terribly wrong! Leave the table, or the casino! If it's 25-30%, this is a cause for concern. Go to another table! If it's 40%, you're under the average of what the computed odds are for you to win, but, it might just be a temporary down cycle.

You'd be surprised at how many players stay rooted to one table, even when they're losing much more than they should! If they were simply aware of this concept – your **table winning percentage** — and what it says about the table, perhaps they would not root themselves to tables come hell or high water, and would not lose as much as they do.

Winning And Losing Streaks

How many winning streaks you have had, and how long they've lasted is another important **X Factor Indicator**. A simple way to keep mental notes on this is to pay attention to how often you've been able to raise your bet and win again, and to what Step within what Level you've been able to get to, with your **3-Unit Notch-Up, Notch-Down Bet Management System**.

At some tables, it's hard to find a winning streak. That's a sure sign of a difficult table, which, depending on how your chips are "doing" (another strong **X Factor Indicator**), might indicate a neutral to bad table. At difficult tables, it always seems that, if you raise your bet, you get clobbered. At other tables, you might find you can raise your bet through all the steps in a particular level and you continue to win (your chips rising as well). That's the other extreme, on the good side.

You want a table that provides you with a healthy number of short and long winning streaks.

Losing streaks are a very good thing to keep track of, because that will keep you focused on how BAD a table is. Two or three hands might not be worthy of scaring you away from a table if you are either way up or staying kind of neutral in chips. But if you lose much more than that, let's say half a dozen hands in a

row, then you should be in gear, moving elsewhere. Don't wait until all your chips are gone!!!

You'd be surprised at how many players recount to me times when they won a good deal of money, but then got frozen in place as they lost hand after hand, until all their winnings were gone – there were two at my last seminar alone. One of those players told me with frustration that, on a recent trip to a casino, he'd been up $2,000, but then threw it right back to the house when a new dealer was brought in. The dealer had "mesmerized" him.

If the principles behind the **X Factor** were so obvious, there would be fewer players telling stories like that one.

Bust Not, Want Not

How often you bust is another good **X Factor Indicator**. It shouldn't happen a LOT. If you're busting 40% of the time or more, it indicates you're getting a lot of "stiffs" — hard totals of 12 to 16 that you have to hit to improve. It's a good indicator something is very wrong. Perhaps there are too many low cards in the **Flow of the Cards** – signaling something might be wrong (see Chapter 11 – Casino Countermeasures and Dirty Tricks). Use this to put your feet in gear. You'll know when that's necessary. Pay attention, as I suggest, to how often you bust percentage-wise. Or, if you find yourself saying "NOT again!" — that's when you leave.

Seen Any 20s and 21s Lately?

How often you draw great scores is also a very telling **X Factor Indicator**. Great scores — good table. Consistently crummy scores — bad table, or perhaps worse. Something might be wrong. Leave that table.

With nearly 31% of the cards being 10s, you should have 2-card hands of 20 points nearly 10% of the time. If you are nowhere near to this figure, there is definitely something wrong – either a random bad card streak, or NOT. LEAVE THE TABLE.

When The Chips Are Down

How your chips are faring is another primary **X Factor Indicator**, and, you'd think, one of the more obvious ones. You'd think everyone would keep track of this – even those who have no concept of the **X Factor** – but you'd be surprised.

Most players haphazardly pile their chips in front of themselves and have no CLUE what they have. Your chips – as I taught you earlier – should be in piles of five $5 chips (**Strategic Stacking**), which will always tell you by sight what you have, and how much you're up or down. (Or – if you are playing at a higher stakes table, of course, stack the higher value chips logically. You would stack $25s in $100 piles of 4, for example.)

If you're up, you stay at the table. If you're down, a light bulb should go off in your head, alerting you to use the **X Factor** to tell you if the table might turn around for you, or if it's hopeless.

First of all, if go down 6 chips within 12 or less hands placing 1-Unit bets, then, invoke my **6-Unit Cheat-Proof Rule** and move on to a different table. Think about it – if you're down 6 or more units within a dozen hands, it means you've lost 75% of the hands! If you have to invoke this TWICE, LEAVE THE CASINO.

Now, if that's not the case — you're simply down in chips after playing awhile – you must ask yourself: is there a persistent "down" pattern or personality to the cards that seems to repeat itself, shuffle after shuffle? Repetitive, bad patterns are a sure sign something is wrong, at least for you.

If, however, you are "up" in chips, and the **X Factor Indicators** are all "go," then you can afford to make more risky moves and increase your **Basic Bet** to Level 2 or 3.

Sometimes down cycles will turn around (by down cycles, I mean both a loss of hands and chips). But not at tables where you have been unable to put together a decent winning streak. And not when you rarely if ever get great point totals. Pay attention to these **X Factor Indicators**.

Your Blackjacks

How often you get a Blackjack is only of use in telling you how GOOD the table is, not how bad. I've been at tables where I'm not doing well at all, and yet I might get two or three Blackjacks! They don't outweigh the effect of the majority of hands, though, which are bad. Plus, at bad tables, you've got your minimum bet down when you get your Blackjacks, so your "take" isn't much. So, this is the least important of all our **X Factor Questions**. I mention this because some players are convinced that this is an important indicator of how good a table is, but it is most definitely NOT.

Splitting And Doubling Indicators

Now, how often you've split or doubled down and gotten horrible hit cards and then lost can be significant. Three times or more, and you should be on your guard. Leave the table, or, at the very least, avoid doubling down and splitting in all but the most safe of situations – against the dealer's 4, 5 or 6 — until you've come to a conclusion as to whether or not to leave that table. If it happens a fourth time, LEAVE.

Especially Watch How "Lucky" The Dealer's Been

*How the dealer is doing is an extremely revealing **X Factor Indicator**.* Does the dealer go on long winning streaks? Many short winning streaks, punctuated by one win for you? That would be a sign of a bad or terrible table. Dealer winning streaks are a sure warning sign, and you should immediately consider leaving the table. If, however, you win one or two, the dealer wins one or two, back and forth, you're at a neutral table.

Or, does the dealer go on moderately long losing streaks? That's an obvious sign of a good to great table. Get more money down.

If the dealer busts rather often, this can be a significant thing

– that is, if you're not busting before him or her. This would say to you: this is a good time to get more money on the table. Stay alert for this kind of thing. However, if you're busting on those hands too, beware!! A card flow where everyone's busting more often than normal might be a tip off of cards that were "arranged" to break that way. You'll learn more about that in Chapter 11.

Believe it or not, ***if the dealer often wins and doesn't bust with up cards of 3 through 6***, this is very revealing; you might be in big trouble. If this is not just a sign of a normal negative count effect, the **X Factor** says: leave the table! Once again, Chapter 11 might hold the answer to what's going on there.

Beware The Dealer's Blackjack

If the DEALER gets more than one Blackjack within a dozen hands, THAT might be an important **X Factor Indicator** (as opposed to *you* getting a Blackjack). If he or she gets 3 Blackjacks in short order, LEAVE that table!! Beware especially if the dealer gets two or more Blackjacks in close succession with up cards of 10! Beware, too, if the dealer gets a Blackjack immediately after each shuffle – if you see this happen twice, shame on you if you stay at that table! Especially if the dealer's repeating Blackjack consists of the SAME CARDS!!! It may be a coincidence, by DON'T STAY AT THAT TABLE, just in case it's NOT!

How often the dealer gets Aces as up cards is also useful **X Factor** information. Too often and you should be "outta there." Remember – Aces only account for 7.7% of the cards!

Beware Of The Dealer's 20s And 21s

Pay attention to how often the dealer gets great scores of 20 and 21, especially if it seems a "constant." That's the pattern you'll run into at tables where the cards are rigged or the dealer is a something of a "magician" (see Chapter 11). Now, it might also be a coincidence, but, just in case, the **X Factor** says: LEAVE that table!

Two-card hands that total 20 points should occur less than 10% of the time! If the dealer is "bucking the odds" and getting those hands much more often, don't stick around!

How Strong Is Thy Dealer?

How often the dealers get weak or strong cards is also very telling. If they get their share of 3s through 6s, and then bust at least 30% of the time, fine. Stay. ***If, however, the dealer gets more than his or her share of strong up cards in a dozen rounds, then that's a wake up call.*** If that's the case, pay attention to other factors that might confirm that it's time that you to leave the table.

Another **X Factor** red flag is the "grouping" of cards. I've seen tables where, miraculously, 3 or 4 Aces always appear in one round, together, from shuffle to shuffle. Coincidence? Grouping of 10s and low cards might be a more serious sign something's wrong. If it coincides with a significant downtrend for you, LEAVE the table.

Why would a rogue casino or dealer want to group Aces or 10s together? So they pass through in a minimum number of hands, affording players a minimum of strong hands. When grouped like that, the dealer's hand tends to offset the players' stronger hands, as well. (See Chapter 11.)

How other players are doing is usually insignificant to us. It's only *when ALL the players are doing poorly* that it really matters. That's an **X Factor** tip-off that it's time to leave.

Applying the X Factor to Money Management

Once you've answered the entire set of **X Factor** questions, you will have a good grip on how the **X Factor** is working for or against you.

Essentially, it answers the question – "How am I doing at this table'?"

These **X Factor Money Managment Questions** will tell you

what Level you should be at in your money management system:

- Are things kind of neutral? You haven't won anything but you haven't lost anything... The cards go this way and that way... The dealer wins some, you win some... Stay at Level 1.
- Are things going well for you? You're winning a good percentage of hands... The dealer is busting on weak cards... Your chips are up... The dealer is getting a good number of weak up cards and not too many strong cards... You've gotten a Blackjack and the dealer hasn't... Go to Level 2.
- Are things going great? You're on a long winning streak... The dealer is busting left and right and never seems to get good cards... Your winnings are piling up... In fact, everyone at the table is doing well... You've gotten a a number of really good hands, some with Aces, as well as doubling and splitting opportunities that won, etc.? Go to Level 3.
- Does the table seem totally cold? You never seem to win and neither does anyone else... The dealer just had 2 Blackjacks and now has a total of 21 after having a weak up card of 6, etc.? Go to Level 0, or leave the table.

The X Factor Goes Where Card Counting Cannot

So, to reiterate, if the point count, for example, is **+10**, who cares, on some level? What is more important to us is what the **X Factor Indicators** tell us.

If the dealer has been winning every hand with incredible scores of 20 and 21, has gotten 3 Blackjacks this round and hasn't ever had a weak up card, then the count means nothing. The **X Factor** then tells you to ignore the count and stay at Level 0, or leave the table. THE X FACTOR GETS YOU AWAY FROM A BAD TABLE WHERE YOUR CARD COUNT MIGHT MISLEAD YOU INTO THINKING THINGS LOOK GOOD FOR YOU (IF YOU ARE ONE OF THOSE WHO BELIEVES A POSITIVE COUNT IS A SIGN THAT THE CARDS WILL TURN IN YOUR FAVOR)!

See how irrelevant the count can be? And how much more relevant the **X Factor** is?

The X Factor Is Powerful But It Takes Time to Grasp

Answering the **X Factor Questions** we've examined in this chapter should provide you with crucial information that will help you immensely, in guiding you safely through the tough challenges you will face. Read and re-read this chapter until you really come to grips with the **X Factor**.

Next up...it's time to take advantage of all the advanced concepts you now have under your belt, by learning *Blackjack The SMART Way* Advanced Strategy!

You are still not ready to enter a casino.

ADVANCED CARD STRATEGY

OK, now you are ready to put everything you've learned together, to become an advanced player!

We will synthesize all of your newfound knowledge and use it to arrive at a higher skill level. The great thing about what you are about to master is that it brings with it a higher win rate, and all the profits that go along with that.

We'll layer *Blackjack The SMART Way* Basic Strategy and concepts with what you now know about:

- The **personalities of the dealer up cards**.
- The mathematical probabilities underlying the game.
- The perils of doubling and splitting.
- Money management.
- The **3-Unit, Notch-Up, Notch-Down Bet Management System**.
- Keeping track of the cards (either by card counting or by **Card Observation**).
- The **X Factor**.

Your goal here will be to achieve flexibility. You will want to draw upon your understanding of *Blackjack The SMART Way* concepts and the mathematical realities you have discovered here, to make more "precise" decisions on the fly — at the blackjack table — based upon the card action you observe unfolding before you. That is, your thinking should now be moving *beyond* the charts, toward a higher consciousness. This is the hallmark of the *Blackjack The SMART Way* advanced player.

In my second book, *Cutting Edge Blackjack* – which will open new worlds for you, when you are ready to go a step further — you'll have even more mathematical information at your fingertips, so you can make even more "precise" decisions, on the spot. You will learn to divorce yourself from the traditional, chart-driven mentality, and do a lot more independent thinking based upon the underlying mathematical realities uncovered in *Blackjack The SMART Way* and the results of my most recent research project.

But, let's not get ahead of ourselves. First, there's a lot of information for you to digest right here and use to your great advantage before you're ready for that more advanced book. Let's take it a step at a time.

For now, you will still need to study charts reflecting the guidelines that will lead you toward becoming a great player. Please take time to review those new, Advanced Strategy Charts now (they appear at the end of the chapter, on pages 207-210).

Looking at the charts for advanced players, you'll see that your options are now greater than they were in the Basic Strategy charts. Now, you can "push the envelope" and make educated choices in "grey areas" that you weren't wise enough to make before.

These extra options will give you the potential to win even more money than might by following Basic Strategy.

How To Play Hard Hands for the Advanced Player

If you take a look at CHART 4 (on page 207) you will see that, unlike the corresponding Basic Strategy chart, CHART 1A, there are now boxes that contain TWO possible moves. These fall in what I call "grey areas," where sometimes the break of the cards makes an unconventional move smarter. The move listed first, often marked with a question mark, is the move you'd prefer to make (often contradicting what you were taught in Basic Strategy) but ***it is only to be done in instances where the card count or break of the cards indicates it can be done successfully***. If **Card Observation**, or the card count instead indicates that that move is likely to cost you the hand, follow the second, more conservative move indicated, instead.

Sometimes the new choice – the one not offered in Basic Strategy — is actually the more *conservative* way to go, by the way! Now that you know something about keeping track of the cards, you can use that added knowledge wisely now in sometimes playing it *safer* than you did with Basic Strategy, in a "grey area" situation. Knowledge is power.

Our goal as an advanced player, therefore, is not to become

more reckless or risky in our approach – far from it! Our goal is to make the smartest move, mathematically speaking. Often, that' s going to involve AVOIDING risk, to conserve our money and protect it from losses! Now, like an experienced sailor, you will be a bit more cautious at times – unlike the younger, inexperienced sailor – you will elect to steer your boat to port when approaching storm clouds appear on the horizon.

The Advanced Player Must Understand Nuances

With added room for discretion, of course, comes the price of having to *think* more (see CHART 4, on page 207). To me, this is the thrilling part of the game, the challenge of out-thinking the cards and the house.

Now, we won't be looking at any of the moves in the Advanced Strategy Charts that coincide with the Basic Strategy Charts. Those you should know by now, by heart.

Let us, instead, talk about the areas in the Advanced Strategy Charts where you will now have choices to make, where you'll have to exercise your judgment to adjust to the **flow of the cards** based upon what you now know about the mathematics that rule the game of blackjack.

You Mean I Can Double On A 7 or An 8?

First, you'll notice that you now have doubling down opportunities even with hands of meager totals of 7 and 8, in four limited cases – if your 8 is against the dealer's 4, 5 or 6, or if your 7 is against the dealer's 5 (which often causes the dealer to bust more than the 4 or 6, especially when the count is positive).

THESE MOVES, HOWEVER, DEPEND UPON THE COUNT OR WHAT **CARD OBSERVATION** TELLS YOU. Making extra money is nice, but ***exercise caution.***

Do these ONLY if you are *certain* that high cards and Aces are due (in the case of the 7, you should have a good idea that 10s and Aces, specifically, are overdue). For card counters, you

should have a relatively high positive count, at least in the range of **+5** or so to double on the 8; it should be **+7** or more to double on the 7, give or take.

But, use your judgment. Otherwise, HIT these totals, as you did before. You have nothing to lose by hitting your 7 or 8 as you did before. In fact, you gain something sticking to what you did in Basic Strategy, and that is the ability to hit your cards again if you pull an unhelpful low card.

Doubling on a 7 or 8 is definitely on the riskier side of things.

Plus, if you're being watched closely by casino management, NEVER do these moves. You'll give yourself away as a smart player.

However, if you have the opportunity, and it seems wise, hey, why not make some extra money? These are the riskiest moves I will suggest that you consider, though, and are a bit "on the edge."

Playing Against the Tricky 2

Ah! Now, as an advanced player, you can really take advantage of the knowledge presented in Chapter 4 regarding the **Tricky 2s**.

Interestingly enough, although the dealer's 2 is a hazardous card, I've added a doubling down opportunity against it – when your total is 9 – but only when you know pretty well that the higher cards and Aces are due to arrive, which would give you a strong winning total. When LOW cards are due (in a negative count), you'll simply HIT your 9 versus the dealer's 2.

I'm placing two former doubling down suggestions into the "grey area" pile, however, recommending instead that you HIT your hand of 10 or 11 against the dealer's 2 if you know that the high cards have been depleted (and the Aces, in the case of the 10) and low cards are likely to fall upon your cards – that is, in moderately to strongly negative counts.

Now come two areas that are cannot be spelled out entirely in the chart (see top of next page):

Number one, if you have 12 through 14 points versus that **Tricky 2**, you should HIT, with a neutral or negative count, or if **Card Observation** tells you that low cards are due. (Even with a 14, the odds are in your favor — you have a 54% chance – with 7 out of 13 cards — of bettering your score without busting. If you chose instead to STAND with that stiff hand, you'll have a greater than 54% chance of LOSING against that 2, so your preferred choice is obvious – you HIT.) However, if the count is positive, or when **Card Observation** says that high cards are due (especially 10s), you should STAND.

Number two, if you have totals of 15 or 16, you'll want to HIT these totals if you can, knowing how often the dealer's 2 results in a score of 17 or more. But, only do so when the count is very negative, roughly **–6** or more, when you're very sure a low card (or, in the case of the 16, an Ace) is coming. *Hitting totals of 15 or 16 here should be done with extreme caution.*

More Caution Against The Dealer's 3

In positive territory, the 3 is our friend. Not so in moderately to strongly negative counts, however.

The dealer's 3 is a better card for the player than the 2, but, as the count sinks to moderately negative territory, it begins to act like a dealer-friendly card, drawing to winning totals. As a result, you'll want to be careful with some of your lower stiff hands in that situation.

So, you really would like to improve your scores of 12 and 13 if you are sure you won't bust. HIT your 12s and 13s against the dealer's 3 if the count is negative. Your chances of improving those hands WITHOUT busting will then outweigh the relative risk.

On the flip side of that point count situation, you should STAND if you have totals of 12 or 13 and and the count is neutral or positive, and **Card Observation** suggests that a 10 (or, also, a 9, in the case of your 13) is likely to be your hit card. That's a more cautious approach than I suggested in CHART 1A, because

now you can make a more informed decision about a more favorable dealer up card.

I'm now also suggesting more caution when you have scores of 9, 10 or 11 against the dealer's 3. You do NOT want to double, as suggested in Basic Strategy, if the count is in that dangerous zone — fairly negative, when high cards have been depleted. With the 9 and 10, you should get more cautious if the Aces – which you should keep track of separately from the count – are depleted, too. Simply HIT your cards in those situations.

The Up Card of 4 Is NOT Always Your Friend

Now, many players incorrectly assume that the dealer's 4 is always a great card for them. You really have to be careful here. Like the 2 and the 3, the 4 is sensitive to card imbalances. When low cards are overdue and start to appear in greater numbers than high cards, they wreak their havoc, turning the 4 into a strong dealer card. That's why I suggest that you do NOT double down on your 8, 9, 10 or 11 against the 4 when the count is –4 or lower. (Also be more cautious with your 8, 9 and 10 in particular, if Aces have been played out).

Don't forget – when you elect to HIT your cards, rather than double, you have NOT given up any edge in your attempt to win. In fact, you are gaining an edge, because you are not limited to taking just one hit card. What you are doing is protecting your money in case the odds turn against you in a risky card count. You may indeed win, but you don't want to jeopardize TWICE as much money by doubling down when your chances of beating the dealer are iffy.

When The Dealer's 5 and 6 Are NOT So Kind

Less so than the 4, the dealer's up cards of 5 and 6 can sometimes become turncoats. That is, when the count is strongly negative, or when **Card Observation** makes it obvious that high cards have been depleted, and low cards are ready to come in a

flood, these up cards tend to give the dealer winning totals. So it is NOT always wise to extend yourself and double down on your score of 7 against the 5, or 8 against the 5 and 6 in those situations – especially if many of the Aces have already appeared. Simply HIT those totals if that's the case.

Standing Against The Silent 7

Remember Chapter 4, regarding the **Silent 7s**? As an advanced player, you are now in a position to take advantage of that information. For example, when you have a hand of 15 or 16 points against the dealer's 7, you might now wisely chose to STAND in certain situations, instead of hitting those cards. This one's tricky, though:

1. If high cards are due (NOT including Aces), yes, you might want to stand to avoid busting, but, if high cards indeed are coming, isn't it likely, then, that the *dealer* got one of those cards as the hole card? So, shouldn't you still take a card here (15 or 16 won't win for you if the dealer has a 17)? That's an interesting question.
2. Or, you might want to pull a card when low cards are due, but if the dealer indeed has a weak hole card, will the dealer not bust? So, in that case, wouldn't it then be smarter to stand on your 15 or 16 than risk busting yourself?

One important key to your answer here is – do you think the dealer's hole card likely to be a 10 or an Ace? If your **Card Observation** skills and the card count suggest strongly that the answer is "YES!," then your decision is easy – you have to hit your high stiff hands of 15 or 16.

If the answer is "NO!" (in other words, the dealer is highly UNLIKELY to have a 10 or an Ace in the hole), then you should definitely STAND...UNLESS you're very, very sure you're likely to get a card that will help you. In the case of your 15, you'd need a 6 or less; in the case of your 16, you'd need a 5 or less.

Your likelihood of busting with a score of 15 if the count is

neutral is about 54%; with the 16, it's nearly 62%. That's a difficult place to be. If the count is +4 or more, your chances of busting go much higher. Plus, keep this in mind — *the dealer only has a 38% chance of having a 10 or an Ace in the hole.* Those are the only 2 cards that will combine with the dealer's 7 for an immediate winning score. So, if the count is strongly positive when your turn arrives, it's worth the risk to STAND.

Now, if your skills have gotten to where you can pretty well figure out when the dealer has a 7, an 8 or a 9 as the hole card, then your choice just became that much easier. You WILL get that good eventually.

If you're certain the dealer has those cards in the hole, DEFINITELY STAND. The dealer will then have a better probability of busting than you will have of improving your score by hitting.

You, as an advanced player, should think this one through and remain flexible. This is one of the more difficult decisions you will have to make.

At a shoe table, you can watch what cards players got as their second cards – those came directly before the hole card. Watch what hit cards players to your right drew — those cards came directly after the dealer's hole card! They might reveal the dealer got a weak hole card, while YOU'RE instead facing the coming 10s.

For example – if players' second cards were K, 10, Q, and 5, and players' hit cards to your right were 4, Ace, and Ace, I'd STAND, wouldn't you? It appears the hole card might very well be a weak card, one that would put the dealer in danger of busting.

Situations like that happen all the time, and – if you exercise the skills I've taught you — questions like the ones posed above will become that much easier to figure out.

Taking Advantage of the Silent 7 With Your 9

OK, folks, here's a move that's NOT conservative, but I

thought was worth mentioning.

We know all about the dealer's up card of 7 now, that it's a player's card. Now, be very careful in executing this move, but, *there are times when it will be wise to double down on your 9 against that 7.*

With a 9, you'd benefit from getting an Ace, 8, 9 or any of the four 10-pointers as your extra card, in a doubling down situation – that's 7 of 13 cards that would be good for you, or 54%, against a weak dealer card. ONLY consider this if the count is **+5** or more, or, by using **Card Observation**, you're pretty certain you'll get a high card or an Ace.

This is only a move for those who have become very skilled and are ready to take advantage of their wisdom, and have some fun "on the edge." It is not for the feint of heart or the overly cautious player, but it is profitable for those smart enough to take advantage of the odds and the friendly nature of the **Silent 7**.

More Caution At Times Against The Dealer's 7

All of that being said, my research shows that the 7 does draw to a score of 17 a high percentage of times. So, in a fairly strong negative count, I'm now telling you NOT to double down on your 10-point hand. If you're going to get a 7 or less as your hit card, be conservative and HIT that hand. You can then take more than one hit card if you indeed pull a low one, and attempt to beat the dealer's anticipated 17.

New Doubling Possibilities With The 8, 9, 10 & Ace

In Basic Strategy CHART 1A, I eliminated five traditionally recommended doubling moves at times when you have totals of 10 or 11 – that is, against the dealer's 8 and 9 in the case of your 10, and against the dealer's 9, 10 and Ace in the case of your 11. I feel strongly that doubling in those cases without the benefit of knowing how to card count or use **Card Observation** is foolish against such strong dealer cards.

As an advanced player, can now understand why doubling against those up cards in a negative count (when low cards are overdue) is an overly greedy move, when your hit card is one of those overdue low cards and the dealer is most likely to arrive at a high winning score. Once again, choosing to HIT your 10 or 11 instead of doubling doesn't limit your opportunity to win — it actually INCREASES your chances. (See Chapter 5.)

That being said, you, as an advanced player, would now be WISE to double down on your 10 and 11 in the five situations listed on the prior page, in *limited* cases — that is, IF the count is moderately to strongly positive. Using **Card Observation**, that means you should double down when you know that high cards (or, in the case of your 10, Aces too) are overdue. You now possess added information you did not have as a Basic Strategy player that makes these somewhat risky moves desirable at times – you now can predict with some certainty when the right cards are due to come.

However, the limitation of getting just one hit card upon these hands makes it mathematically unwise to double down in neutral or negative territory when facing such strong dealer up cards – we saw why in Chapter 5. Simply HIT your 10 or 11 in those cases.

A Fresh Look At Surrender

A word about Surrendering – now that you're an advanced player, DON'T do this if the count is negative. Similarly, with **Card Observation**, DON'T Surrender if low cards are overdue. To be more specific, then: you would want to HIT your 13s to 16s against the dealer's Ace, your 14s to 16s against the dealer's 10, and your 15s and 16s against the dealer's 9, if the count is negative, or if **Card Observation** tells you that low cards are coming.

On Insurance

Insurance is not recommended in the Advanced Charts. It's

most often a losing bet. Don't forget – the dealer has roughly a 31% chance of getting a 10 under the dealer's Ace. This does not mean, however, that you won't want to use this option on rare occasions. (This is one area that cannot be covered well in the context of a rigid chart situation.)

If the card count was very positive when the dealer dealt the hole card, or if **Card Observation** tells you that the hole card is super likely to be a 10, you might consider taking Insurance *even if you do not have a Blackjack*. (Of course, if you DO have a Blackjack, you can also elect for Even Money, which is just as good.)

Insurance, after all, is a separate bet, and – if you're sure you can win it – it is, on occasion, a smart move. It would spare you a loss if you are right and the hole card is a 10, when you have a non-Blackjack hand.

I'll leave that up to you. For card counters — consider doing this perhaps when the count is **+6** or more when the hole card is dealt. If you're confused about when to do this, DON'T ever take Insurance. It's a move for a seasoned advanced player.

Additional Soft Hand Opportunities

You'll notice that the Advanced Players CHART 5, for soft hands (on page 208), differs in only 14 boxes from CHART 2, and we already discussed one of the boxes, regarding Insurance (that is, you should STAND on a Blackjack, UNLESS the count was very positive when the hole card was dealt, because – if you stand, for a probable win – then you will get the full payoff of 1.5 times your bet).

Here are the other items in CHART 5 that are new (you'll probably not see the following in any other book):

For one thing, we're taking advantage of what we know about the dealer's **Silent 7** – that it's really the player's card. So, if **Card Observation** tells you that 10s are overdue (and Aces as well), or the lowest of the low cards (when it's your turn), then double down on your Ace-4, Ace-5, Ace-6 and Ace-7.

Both the Ace-4 and Ace-5 draw to winning totals with 9 of the 13 possible hit cards – the Ace-4, with an 2, 3, 4, 5, 6 and the 10s; the Ace-5, with an Ace, 2, 3, 4, 5 and the 10s. Your Ace-6 and Ace-7 draw to winning totals with 8 of 13 possible cards – the Ace-6, with an Ace, 2, 3, 4, and the 10s; the Ace-7, with an Ace, 2, 3, 9 or the 10s. Not bad! Once again, the **Silent 7** is a weak card for the dealer, so – although these doubling moves are radically new to you – obviously they make total sense.

Now, with the Ace-8 combination, you can DOUBLE DOWN against the dealer's 4, 5 and 6, PROVIDED that high cards are moderately to strongly overdue — that is, the count is **+5** or more. Better yet if your independent tracking of Aces tells you they're also likely to start appearing soon. If the count is less than **+5**, or **Card Observation** cannot confirm the conditions spelled out above, STAND as you did before.

The Lower Ace Combinations

Another difference in this Advanced Chart is that you will sometimes be *more cautious* when you have any of the lower soft hands — the Ace-2 through Ace-5 — versus the dealer's 4, 5 or 6. Double ONLY if the count is roughly neutral or in positive territory. Otherwise, HIT them. The dealer's 4 through 6 are much more likely to score winning totals in negative territory and these small Ace combinations have a smaller than even chance to score winning totals if restricted to the one hit card you'd get with doubling down.

However, you have two NEW doubling opportunities here, with the Ace-4 and Ace-5, against the dealer's 3 (and, as mentioned before, the 7), IF the count is NOT negative — if high cards or Aces are NOT depleted, when the dealer would likely score well.

Splitting for the Advanced Player

OK, CHART 5 was easy! Now, CHART 6 (on page 209) differs from Basic Strategy CHART 3A, surprisingly enough, in that it is

largely *more conservative!*

Take a moment now to peruse this chart. You will undoubtedly notice that you will be doing LESS splitting as an advanced player than you did with *Blackjack The SMART Way* Basic Strategy. Interesting.

Most players think that being an advanced player means, inevitably, taking more risks. Where appropriate, that's great, but it's just as useful and profitable to cut back where you can on possible losses, to end up with more winnings when the day is through. As indicated in Chapter 5, "Dangers In Doubling Down And Splitting," those options can often prove to be the casino's friend, and not yours.

Think about it. It's the hands where you split and double down that can lead to your biggest setbacks. You've got more money on the table. If you don't exercise proper caution, you'll end up chasing deficits instead of building gains.

Re-Think Splitting Against The Tricky 2s

The dealer's **Tricky 2** is reason for caution when you are considering doubling or splitting – moves that require you to increase your bet.

You should still split your 8s, because my research shows that splitting your 8s will do better for you than either hitting your 16 or standing on it. Keeping the two 8s together as a hand of 16 is NOT a good option in this case.

However, you will want to become more cautious with your pair of 2s. In a negative count, or when high cards have been depleted, simply HIT your 2s. You will save yourself the extra money you'd probably lose if you split your 2s. You're unlikely to win here either with your un-split deuces or your split hands of 2 in that situation, when the dealer's 2 is less likely to bust.

There's another instance where you should play it safer – if you have a pair of 5s, in moderately negative territory. Instead of doubling here, HIT those cards if the count is –4 or lower, or if **Card Observation** tells you low cards are overdue.

Doubling on a 10 is no picnic if low cards are coming in large numbers. You're then likely to draw a stiff when the dealer's 2 is likely to draw to a winning score.

You will also want to play it safer with your pair of 9s. *STAND on your pairs of 9s if the count is negative, or* ***Card Observation*** *tells you both that high cards and Aces have been played out more than other cards*. The 9s – with a total of 18 – provide a good score. No need to risk splitting them and placing more money on the table when the dealer's 2 becomes even stronger, and your chances of drawing strong winning hands with the split 9s becomes less.

When You Should Play It Safer Against the 3

As mentioned above, the dealer's up card of 3 acts more like the dealer's friend than the player's, once the count gets down to –4 or lower, or when **Card Observation** tells you that low cards are coming. So, you don't want to take on any more risk than you have to if you think the 3 will give the dealer a winning total.

So, DON'T split your pairs of 2s or 3s in that situation. HIT them. There's no clear advantage to splitting these cards, if the dealer's 3 isn't likely to bust.

Also HIT your pair of 5s when the count is moderately or strongly negative as outlined above — don't double down. As we saw earlier, you don't want to double your money on your 10 when your hit card is likely to produce a stiff, and the dealer's 3 looks like a winner.

A More Lucrative Possibility With Your 4s

For some psychological reason, when you hold a pair of 4s, it isn't immediately apparent that they should be treated simply as a hand totaling 8 points, but this is the smartest thing to do! That's because, of course, you NEVER split them.

So, against the dealer's 4, 5 and 6, you are not going to want to hit your pairs of 4s, as you did in Basic Strategy – you will want

to double down, if conditions are favorable. Since you know now that those weak dealer up cards are only dangerous in negative territory, the wise thing to do is to double down on your pair of 4s when the count is either neutral or positive. If you're using **Card Observation**, you should double on the 4s when you determine either that the card flow has been rather balanced (neutral), or if it tells you that high cards (especially 9s and 10s — and Aces too!) are due. Otherwise, HIT.

Something You Should Know About The 4, 5 and 6

Somehow, the dealer's up card of 6 has gotten the reputation of being the best card for the player. In fact, I am going to pop this balloon, as I have popped many others in this book. (We'll see justification for my saying this in much greater mathematical detail in my second book, *Cutting Edge Blackjack*.)

For instance, when the count is positive, the dealer's 5, and then the 4 are the two best cards for the player, causing the dealer to bust more than the 6. When the count is neutral, the dealer's 5 causes the dealer to bust more than the 6. When the count is negative, the 6 indeed might make the dealer bust most often, but, still, the dealer's 7 will provide the most victories to the player.

That being said, the dealer's 4 is to be respected during moderately to strongly negative counts, as you saw earlier in this chapter. DON'T double on your pairs of 4s and 5s against the dealer's 4, when the count gets down to –4 or lower, or when **Card Observation** says high cards have appeared in much greater numbers than low cards. Simply HIT them.

And, similarly — although the dealer's 5 and 6 are not to be feared as much as the 4 in negative counts — you should NOT double on your pairs of 4s against these cards when low cards are overdue (as mentioned above in the section discussing hard hand totals). You'll have a much better shot at winning in that case, starting with your total of 8.

When To Respect The Silent 7

There's one change you should make in your approach to the up card of 7 from Basic Strategy.

Think twice about doubling down with two 5s. Use the same criterion we used earlier in this chapter with your hard hand of 10, which is really what you have here – once the count gets down into fairly negative territory, simply HIT these cards.

A Word About The Dealer's 8

Now, we won't radically change our strategy with regard to the dealer's up card of 8, but you should know that my studies have shown the 8 is neither great for the dealer nor the player.

It, perhaps, should be off in its own category. When your wins are compared to the dealer's, the 8 is not a killer up card.

Why?

The 8 most often causes the dealer either to reach a point total of 17 or 18, or to bust. Since 18 points is a fairly weak winning total, you will often outscore the dealer (with a 19, 20 or 21), push, or win because the dealer busts. (We will look at this in much greater detail, in *Cutting Edge Blackjack*.)

Therefore, when the dealer has an 8 as the up card, you should NOT throw in the towel. To the contrary, you should feel fairly lucky. How do we use this information?

Now, you can consider doubling down on your pairs of 5s when the count gets up at least into moderately positive territory, or when **Card Observation** tells you low cards have been depleted. This is what I recommended for your hard total of 10, earlier in this chapter, for the same reasons.

Where Does That Leave The 9?

The up card of 9 is no weakling for the dealer. That is definitely a heavyweight contender.

And yet, you can now consider – as you did with the 8 – doubling down on your pairs of 5s against this card, as you did with your hard totals of 10. You still want to wait, however, until you really have the edge here, where the odds make this an obvious move. That would be when the count is strongly positive, or **Card Observation** tells you that the one extra card you'll be given will be a high card, or an Ace, producing a strong, winning hand.

You Mean I Should Sometimes Surrender Pairs of 8s?

My advice regarding your pairs of 8s is probably going to raise some eyebrows, but, as you will see, it makes total mathematical sense.

Always SURRENDER your pairs of 8s against the dealer's 10 or Ace, if it's allowed. If it's not permitted, split them into individual hands of 8, because that would give you a better chance of winning than if you simply hit your hard combined total of 16, which is a very treacherous total indeed.

Your 8s are up against the dealer's strongest cards when you're facing the dealer's 10 and Ace, which tend to draw to very high winning totals – better totals than your 8s will achieve. It's much better here to get half your bet back, if surrender is allowed. Any way you cut it – split them, keep them together – you stand a very good chance of losing here. Understand that, in the long run, this will be a losing situation for you.

You want to maximize your gains through a complete understanding of the odds, the mathematics that rule the game.

Therefore – although it will raise the eyebrows of those who haven't read *Blackjack The SMART Way*, stand firm and do what you know is right. It's your money, and you'd be foolish not to protect it if possible, in a no-win situation.

But Don't Abandon Basic Strategy

OK, so now you're a lot wiser. But, you know what? There

will be times where you still need to return to Basic Strategy! So don't forget it! When would you, as an advanced player, want to play according *to Blackjack The SMART Way* Basic Strategy, and why? Easy! When you don't know the count, or it's neutral. With **Card Observation**, it would be when the card flow is balanced.

So, when, specifically, would this occur?:

- When the dealer is dealing the first round after a shuffle. You probably haven't seen enough cards to draw enough conclusions.
- When you join a new table, in mid-play. You have no idea what cards were played before. Play Basic Strategy, but use **Card Observation** to fine tune it.
- If the count, during play, returns to a neutral or only mildly positive or negative count. For **Card Observation**, it would be when the cards seem generally balanced.
- If you momentarily forget the count.

The lesson here is – *Blackjack The SMART Way* Basic Strategy is not just for beginners or intermediates. It works great, and is a super tool for the advanced player, too, when appropriate.

Practice Makes Perfect

Well, that wasn't so bad!

Study the charts on the following pages, until they become second nature to you. You should know, on sight, in a practice situation, what to do in every card situation.

Practice, practice, practice!

Plus — *review your charts and notes at least an hour before you play, and get your strategy down COLD*.

Or, if you just can't seem to do it on your own, you might consider obtaining my audio book, *Preparing YOU To WIN*, which does your one-hour review for you!

It goes through every situation you'll need to remember at the casino, with fun quizzes at the end of both the Basic and the Advanced Strategy sessions.

It's your money!

But you're not done yet — in the next chapter, I am going to fill you in on something you need to become aware of: casino countermeasures and dirty tricks.

You are going to want to thoroughly familiarize yourself with that chapter, especially so that you can avoid becoming victimized by the few dishonest dealers and casinos who are, unfortunately, out there. Hopefully, someday these people will no longer be allowed to spoil the casino world, but, until then, knowledge is power.

You are still not ready to enter a casino.

CHART 4: HOW TO PLAY HARD HANDS

FOR ADVANCED PLAYERS

	A	10	9	8	7	6	5	4	3	2
4 - 6	H	H	H	H	H	H	H	H	H	H
7	H	H	H	H	H	H	**D?** or H	H	H	H
8	H	H	H	H	H	**D?** or H	**D?** or H	**D?** or H	H	H
9	H	H	H	H	**D?** or H	**D**	**D**	**D?** or H	**D?** or H	**D?** or H
10	H	H	**D?** or H	**D?** or H	**D?** or H	**D**	**D**	**D?** or H	**D?** or H	**D?** or H
11	**D?** or H	**D?** or H	**D?** or H	**D**	**D**	**D**	**D**	**D?** or H	**D?** or H	**D?** or H
12	H	H	H	H	H	S	S	S	H or S?	H or S?
13	H? or Sur	H	H	H	H	S	S	S	H or S?	H or S?
14	H? or Sur	H? or Sur	H	H	H	S	S	S	S	H or S?
15	H? or Sur	H? or Sur	H? or Sur	H	H or S?	S	S	S	S	H or S?
16	H? or Sur	H? or Sur	H? or Sur	H	H or S?	S	S	S	S	H or S?
17-21	S	S	S	S	S	S	S	S	S	S
BJ	S	S	S	S	S	S	S	S	S	S

CHART 5: HOW TO PLAY SOFT HANDS

FOR ADVANCED PLAYERS

	A	10	9	8	7	6	5	4	3	2
Ace-2 & Ace-3	H	H	H	H	H	D? or H	D? or H	D? or H	H	H
Ace-4 & Ace-5	H	H	H	H	D? or H	D? or H	D? or H	D? or H	D? or H	H
Ace-6	H	H	H	H	D? or H	D	D	D	D	H
Ace-7	H	H	H	S	D? or S	D	D	D	D	S
Ace-8	S	S	S	S	S	D? or S	D? or S	D? or S	S	S
Ace-9	S	S	S	S	S	S	S	S	S	S
BJ	S? or Eve-n	S	S	S	S	S	S	S	S	S
Ace-Ace	Sp	Sp	Sp	Sp	Sp	Sp	Sp	Sp	Sp	Sp

CHART 6: SPLITTING

FOR ADVANCED PLAYERS

	A	10	9	8	7	6	5	4	3	2
Two 2s	H	H	H	H	Sp	Sp	Sp	Sp	Sp or H?	Sp or H?
Two 3s	H	H	H	H	Sp	Sp	Sp	Sp	Sp or H?	H
Two 4s	H	H	H	H	H	D? or H	D? or H	D? or H	H	H
Two 5s	H	H	D? or H	D? or H	D? or H	D? or H	D	D? or H	D? or H	D? or H
Two 6s	H	H	H	H	Sp	Sp	Sp	Sp	Sp	H
Two 7s	Sur/H	Sur/H	H	H	Sp	Sp	Sp	Sp	Sp	Sp
Two 8s	Sur/Sp	Sur/Sp	Sp	Sp	Sp	Sp	Sp	Sp	Sp	Sp
Two 9s	S	S	Sp	Sp	S	Sp	Sp	Sp	Sp	Sp or S?
Two 10s	S	S	S	S	S	S	S	S	S	S
Two Aces	Sp	Sp	Sp	Sp	Sp	Sp	Sp	Sp	Sp	Sp

Sur/H = Surrender if allowed; if not, HIT. Sur/Sp = Surrender if allowed; if not, Split.

CHART 6B: SPLITTING WITH RESTRICTIONS

IF POST-SPLIT DOUBLING & SPLITTING NOT ALLOWED

	A	10	9	8	7	6	5	4	3	2
Two 2s	H	H	H	H	**Sp**	**Sp**	**Sp**	**Sp**	**Sp** or H?	H
Two 3s	H	H	H	H	**Sp**	**Sp**	**Sp**	**Sp**	H	H
Two 4s	H	H	H	H	H	D? or H	D? or H	D? or H	H	H
Two 5s	H	H	D? or H	D? or H	D? or H	D	D	D? or H	D? or H	D? or H
Two 6s	H	H	H	H	H	**Sp**	**Sp**	**Sp** or H?	**Sp** or H?	H
Two 7s	Sur/H	Sur/H	H	H	**Sp**	**Sp**	**Sp**	**Sp**	S	H
Two 8s	Sur/Sp	Sur/Sp	Sur/Sp	**Sp**	**Sp**	**Sp**	**Sp**	**Sp**	**Sp**	S
Two 9s	S	S	**Sp**	**Sp**	S	**Sp**	**Sp**	**Sp**	**Sp**	**Sp** or S?
Two 10s	S	S	S	S	S	S	S	S	S	S
Two Aces	**Sp**	**Sp**	**Sp**	**Sp**	**Sp**	**Sp**	**Sp**	**Sp**	**Sp**	**Sp**

A
CASINO
COUNTERMEASURES
&
DIRTY TRICKS
A
211

I felt it my duty to include this chapter in *Blackjack The SMART Way*, after witnessing many things at casinos that can make playing hazardous. The deciding factor was when I witnessed a casino dealer cheating players out of their money. That's when I decided that I couldn't in good conscience send you out into the treacherous modern casino environment without warning you about the few rogue casinos and dealers whom you must learn to detect and avoid.

If I believed cheating and unfair countermeasures were the norm at every casino, I never would have written this book, nor would I encourage you to play blackjack. I still feel the cheaters are in the minority, but, nonetheless, you will ultimately run into them, and so you need to be aware of this issue.

I had long thought that some dirty tricks were going on at one or two casinos along my journeys, but it took me awhile before I figured out what was actually being done, and what to look for, to spot the schemes.

I decided to do some research to help me ferret out the cheaters, and I discovered that others had experiences in the same vein. The stories corroborated what I have experienced from time to time.

I Had Been Warned

Many years ago, when I started playing casino blackjack (and was winning much more than I was losing), I tried to interest an older friend of mine into learning my system and coming with me to Atlantic City. He surprised me by saying vehemently that he refused to play blackjack, because his theory was that many casino dealers are crooked. He told me he feels that they are universally a bunch of card sharks who can pull an Ace or 10 out of a "hat" and ruin your hand, or grace theirs. Well, let me say that while I still enjoy the game and do not agree with my friend's totally bleak assessment, my eyes certainly have been opened.

The Bigmouth Bertha Who Opened My Eyes

I had nearly finished the First Edition of this book when I

came across a dealer who forced me to rethink my approach, from start to finish, so that I would not send you into the clutches of such a dealer unaware that you might become a sheep to be shorn.

I had been field testing the blackjack system I am teaching you in this book at low stakes tables and had won well over a thousand dollars in 11 straight trips to various casinos, when I finally ran into a losing night.

I went with a friend, and we kept running into awful tables. So, without much delay, we'd get up from those tables and move to other ones. Unfortunately, the casino had a limited number of tables. Not a single table was any good, and not a single player was winning. That was definitely a tip-off!

We moved to a 2-deck pitch game table where a middle-aged woman with a real bad attitude was dealing. I immediately disliked her. As she shuffled and play was at a standstill, I politely asked a player in the second baseman's seat if he would kindly move to his right one seat, so I could watch my friend's cards and help him out with the difficult decisions.

"Awww," the dealer snorted in sarcastic baby-talk. "He wants to sit next to you."

I call these types of dealers **Bigmouth Berthas** (or, if the dealer is male, **Bigmouth Barneys**).

I shot her a withering glance and ignored the remark.

Later when my friend – almost sheepishly – turned his dealt cards over and told her he wanted to double down, she retorted:

"I've worked as a dealer for 20 years; I know when a player wants to double down!" That was a totally gratuitous insult.

A player has no choice in this matter, because the casinos REQUIRE you to follow the procedure my friend followed, and verbally tell the dealer you want to double. You cannot simply let the dealer assume what you want. You MUST say "double down" or "double."

Anyway, as my pile of chips sank below a $100 loss, I began to suspect that this dealer was not on the up-and-up. She was constantly drawing improbable streaks of great hands — 20s, 21s, and Blackjacks — and never busted. I was determined to ferret out what my sixth sense was telling me. So, it finally dawned on

me — she has to use her hands to pull off any trickery she might be doing — so I decided to watch her hands very closely.

That's when I discovered she was peeking at the top cards!!!

Whenever she found an excuse to use her right hand, whether to cash in a player's money for chips, or collect a player's busted hand and bet, *she would turn over the pile of cards she was holding with her left hand, pretending to scratch her chin with her knuckles. In reality, what she was doing with that scratching motion was to fan the top cards out a ways and peek at them, while she distracted the players with her right hand activity!!!*

Then she'd deal cards with the pack of cards held up toward her face at a peculiar 70 degree angle, so players couldn't see the top of the cards. Her left thumb then pulled the top card back a little, as her right thumb simultaneously dealt SECONDS – pulling cards from under the slid-back top card, from the upper end of the deck! Then she plunked the top card she was saving down on her cards, which would miraculously draw to a great score, or she would use it to bust a player's hand!

Repeatedly, she'd turn over the cards and hold them right by her face, while distracting players by doing something with her right hand, and once again players would bust and she'd get great point totals and win!

No one else seemed to notice what I was observing, or sensed that anything was wrong!

When I discovered this, I sat back and glared at her. She gave me a cocky look and, talking out of the side of her mouth, nastily asked me "aren't you playing"? Her head shook with cockiness, and her eyebrows were raised as if she was hot stuff.

Livid, I shot her back a look that let her know "woman, I am on to your sleaziness," and pointedly responded: "No, I am waiting for the *next* dealer."

That's when she did something shocking. She immediately turned to her left, where another dealer was just standing, cooling his heels, made a clicking noise with her tongue signaling him to take over, and she then hastily made her getaway!

Now – if you think I'm paranoid, YOU try to get a dealer to leave by simply telling them you are going to wait for the next

dealer to arrive! Boy, that would be great if that was how it worked! You don't like a dealer, you just tell them so, and they'll leave! Fat chance!

I glanced at my watch to see that this Bigmouth Bertha had been there SEVEN MINUTES LONGER THAN WHEN HER SHIFT WAS SUPPOSED TO HAVE ENDED. When have YOU seen a dealer do that? That was all the confirmation I needed. They had left her in longer than dealers normally stayed, so she could work her "magic." That was one case where I truly felt the casino was in on it. For, there was that dealer who eventually took over for her, standing right next to her, ready to take over, but he did not make a move, nor did any casino boss tell him "hey, buddy, get to work!" He waited for her signal, and that was OK with the pit boss and the floor managers.

When have YOU seen a dealer WANT to stay beyond her shift? When have YOU seen a dealer NOT working, just hanging out by the side of your table, waiting for your dealer to signal them? No, there's a protocol, executed with regularity. Any change in that protocol — look out!

I turned to my friend, recognizing that we'd just been "had" by what those in the industry call a **card mechanic** – a dirty dealer – and told him it was time to take a break. Of course, I will never play at that casino ever again. I left with $125 in losses, which, although manageable for a losing day, was egregious in that it came at the hands of a cheating casino. It was a lesson I will never forget. I swore right then and there I would get the word out in this book.

That Wasn't The First or Only Time

In fact, that casino had long been suspect in my mind. I'd seen a dealer attempt to palm a card there. She was so clumsy that the card she was palming got stuck in the creases of her left hand when she tried to be slick and use it to win her hand. She wound up having to put the card FACE DOWN on the table before being able to flip it over! She even laughed when the card got stuck! I looked at the other players, who were busy chatting and didn't notice a thing!

Another dealer I suspected was cheating there got very nervous and clumsy with the cards when I focused my eyes directly on his hands at all times. Suddenly he couldn't shuffle without spilling cards and making a mess of it. Why did I make him so nervous? I caught yet another dealer there only *pretending* to shuffle the cards properly. As she distracted the players by making small talk, she was actually just dropping clumps of cards from the halves she held in her hands rather than intertwining the two decks, keeping the order of the cards largely intact!

Low Cards Runneth Over

My first concrete encounter with dirty tricks happened many years ago, at a large Atlantic City casino. I'd long thought that there was a smattering of some cheating or unfair practices going on, but I couldn't figure out how it was being done.

I was playing at a 6-deck shoe table, and it quickly became obvious to me the shoe was unnaturally heavy with low cards (2s, 3s, and 4s) while being short on high cards, especially 10s. I sat there for three hours, during which I proved the fact that the cards were crooked, to the satisfaction of all of the players at that table.

I got cocky after awhile and started hitting 17s and 18s to prove my point, saying loudly something like "Well, I'm not supposed to do this, but something tells me I'm gonna get a low card here," and I'd pull to a 20 or 21 every time. I NEVER BUSTED DOING THAT! It was ridiculous how lopsided the shoe was with low cards, but, until I pointed it out repeatedly and loudly, NO ONE ELSE NOTICED! And, even then, it took the other players awhile to believe me!

I'd pull cards with a 14 against the dealer's 5 or 6, and always improve my score. Of course, the parade of dealers who dealt at that table over the course of the three hours I was there were always getting winning totals, too, usually with hands that ran to 6 or more cards! They never seemed to bust! It was obvious to me the shoe had been rigged. If you didn't notice it, and continued to play according to your normal strategy for an honest table, you would certainly lose much more than normal.

The players laughed at first, but then they started leaving the table when they realized I was right. They left grumbling about "all the low cards." One of the players then starting counting the 10s and other cards – out loud! – and suddenly everyone who had come to play at the table was doing it! I was a bit embarrassed, because this was undoubtedly a practice that was not allowed by the casino, and I had prompted it.

Nonetheless, the other players determined that I was right. It was a crooked shoe, with too few 10s and too many low cards!

Finally, I offered to buy the cards for $50.

"No, sir, I can't sell you the cards," replied the dealer.

"OK," I said, "I'll give you $100!" I was up to $200 when the dealer called over a pit boss and two burly types who refused to sell me the cards and warned me they'd throw me out physically if I didn't stop talking about the cards.

"You're scaring the players," said the pit boss. (By the way, it was strange that they claimed they didn't sell their cards, because you could buy cards that had been used at the tables in their gift shop!)

You know, I realized something else, at the moment the dispute turned into a confrontation. It was stupid of me to have made such a show of it. Number one, that draws too much attention to you — you want to remain anonymous. Number two, you never know with whom you're dealing. So, my advice to you is: If you catch a dealer or casino doing something wrong, simply leave. Don't say anything.

Other Dirty Tricks

I am now on guard for anything unusual that might be suspect. For example, not too long ago, I noticed a dealer doing something funny as she picked up her cards after the round was finished. She had these cards:

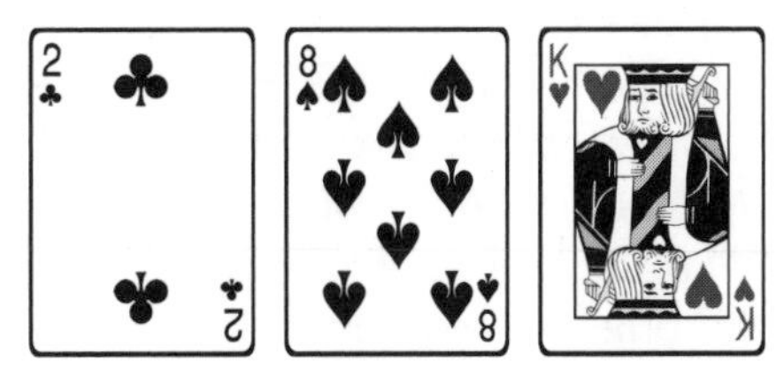

Instead of taking her cards in order, *she slipped the players' cards she'd picked up under her 2 and flipped it over her 8, on top of her KING (see the illustration below)!*

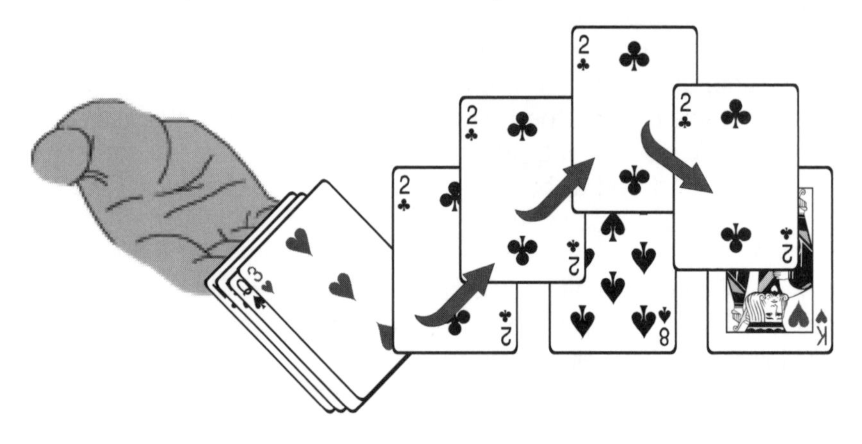

She then gathered the cards with her right hand, this time with a more understandable right to left sweeping motion, slipping the 8 under the KING on the table!

She was interspersing 10s between lower value cards!

When dealt later, the high-low-high-low sequence causes a very bad flow of cards to develop.

It also makes dealing seconds that much easier, because the dealer then knows which of the two top cards to deal to players he or she wants to bust, not to mention the card the dealer wants as his or her hit card, to make a winning hand.

Now, try this at home. When you pick up these cards, what

would be the most natural way to do it? In order, correct? ...Sweeping your hand from the right of the 2, picking up the 2, 8 and King, in that order, by sliding one on top of the other. In fact, this is not only the natural way to do it, this is the way dealers are SUPPOSED to do it — in a standardized fashion, each time. (One reason for this is that, if there's a dispute — as I had once with a dealer — management can then have the dealer re-create the round and determine who's right and who's wrong.)

Casino Countermeasures

I have also been targeted at times for casino countermeasures which — although not illegal like the out-and-out cheating I described above — are certainly not what I would call fair play.

For example, one time I went up more than $100 in 20 minutes, but during that time the pit boss brought in TWO new dealers! To do this without alerting players too much to the unusual frequency of dealer changes, she created a ruse. She pretended to find fault with the first dealer, a nice woman who, to me, was obviously dealing properly and professionally. The pit boss then replaced that dealer — outside of the normal shift change time — commenting to the dealer in an exasperated tone, "No, you're doing it *wrong!"*

The new dealer she brought in was a Quick Rick type, who threw the cards at us at the speed of light, the cards sometimes winding up on the floor. I guess the pit boss suspected I was card counting, and that speeding up the game would hurt me.

Nope. I kept going up. The dealer then began to make "mistakes". He nearly took my bet when I beat him with a 21. "Ah, ah, ah! Isn't that a 21?" I asked him. He apologized and paid off my bet.

But he continued to make "mistakes." He hit my pair of deuces when I wanted to split them. Although he apologized, he also told me he could not take back his error. I had to play my 2s un-split. I lost that hand. I can't remember why I didn't protest this error to the floor manager or pit boss. Perhaps it was because I felt they were "in" on it.

Another thing he was doing, I noticed, was reshuffling after

only about 35% of the cards had been dealt! That's very unusual and very suspect. I kept winning, however, and so I kept playing.

This latest dealer didn't last but 5 or 10 minutes before another dealer was quietly brought in. I suddenly turned around from a conversation and noticed that *they were bringing in new cards too!*

I got up and cashed in my chips. I was up about $300 by that time, and knew it was time to leave!

Jealously Guarding Those Chips

On another occasion, when, within 15 or so minutes , I was up about $150, I decided to pocket some of my chips and move to a new table. The action had become rocky at the table at which I'd been playing. All of a sudden, the dealer at that new table was immediately replaced by a female dealer, OUTSIDE THE NORMAL SHIFT CHANGE TIME. I had never seen this woman before.

It was odd because the other dealer's shift was not over. Casinos have dealers at the table for regular shifts. Depending on the casino, that could be 20, 30 or 60 minute shifts, which change like clockwork. It should never vary.

The new dealer was another one of those Quick Rick types, chucking the cards at high velocities haphazardly all over the place. Some were hitting the floor, because she was not talented enough to deal at the speed at which she was apparently ordered to deal.

(Casino bosses must think a quick dealer throws good players off. That's ridiculous. It only spoils the game for all the players. Especially when they're going faster than they're capable of doing well. It's not fun.)

Anyway, she suddenly singled me out – after not saying a word to any of the other players – and asked me: "How are you doing?"

"Not very well," I said, lying. "I'm down."

"Oh really?" she said. "You must have gotten more cash from the money machine then!"

It was pretty stupid of her to be so brazen! She could have tried some small talk first, to hide her purpose! I was shocked.

It was obvious to me what was going on.

I ask you: HOW did this new dealer know how much I was up? I had pocketed many of my chips from a prior table, and only put a small amount out on her table BEFORE she arrived. I had never seen her before, and she had never seen me.

The conclusion is inescapable. Some casino boss sent her to my table to try to win back my winnings. She was told EXACTLY HOW MUCH I WAS UP IN WINNINGS, THUS EXPLAINING HER SURPRISE WHEN I TOLD HER I WAS DOWN.

This was one of the first times I became aware of casino countermeasures that are sometimes used against winners.

I picked up my chips and left. In fact, I did not return to that casino for well over a year, when a friend told me the action had become more honest there. I refuse to play at casinos that play unfair. I only like to play when it's fun, and the action is honest.

One thing that surprised me about this incident was that I was not up a huge amount when they resorted to countermeasures! Since then, other players have confirmed what I am about to tell you: some casinos jealously guard every chip that might go out the door with a winner.

Beware the Shill

For many years, I suspected I'd been victimized on occasion by casino employees who were pretending to be players, who, I surmised, were sent to my table to louse up my game. I later found out that I was right, and that these phonies are known as "shills," or "house players."

I found a reference to them in an article called "Jimmy the Greek's Crash Course on Vegas" in the July 1975 issue of Playboy. He wrote:

> "Finally, a word about shills. They are not, contrary to general opinion, designed to lure you into anything. The casinos know that a lot of gamblers don't like to play head to head with a dealer, so shills provide the social framework for a game."

Others disagree. John Scarne, in *Scarne On Cards* talks of shills who are what he calls "**anchormen**" who facilitate cheating by the dealer. The dealer peeks at his topmost cards, and signals to the shill whether he wants the shill to take a card or not. The dealer might, for instance, place his right hand, palm up, on the table to signal to the shill to take a card, or palm down, to pass. In that way, the dealer gets the card *they* want, to get a great score. This practice is said to be done by dealers who are not slick enough to deal seconds.

And Dr. Thorp, in *Beat the Dealer,* informs us:

> "Shills generally follow "shill rules;" i.e., they never double down, split pairs, or insure, and they stand on hard totals of 12 or more. If the shill does not follow a fixed strategy he may be helping the dealer and/or house to cheat the players."

The Incident That Woke Me Up To Shills

Earlier in this book I spoke of **One-Hand Harrys and Harriets**, who come to your table in mid-play, play a few hands at most and then leave. They often make stupid moves and louse up the card flow. Well, one day, one of these **One Hand Harrys** made the mistake of tipping me off that he was a casino employee.

I was up about $200 shortly after arriving at a casino where I always found the employees to be very unfriendly. The pit boss sent over a new dealer who was apparently instructed to be a Quick Rick. She sped up the game in an apparent attempt to thwart my winning cycle. I nearly laughed out loud, however, as she clumsily sent cards flying off the table, to the wrong players, all over the place – I mean, she just wasn't skilled enough to pull it off.

Suddenly, a guy in a suit sat down in the third baseman's seat. I'd essentially been the third baseman until that time. No one had been to my left.

He looked out of place from the start. No one at this casino wore anything but casual clothes, and HE WORE A DARK, PIN-STRIPED SUIT WITHOUT A TIE! I immediately recognized this

as his attempt to "fit in" and look like the rest of us. It didn't work.

He was looking right at me with a malicious grin as he placed his small bet of a chip or two. Still looking at me with his peculiar smile and not even pretending to look at or care about his cards, he casually hit the table, indicating to the dealer to hit his 16, a totally wacko move, because the dealer had a 6. The guy busted and the dealer "miraculously" beat us all with a 21.

Continuing to glare right at me, he placed a second bet, made a similarly stupid move (I forget what it was, but only a fool would have made it), and the dealer, once again, drew to a strong winning score and beat all of the players at the table.

The funny thing about it, was that it appeared *he was intentionally playing stupidly* – he made his moves with confidence and without hesitation. Plus – *he did not seem to care that he lost both bets*. And he never seemed to look at his cards — he kept looking at me!

After those two hands, he promptly got up to leave, staring at me with his evil smile every inch of the way. It was kind of a "take that!" smile. He had given himself away.

I knew immediately that he was a casino employee, perhaps a boss, who came to spoil my winning streak, which he did, in cahoots with the dealer. But he was a fool, because he revealed himself to me, and, in so doing, convinced me of what my sixth sense had told me long ago about shills and their purpose. I promptly left the casino.

A Strange Pair

Not too long ago, I had another uncomfortable experience which I believe also involved shills. I was in a rather empty, small casino mid-day, the same casino, in fact, where I'd later catch that Bigmouth Bertha dealing seconds. I was up about $50 within 10 minutes, when the two players who'd been playing at the table, a young couple, decided they had to leave.

Suddenly, two guys came from nowhere, two loud jerks, and sat down on either side of me. The whole table was empty and they sat on either side of me! I was on alert right away, because that was strange!

They kept looking at my cards, *leaning their heads over my shoulders (I found myself leaning back to avoid contact).* As if that weren't bad enough, they passed chips between themselves, their hands going right over my pile of chips!

Naturally, I watched their hands closely on these occasions to make sure they did not take my chips, but I don't believe all of the chip exchanging that they did was what it seemed.

I think their real purpose was to create a distraction to take my eyes off the dealer, so that the dealer could manipulate the cards, or peek at the cards, to spoil my winning streak. I say this because I now know that cheating goes on at that casino. The guys were definitely interested in knowing what my cards were, that's for sure.

"Miraculously" I say facetiously, "miraculously" the cards started turning in favor of the dealer, with the arrival of these clowns. He suddenly went on a super winning streak, pulling great cards every hand. Before very long, I knew something was wrong and I picked up my chips and got up to leave.

As I began to walk away, one of the two jerks I strongly suspect were shills or anchormen urged me to keep playing!

"C'mon, why are you leaving?" he asked, or something to that effect, as if we were buddies. Would a real player do that? I couldn't WAIT to leave!

My Experience Is Not Isolated

My experiences have been echoed by a number of other blackjack authors who, like myself, are regular players. There has been ample documentation about this subject.

The one new development in recent years has been the advent of hidden video cameras, which have supplied us with undeniable documentation of the shady practices of rogue dealers.

In fact, recently, there have been a spate of excellent cable TV documentaries, in which they have aired footage of the hanky-panky caught by casino surveillance cameras.

Some of the footage I saw involved cheating and thievery by players. But some of it involved cheating by dealers.

Making Blackjacks

I have got to share this incredibly ballsy scam which was caught on videotape and then shown in an excellent documentary on The Learning Channel.

Get this. The male dealer involved was so good at manipulating the cards that the show's host had to pause the video several times to show how the sleight-of-hand dirty trick was pulled off!

Here's how the scam worked: the dealer had an Ace as his up card. He then curled up one edge of his hole card, to peek to see if he had a Blackjack. The camera caught him exposing a 6, giving him a weak score of 17. That was legal. However, he was simultaneously squeezing the undealt cards in his left hand, bending the top card and peeking at it! The camera clearly showed what the dealer then saw — that the top, undealt card, was a face card.

In a flawless motion worthy of the best magician, he then indicated he had a Blackjack, by immediately proceeding to turn over the hole card. That is, he PRETENDED to turn over the hole card. Here's what he REALLY did: with blinding speed, he picked up his Ace and the hole card with his right hand. He then slipped the 6, the hole card, onto the top of the deck of undealt cards in his left hand! In a fluid motion, his left thumb then skillfully held the 6 apart from the face card, the former top card which was now below the 6, releasing it. Then, quickly snapping his left wrist, he flipped the face card over, face up, onto the table, as if he were revealing his hole card. Voila! A Blackjack!

THE DEALER WAS MAKING HIS OWN BLACKJACKS OUT OF LESS THAN PERFECT HANDS!

The Card Clumpers

Interestingly enough, there's a whole school of players who believe that most every casino is crooked, and have fashioned a system that is meant to deal with that perception. I'm referring here to the "card clumpers," as I think they call themselves.

Their theory, apparently, is that casinos routinely rearrange the cards into "clumps" of high and low cards, thus making it very hard to win. (I say "apparently" only because I have not read any of their books. I have just read their promotional literature, on the Internet.) They say the dealers arrange the cards in this way, by incomplete shuffling.

Although I disagree with them on two counts – I believe there *are* honest games out there, and that cheating (if it's being done) comes in many forms, not just through shuffling "tricks" — I *have* noticed some evidence of shuffling trickery going on at a number of occasions at a few suspect casinos.

At those casinos, I have noticed that Aces frequently seem to appear in groups of 3 or 4 close together, so that they're all dealt in one round. That would benefit the casino two ways: 1) no one player would win too often with the aid of a Blackjack or other Ace combination; and, 2) the dealer would tend to get one of those Aces for a strong hand.

I have also noticed times at those casinos when 10s seemed to come grouped together. And low cards. When 10s are grouped closely together, spaced by a few low cards, it has the same effect as grouped Aces does. And when low cards are grouped together, it spoils players' efforts to win when they double down (leaving players with low, losing totals) and tends to give the dealer a winning hand. So, if you see a dealer constantly winning by pulling 4, 5, 6, sometimes 7 cards, yes, it could be a sign that the 10s were shuffled into groups so that there would be protracted streaks of damaging low cards. Or, it could be symptomatic of other scams, such as ones I described earlier in this chapter.

That being said — let me make it clear that I disagree totally with the approach these "clumpers" are apparently taking.

Number one, it seems that they are altering their card strategy to anticipate just one possible unfair casino practice, whereas there are many other ruses going on that do not involve that practice. Plus, there are definitely honest casinos worth playing at that do NOT engage in shuffling tricks or other improper behavior. Number two, I feel it's crazy for them to encourage anyone to play at casinos where wrongdoing is suspected. My advice, instead, is: LEAVE at the first sign of trouble!

You have to become very discriminating about where you play.

That's very important if you want to get your win rate up to its maximum possible level.

Other Authors Have Been Victimized

Lawrence Revere, author of *Playing Blackjack As A Business*, spoke of having been cheated by a dealer in a downtown Las Vegas casino. (Interestingly enough, he says he later found out that the dealer had previously been discovered cheating at a Northern Nevada casino!) He wrote:

> "As the dealer picked up the cards from the previous hand, I saw him "peek" at the top card on the deck. He then dealt four "seconds" and took the ace of clubs for himself. (In dealing a second, the dealer slides the top card back, then deals the next card, keeping the top card for himself.)"

Revere complained to the casino management but he says they did nothing.

He later downplayed this incident, though, saying that it was a rare occurrence "at a large casino":

> "Word gets out whenever a casino is cheating or "Running Flat," and it is only a short time until the casino is closed by Nevada authorities."

And If You Need Further Proof...

Both Edward Thorp's book *Beat the Dealer* and John Scarne's book *Scarne on Cards* are great resources if you want to read more about others' experiences at the hands of crooked dealers. In fact, Dr. Thorp estimated back in the 1960's that a blackjack player would run into a cheater 5 to 10 percent of the time. He stated though, that there are definitely casinos that are entirely honest.

I hasten to add that, in my experience and judging from others', the percentage of honest casinos depends on what state or country you're in.

Countermeasures Vs. Cheating

Dr. Thorp's system was so successful against the fully-dealt, 1-deck blackjack games of his day, by the way, that casinos actually changed the way the game was played! Many of those changes became standardized — such as the imposition of multi-deck games, and the practice of reshuffling the cards well before they have been completely dealt out.

Casinos also instituted all kinds of unfair countermeasures to deal with the winning players who were unfazed by the game changes. In the decades since Dr. Thorp's book first appeared, casinos have only gotten better at these practices, and so it's important for you to understand what you might experience in this regard.

First, let me make this distinction: countermeasures are different than out-and-out cheating, or what I call dirty tricks. *Countermeasures* are legal but unfair. They are often detrimental to your game, and they are certainly *meant* to be. *Casino cheating*, however, refers to serious offenses that are *illegal*, and, if documented by local gaming officials, could cause a casino to be shut down. Cheating will ALWAYS be detrimental to your game. You cannot win in the face of it.

Dr. Thorp reports that more than 20 Las Vegas casinos had been put out of business in the first 5 years of the Nevada Gaming Commission's existence alone, for playing dirty. One of those casinos had been caught removing a significant number of 10s from the deck and increasing the number of low cards. Another of the offending casinos had instructed dealers how to cheat players.

Dr. Thorp himself discovered many irregular practices, as a player — decks that had too many cards (one 1-deck game featured 58 cards!), a shoe that dealt seconds (and when he moved to a different table, they moved the shoe to his table!), shills that followed him from table to table, and dealers who peeked at their top cards and then dealt "seconds."

He then went on a trip to Reno and Las Vegas with card experts in tow to see how much cheating he would uncover. He wrote:

"There was cheating at large plush casinos, as well as smaller out-of-the-way places. There was cheating at all betting levels, even for 25¢!!"

He spoke of a situation at the hands of a crooked dealer where he'd lost 22 out of 24 hands, the probability of that happening by chance, he said, was TWO MILLION TO ONE! He later discovered the dealer was rearranging the cards in a high-low-high-low sequence, when he picked up hands that had been played out (just like the dealer I saw flipping the 2 onto the 10, which I illustrated earlier in this chapter). That created a flow of cards that was a killer to the player.

Why You Should Know About A "Sizz"

So, I hope I've made my point. By now you should see that you're not just playing against the *game* itself. You're also playing against casino employees, who just might make things difficult at times. A minority of times, yes, but often enough, and at enough casinos, that you must learn to spot their intrusion and know how to react.

Speaking of which — do you know what a "**sizz**" is? If you hear the pit boss or floor managers talking about a **sizz** while you're playing, you had better look out. A **sizz** is the casino bosses' way of telling each other that a player — maybe you — is on a good winning streak, a **sizz**. If they're discussing it, and doing so in code, it's likely they're considering instituting countermeasures against that player. Pay attention, because that player might be YOU! Leave immediately if you believe they've noticed and targeted you.

How To Alter Your Approach to Avoid the Cheats

In sum, I've listed some of the major ways you might be cheated and treated unfairly, in charts you'll find at the end of this chapter.

Some forms of cheating are done only when a player places a large bet, so it might not be a constant factor you would notice all

the time. Be on your guard!

Here are some things you might make a habit of, to avoid becoming victimized:

- *Use my **6-Unit Cheat-Proof Rule** (first described in the Money Management chapter): If you lose 6 Units while making 1-Unit minimum Basic Bets, within a dozen or so hands of arriving at a table or with the arrival of a new dealer or new cards, leave the table. (At a $5 table, this would stop your losses at $30 maximum; at a $25 table, you would apply this rule after going down a maximum of $150.)* You might or might not have been victimized, but, then again, moving saves you both from victimization *and* a table where the cards are breaking badly, so it's smart in two ways.
- *Pay attention to any changes or distractions going on at your table* – dealer changes, card changes, shift time changes, player changes, sudden commotions, sudden noises, objects falling off the table, noisy or annoying players, etc.
- *Find out when dealers are supposed to change shifts, and then check your watch to make sure this regular pattern is not being disrupted, which would be a telltale sign.* Any unusual change might reveal the presence of a **card mechanic** or other dirty dealer.
- When approaching a new table, ask players how the table's been doing, and if there have been any winners lately. If the answers are "bad" and "no," don't play there.
- *Watch the dealers very closely.* Watch their hands, how they hold their cards, their eyes, how they shuffle, how they pick up the cards. Watch for dealer "mistakes" in paying off your bet or playing out your cards.
- Be on the lookout for **shills** and the use of an **anchorman** or **anchorwoman**.
- *Always stay alert.*
- ***Remember the faces and names of the dealers you lost against and avoid them in the future.***
- *Remember the faces and names of the dealers you've won against, and seek out their tables the next time you play at their casinos.*

A player has powerful ways to respond to casino dirty tricks and countermeasures – lower your bets, leave a table, or leave the casino. If cards are being shuffled when you raise your bet (the casino assuming you'd only do so when the cards are favorable to you), raise your bet whenever the cards are BAD for you. Then, the dealer will shuffle them away! A player can respond to nasty dealers by withholding tips and, finally, leaving their tables. *But you must be alert to possible trouble, and then be quick to react to factors that turn against your favor.*

All of Which Proves a Point About Betting

The other day, a fellow I met recounted his experiences at a casino. He said he noticed — sitting in the first baseman's seat — that it seemed as if he always won the first hand he was dealt after the cards were shuffled. Thereafter, he was very tempted to a very large bet on those hands. He seemed like a smart, observant man, and he wanted to know what I thought of this.

First of all, I told him there was no plausible reason his first hand after a shuffle invariably would be good — unless he was being suckered.

Now, especially in light of what I've told you in this chapter alone, I think you can guess what I then told him regarding very large bets. This man was totally unaware of casino countermeasures and the rogue dealers he might occasionally run into.

How does he know that, once that large bet was down, a rogue dealer might not show his or her stripes? If you're unfortunate enough to encounter these people, they often wait until you have a large bet down to dip into their bag of tricks. So, while, on the one hand, this fellow was contemplating a money management mistake (he was thinking of betting on hands as if he was playing roulette!), he was also, unwittingly, courting a bigger danger.

In fact, I happen to know of one or two dirty dealer tricks that specifically target the first baseman — those particular scams depend upon the top cards being set up to deal the first baseman a bad hand. It's easier for some dealers to pre-plan a scam on the first baseman during a lull in action than it is to target all the

players with more sophisticated sleight of hand tricks. So either be on guard when you sit in that seat, or, if you're like me, you will avoid sitting anywhere near it.

The Ultimate Countermeasure

An interesting thing happened to me other night.

After having won $112.50 in less than 15 minutes at a $10 minimum bet table, a new dealer was brought in. Suspecting a casino countermeasure to relieve me of my winnings, I asked the new dealer to "color me in" after losing the first hand to her. As she was exchanging my stacks of red $5 chips for two black $100 chips, a very pretty floor manager suddenly showed up at my left elbow.

"What's your name?" she asked. The table was packed, but she ignored everyone else to pick me out. I noticed right away she was holding a pad with a pen ready to write my name down. Oh boy, I thought, someone wants to know who I am.

"Why do you ask?" I responded, politely.

"I just want to know," she retorted. That didn't make any sense. Most people have a *reason* for asking such pointed questions. And she certainly seemed anxious to get my name.

"I'd rather remain anonymous," I blurted out, not really prepared (shame on me!) for such a blunt approach as hers.

Realizing I might have raised a red flag, I added, "but *you* can call me Richard," and I placed my hand on her arm in a friendly fashion as I walked away. Obviously, one of her higher ups sent her over to find out who I was. Perhaps someone watching via the "eye in the sky" – the hidden camera in the ceiling, above the tables.

Later that night she sidled up to me and asked me where I was from. "Santa Fe?"

"No, locally."

"Oh, I thought you were from Santa Fe," she said. Yeah, right! How would she know if she'd never met me? She was just fishing for an answer to the question someone wanted answered.

"I think I've seen you here before," she continued. Ah ha. Someone had taken note of the fact that I was a regular winner.

I certainly had never taken notice of her before.

"Yeah, I come here from time to time," I responded. "My friend's wife loves to play the slots – and I come with them sometimes, but I don't like to play too much, because I don't have the money." I don't know if she bought that explanation, but I hope it threw her off somewhat. Probably not.

I related this story to a friend of mine who used to work at a large casino in Reno, and his reaction was "They're starting a file on you." Then he added, "But isn't that ridiculous? It's OK if the casino wins *your* money, but YOU'RE not supposed to win from *them!"*

I'd been identified as a smart player. Many casinos don't like smart players. They jealously guard every chip that leaves the dealer's tray and actively work against winners when they're spotted.

Some casinos have even been known to secretly photograph players, and pass those photos with identifying names written underneath to other casinos, if they suspect someone's a card counter, or just a smart player who wins a lot. In fact, there are now computers in some casinos that can scan your face and identify you if your features have already been placed in a computer file as someone to watch. You might ultimately be barred from a casino just for being a good player! There have been court challenges to this insidious practice, but, so far, the courts in most jurisdictions have ruled in favor of the casinos (not so in Atlantic City).

I'll have to be more careful in the future, and probably play less at that casino with the nosy floor manager. In any event, it sure is a nice ***compliment*** to have been noticed by the casino bosses! I consider it an ***honor***.

Passing The Bar Test

For those who would not be happy if they were barred by casinos for being smart players, I offer you some useful tips:

- ♥ If you've drawn the unwelcome attention of a casino boss, play there at a time when the boss who took note of you isn't there.

- DON'T play with friends. That might raise a red flag, because there are some unscrupulous players who actually try to cheat the house, and they often come in pairs. The house is on the lookout for them, naturally.
- Practice card counting and **Card Observation** at home until you can do these with finesse, without being noticed.
- Play the 4-deck shoe game if you've been playing the 1– or 2-deck pitch games. The pitch games are being scrutinized more than the shoe games, because those are the games smart players prefer.
- Wear different attire each time you play. The more radical the shift in appearance, the better.
- Find other casinos to play at, and lay off playing at the one where you've drawn some "heat" for awhile.
- Play at as many good casinos as possible, so you won't become too familiar at any one of them.

Study The Charts

There's a lot to absorb in this chapter, so I've distilled the information on dirty tricks and countermeasures into two easy to use charts. You'll find them immediately following this chapter.

These should be very helpful to you. They list the various forms of cheating and countermeasures that you should learn to detect and avoid. You'll want to review these charts before you head to the casino, so you're on guard for the rogue dealers and casinos that are out there. Even if they don't by any means comprise the majority of dealers and casinos at which you'll play, they can cause you to lose a LOT of money if you are not vigilant about ferreting them out.

The left column of the charts list some (but not all) of the practices that pose a threat to your game. The middle column describes some of the things that might tip you off that a particular cheating scheme or countermeasure is going on. And, the right column tells you how to confirm what you suspect. Once confirmed, your response in most cases should be to LEAVE. With some of the more benign countermeasures, you might

choose to stay if you are still winning. But be on a heightened state of alert, and LEAVE the moment they start to affect your game negatively.

You have now completed your introduction to the Blackjack The SMART Way system. If this is your first time through this book, you'll want to go back, take notes, and periodically re-read the chapters whose material you' have not yet fully absorbed, until it all becomes second nature to you. Then, PRACTICE, PRACTICE, PRACTICE.

If, at some point, you think you would like to attend one of my seminars, let me know and I will put you on my mailing list. The best way to do so is probably by going to the Mystic Ridge Books web site, and sending me an email message, at:

www.blackjacktoday.com

Countermeasure	What To Do
The cards are shuffled more frequently than normal.	Leave the table if your winning streak has now becoming a losing streak or if the cards have become erratic.
A Quick Rick dealer has been brought in, greatly speeding up the game.	If you start losing, leave the table. Don't tip Quick Ricks. Move to a table where a dealer you like is dealing.
A new deck of cards has been brought in at an odd time.	You should get to know when cards are supposed to be changed. Leave the table right away.
A new, nasty dealer has been brought in.	If you start losing, leave the table. Never tip these types. Move to a table where a dealer you like is dealing.
The new dealer puts the shuffle marker very high up in the cards, so that players will only see 40 percent or less of the cards.	Leave the table.
A pit boss suddenly shows an interest in you, asking your name, or telling the dealer to shuffle up more, or changes dealers unusually frequently, or tells the dealer not to allow you simple things like coloring up some of your chips while you're still playing.	Leave the casino and slack off on your visits there for a month or so.

Countermeasure	What To Do
You think a shill is at the table.	Leave that table.
The dealer shuffles up whenever you place a higher bet.	This one is wonderfully easy: only place a larger bet than normal if the cards are BAD! That way, you'll get neutral or good cards, and can force the dealer to shuffle if the cards are bad.
The dealer singles you out from all the players and either seems too "interested" in how much you have won, or makes nasty comments. It seems as if they were told to do so, to ruin your concentration.	Leave the table.

Dirty Trick	Tip Off	Confirmation
The dealer is dealing the second card from the top of the deck. This is otherwise known as "dealing seconds."	The dealer holds the cards up at an angle so you can't see the tops of the cards (at a pitch game). The dealer always seems to win, even with the weakest up cards, scoring 20s, 21s and Blackjacks more than probable. Often the dealer holds the cards very tightly, with the index finger held along the shorter end of the cards, at the top. This is known as a "mechanic's grip." A less-skillful dealer might fumble in attempting to pull this off. Look for one or more times when the dealer "acciden-tally" deals more than one card at a time to a player.	Watch the dealer very closely. He or she might peek at cards on the top of the stack, either by turning the cards upside down, or by "bubbling up" the top card, or by fanning the top card out a bit and peeking at its reflection in a mirror or shiny object lying on the table, or in any number of other ways, at a pitch game table. Also, *their thumbs never leave the top card.* At shoe tables, there are crooked shoes that have a mirror-like device that lets the dealer peek at the top card. Or, marked cards might be used (usually with braille). The dealer would then raise the top card deftly, and deal you the second one.

Dirty Trick	Tip Off	Confirmation
The deck(s) are rigged with too many low cards, especially 2s to 4s, with some 10s, and perhaps other high cards, such as 9s, removed. The number of cards might actually be less or more than there should be.	The dealer rarely busts, and often draws winning hands consisting of 4 or more cards with weak up cards. You, on the other hand, are losing whenever you double down, getting weak hit cards.	Over time, from shuffle to shuffle, this will become apparent, if you are observant. Watch the cards carefully. If cards have been added, they're bound to show up — for example, you might see three 4s of the same suit, in a 2-deck game! If no cards have been added but 10s are reduced in number, you might try simply counting the number of 10s (silently) that appear between shuffles, and see if the number appears to jibe with the right proportion you'd expect. This is hard to confirm, however. The flow of cards will mimic the same symptoms as with another scam, the shuffling away of the 10s.

Dirty Trick	Tip Off	Confirmation
Shuffling away the 10s.	The 10s don't show up very often, or in the correct proportion, from shuffle to shuffle. The higher proportion of low cards that then are dealt results in fewer busts for the dealer, and a higher number of dealer winning scores than normal.	This can only be confirmed at the time when new cards are brought in and first shuffled. This is done when the cards are fanned, face down. Most often, it is done by the dealer separating the cards in the very middle of the arc of cards from the rest, and then arranging it so that they wind up on top of the cards to be cut by a player. Most players will put the shuffle card in the middle of the pile, and those 10s on the top will therefore not find their way to the table.
The cooler deck: the cards are rigged in a specific order, to guarantee players will lose to the dealer's total.	The cards come out often in a sequential order, according to card values, with the dealer beating the player(s) by one or two points each time.	This is usually only effectively used against players who newly arrive at a table. The dealer has already "shuffled" the cards before you arrive. Hard to confirm, but the 6-Unit Cheat-Proof Rule will protect you.

Dirty Trick	Tip Off	Confirmation
The cards are marked. The dealer then sometimes will deal players cards other than the ones they should have gotten in an honest game, in order to cause them to bust; and deal themselves cards other than the ones they should have gotten in an honest game, to draw to a winning score.	With a sophisticated dealer, there's no easy tip off, except that the dealer wins way too much, and players (especially those who are winning, and/or who are making big bets) are busting more than should be expected.	This is very hard to confirm, with the clever markings in use. (Plus, shoe-game-table players never get to see the backs of the cards closely.) While you can casually look for any flaws on the backs of the cards with a pitch game, they would be hard to detect. Basically, your protection here is in watching the dealer's hands closely, to detect the dealing of seconds, or any dealing of improper cards in general (cards other than the top one).
The selective up card.	This is easy to spot. Watch which of the cards the dealer turns over to become the up card. In most casinos, it should be the first one dealt. It should be the same one each time.	Always watch the dealer's hands to confirm that the right card has been turned over to be the up card.

Dirty Trick	Tip Off	Confirmation
The cards have been "stacked" in a high-low-high-low etc. sequence.	The cards break unusually. Once you notice something is wrong, this cheat is perhaps the easiest to spot, now that you are aware of it. Just watch for the sequence of the cards as they are dealt.	The cards may have been pre-arranged, but, often, you'll *see* the dealer re-order cards as they are picked up, as described in Chapter 11. This is clearly improper.
The cards have been "stacked" such that the 10s are grouped together, as are the low cards.	The cards break unusually. The predictability of the cards seems gone.	This one might have been pre-arranged or done through clever shuffling. The confirmation that the problem exists is through observation — the 10s seem to come togther in just one round, separated by devastating rounds consisting primarily of lower cards.
Making blackjacks. The dealer, in a pitch game, switches the hole card to give themselves a blackjack.	Hard to detect with a dealer who's good with sleight-of-hand tricks, although the dealer will get more blackjacks than is probable.	Watch the dealer's left hand; if it's the one that turns over the hole card, look out! Watch also for for dealer peeking at the top card.

Dirty Trick	Tip Off	Confirmation
The dealer is a "card mechanic" (a term for someone with sleight-of-hand skills like a magician), but it's not immediately apparent how they are scamming the players.	Card mechanics typically deal fast. They often act as if they know they're going to win. They continue to deal, although their shift is over; or, they are brought in before the prior dealer's shift was over. They win way too often, beating all the players in numerous rounds. Someone might be overhead to say "I never win against this dealer!" All of the above is circumstantial evi- dence and not proof.	Although the best are hard to uncover, watch them very carefully, especially their hands. Watch any funny behavior, such as continual scratching while turning over the cards (at a pitch game table). Pay attention to when they are brought in, and if they continue to deal beyond their normal shift. See if you can catch the dealer peeking improperly at their cards.
There's a shill at the table.	Watch for players suddenly show up when you're ahead; they typically have just a few chips and make stupid moves. Watch for players who don't seem to care they're losing.	Watch for a new player who makes stupid moves, while the dealer gets great totals (especially if the player sits in the third baseman's spot). Watch for new players who are overly eager to see your cards.

Dirty Trick	Tip Off	Confirmation
There's an anchorman or woman at your table working in cahoots with the dealer to cheat players.	The player in the third baseman's seat is making goofy moves, following which the dealer draws strong winning totals.	Watch for any subtle signaling going on between that player and the dealer. If the dealer is using marked cards, this might go on undetected, but, if not, look to see if the dealer is peeking at the top cards. Beware of any distractions that might cause you to take your eyes off the dealer.
Palming cards. The dealer has chosen a card he or she wants, either to bust a player, or to improve their own hand, palming it in their left hand, to turn the trick later. (Used more at a pitch game table.)	The dealer uses his or her left hand to flip over a card that either busts you, or "miraculously" gives the dealer a great score.	Watch the dealer's left hand. The dealer should be dealing cards with the right hand.

PRACTICE,
PRACTICE,
PRACTICE

Now that you've completed your first read-through of *Blackjack The SMART Way*, you're probably very eager to put all the information to good use!

How To Practice

To get a full command of the skills you've acquired in this book, you absolutely have to practice them first, at home. You been handed an awful lot of material to digest, much of which was entirely new to you. All of that doesn't fully sink in until you've played a good number of blackjack hands, and your decisions become flawless and quick.

At first you will find you are having trouble remembering some of what you thought you had down pat. It's better that you have your moments of uncertainty at home, where you're not under the gun to make the right move and make it quickly, with your money on the line. With all of the distractions you'll face at the casino, you don't want to be struggling to remember your strategies and methods under that kind of pressure.

You have a lot to memorize, initially, above and beyond the *Blackjack The SMART Way* Basic and Advanced Card Strategies.

Study up on the **3-Level, Notch-Up, Notch-Down Bet Management System** and the **X Factor** (which work together), until you understand exactly how to apply both of those at the table. Practice card counting, with the idea in mind that you'll need to be able to keep up with the fast pace of any Quick Rick dealer that is sent to your table. Practice **Card Observation**, until you can analyze the cards on the table speedily, remembering all the **Card Observation Questions** you need to ask yourself, and then use the information properly in making your move.

There's an especially important reason why you need to have your playing skills down pat before entering a casino. Because, once inside, you will need to keep track of more than just the cards.

You must keep a watchful eye on the dealer, to make sure everything is on the up and up. You'll want to pay attention to

the pit boss and the floor managers, casually, to make sure there are no countermeasures in effect. You should pay attention to anything unusual at your table – players who might be shills, any distractions that might be staged to divert your attention from the dealer, and so on. You won't be able to do all of this, if your head is filled with confusion about how to handle card strategy and implement the *Blackjack The SMART Way* system components.

The Advantages Of Working With Cards

Now, here's what you should do. If you don't already own a good set of cards, go to the store and buy a dozen decks of good-quality cards, like the casinos use. (If a casino is near, you can usually buy decks that had been used at their tables, for cheap. Another place you can find quality cards at a discount price is at those huge, warehouse-style stores.) If you have some spare cash, buy yourself an inexpensive blackjack layout, either on a large piece felt or a roll-up mat. Gambling supply stores typically have these for between $15 and $35, depending on the materials used. Buy some inexpensive betting chips, too, so you can practice your betting system.

I have come to the conclusion, after practicing my theories for many years at the computer and at a simulated blackjack table, that nothing substitutes for practicing with cards. The action is slower using cards, and you will tend to notice things you do not when you're whipping through hands with a super-fast computer program. Plus, nothing beats the feel of real cards, which will prepare you for the casino environment.

Take those 12 decks you've purchased, and deal out rounds with various numbers of players, using, alternately, 1, 2 and, then 4 decks. If you plan on playing at 6-deck tables, practice with 6 decks, too (I don't play at those tables). Play all of the players' hands until you have the strategy charts down cold. Place bets on each of the hands, and play according to your **3-Level, Notch-Up, Notch-Down Bet Management System**, while applying the **X Factor**. When you are ready, try your hand at card counting and **Card Observation**.

Then, see what you might learn from patterns that tend to make themselves apparent as the cards unfold during each round. Stop and study the cards that have been played. (You'll want to replace the decks with fresh ones periodically, because each set of cards tends to develop its own personality, as I've suggested!)

Preparing YOU To WIN

I also recommend you obtain my audio book, *Preparing YOU To WIN*. It is essential that you review your game just before you play, but, unfortunately, few players do so. This fabulous 70-minute audio book does the job for you, so reviewing becomes fun and almost effortless. If your favorite bookseller does not yet carry the full line of Mystic Ridge Books, ask them to call, toll-free: **877-977-2121**, and put in an order for you! (Or, you can order *Preparing YOU To WIN*, by sending $14.95 plus $3 S&H to: Mystic Ridge Books, P.O. Box 66930, Albuquerque, NM 87193.)

What's Next?

Once you've integrated everything you've read in this book, and have used it to great success, you'll probably hunger for more information on becoming yet a smarter player and bigger winner.

At that point, you can take your game to an even higher level, with my latest book, *Cutting Edge Blackjack*. It contains the startling results of my latest research project, along with many powerful new concepts from which you will profit greatly.

And check out my website, **www.blackjacktoday.com** regularly, for free tips and updated information!

Congratulations and Good Luck!

You are now armed with enough information to become a very good player. Once you have studied, practiced and perfected your skills to your satisfaction, then, by all means, it's time to go to the casino!

I wish you the very best! But, most of all, have fun!

Glossary Of Terms

Glossary of Terms

(Note: Terms starting with numbers are listed under the letter that starts the alpha-numeric spelling of those numbers.)

Advanced Strategy Charts: A diagram or spreadsheet showing suggestions as to how the Advanced Player might play his hands in every card situation. They sometimes contain two suggestions per situation, if judgment needs to be exercised according to the card count, or card observation.

Advanced Strategy: What Advanced Players use in deciding how to play their hands. It's arrived at by these players, through the use of the Advanced Strategy charts, in combination with their application of card counting and/or **Card Observation**, the realities regarding the behavior of the dealer up cards, the **X Factor**, and advanced players' understanding of the mathematical probabilities they face in every card situation.

All-Inclusive Counting System: The *Blackjack The SMART Way* card counting system which takes into account every one of the 13 possible cards. (See Chapter 8 for details.)

Anchorman or Anchorwoman: A shill or buddy of the dealer's, who, sitting in the third baseman's seat (or, simply to the left of all the players), works in cahoots with the dealer to cheat players out of their chips. Most often, the anchorman or woman is told by the dealer, through the use of signals, whether or not to take a card, so that the dealer might draw the card he or she needs to achieve a high, winning score.

Barring a Player: The controversial practice in which a casino sometimes bans a player from playing there anymore. Always done against players who cheat, it's controversial when it's done against card counters. The courts have ruled in favor of the casinos so far in allowing this practice to continue (except, I

believe, in New Jersey).

Blackjack: When your first two cards contain an Ace and a 10-point card, for 21 points. It pays 1-1/2 times your bet (unless you tie with the dealer, in which case you win nothing unless you've chosen to take Even Money or Insurance; if you've chosen one of those options, you're paid an amount equal to your bet).

Basic Bet: The name I give to the minimum bet you want to play, whatever Level you're at. If you're at Level 0 or 1, the Basic Bet is 1 Unit. If you're at Level 2, the Basic Bet is 2 Units. If you're at Level 3, the Basic Bet is 3 Units. At no point during play at any Level will you place a bet that's lower than the Basic Bet.

Basic Strategy: What beginners and intermediates use to decide how to play their hands. It's dictated by the Basic Strategy charts and players' understanding of the behavior of each the dealer up cards.

Basic Strategy Charts: The diagrams or spreadsheets which dictate to Beginners and Intermediates how to play their hands in every card situation. These diagrams contain only one suggested move per situation.

Betting Spot: The place on the table, in front of your seat, denoted by a circle or square usually, where you must place your betting chips.

Bigmouth Barneys & Berthas: The nickname the author gives to dealers who are verbally abusive and/or insulting.

Burning A Card: After shuffling, the dealer usually discards the top card into the discard rack. That's referred to as "burning" a card. It means "to discard." Some casinos burn as many cards as there are players, before the dealer starts dealing from the newly

shuffled stack.

Bust: To go over the maximum allowed point total of 21 when drawing a card. Whomever busts — the player or the dealer — loses instantly.

Card Counting: The practice in which cards are assigned either a positive or negative number, and counted as they are played, in order to keep track of the proportion of low and high cards played, so as to predict what cards might be dealt next.

Card Mechanic: One of an estimated 300-400 dealers nationwide who, like magicians, employ sleight of hand tricks to cheat players out of their bets. Also referred to in this book as "rogue dealers," they have developed very specialized skills that cannot be pulled off by the average dealer. (Nor is the average dealer, by any means, crooked.)

Card Observation: An alternative to card counting, and one of Richard Harvey's innovations, this practice enables the player to figure out what cards are due – low or high – and what the dealer's hole card might be. It's based upon mathetmathical probabilities, much like card counting, but is easier to implement and often more telling regarding the dealer's hole card, your next hit card, and situations where 10s and Aces are either depleted or overdue.

Card Observation Questions: The five questions you must ask, in analyzing what the cards dealt during a particular round tell you about the dealer's hole card, and your next hit card. (See Chapter 8.)

Casino Countermeasures: Moves made by casino bosses and dealers to win back the money won by players. Often unfair, these moves include, among other things, frequent reshuffling, the speeding up of action, and changing of dealers.

Cashing out: Taking your chips to the cashier's window (found off to the side somewhere in the casino) in exchange for their cash value.

Charts: The diagrams or spreadsheets in this book in which suggested moves in particular card situations are displayed.

Chips: The colored "coins" you use instead of money to place your bet. Although the colors of the various denominations — $5, $25, $100 and $1,000 – are usually the same from casino to casino (red, green, black and pink), the graphics and writing on each coin is peculiar to each casino, and always contains the name of that casino.

Circle of 13: A concept found in the author's second book, *Cutting Edge Blackjack*, the audio book *Preparing YOU To WIN,* and seminar material. This is used to help determine what the mathematical probabilities are, to make smart moves.

"Color me in": What you say to the dealer to exchange your lower denomination chips for easier-to-carry higher denomination chips. Low stakes table players -- who play with red, $5 chips -- will be exchanging those chips for green, $25 chips, or black, $100 chips. How to do this: Wait for the dealer to finish collecting the cards from the last round, or finish shuffling the cards, and then place your chips on the table, just beyond the Insurance circle, and say "color me in, please." The dealer will then make the exchange. The dealer decides which of the higher denomination chips to give you. The reason this is done is that the casino does not want the dealer to run out of the more commonly used red or green chips.

Cooler Deck: Cards that have been secretly pre-arranged in a certain order before being dealt so that the dealer beats all of the players at the table.

Coupon Charlies & Charlenes: The name the author gives to players who come your table, with newspaper coupons in hand, only to play one or two hands to cash in their coupon and then leave. They are often not even blackjack players – they are often slots players who sat down to play simply because of the coupon. They usually play poorly and louse up the action. Take note of their arrival.

Cutting the Cards: After the cards are shuffled, the dealer offers the shuffle marker to a player, who then pushes that marker into the cards wherever they choose, thereby cutting the cards in two. The cards above where the player places the marker go to the bottom of the stack; the card directly below the marker becomes the top of the stack, to be the first card played (and that card is "burned," or discarded by the dealer; the card below it usually then becomes the first card dealt).

Dealing seconds: When rogue dealers cheat players by first peeking at the top undealt cards; they decide which card they want; then, holding onto that card once it reaches the top of the stack, they deal cards from below it until they use it either to bust your hand, or to make their hand reach a great total, usually 20 or 21.

Double Down or Double: Placing an amount of chips equal to your bet (doubling the amount of money you have on the table), in exchange for just one more card dealt upon your hand. You may do this only immediately after having been dealt your first two cards. Once you've taken a third card, it's too late. Obviously, you only want to do this when you have a point total that won't bust with the taking of an extra card. You usually do this when you think the dealer will bust.

Even Money: When a player who has a Blackjack asks the dealer to be paid off right away, in even money (chips equal to the players bet, instead of the normal 1-1/2 times bet winnings),

after the dealer's up card turns out to be an Ace. This prevents the player from being "robbed" of a win if the dealer comes up with a Blackjack. To do this, the player says "Even money" when the dealer asks "Insurance?" after getting an Ace up card. (Not allowed at all casinos.)

Eye In The Sky: The camera that's focused on the table you're playing at. Somewhere, off in a casino office, an employee trained to identify cheats, card counters and winning, smart players, is observing you through that camera. If he or she decides you fall into one of those categories, he or she will contact floor managers and pit bosses to initiate countermeasures, or, possibly, bar you. It's also sometimes used to resolve betting disputes.

Face Card: A Jack, Queen or King.

50-50 Rule: If a player has the same point total as the dealer's up card, the player will have roughly a 50-50 chance of winning that hand.

First Baseman: The player who sits in the seat immediately to the dealer's left (on the right side of the table from a player's perspective – see DIAGRAM A, p. 55).

Floorman or Floor manager: The lowest level casino boss, directly under the pit boss, who supervises a certain number of dealers and watches over the action at their tables.

Flow of the Cards: the author's term for the order in which the cards you're analyzing were dealt, particularly with regard to the placement of 10s, Aces and high cards. The **Flow of the Cards** is of concern to you when you are using the practice of **Card Observation**. (See Chapter 8.)

Hand: Your, or the dealer's, first two cards. Secondary meaning:

how your cards played out during any one round of action.

Hard Hand: Any hand that does not contain an Ace.

Hard Total: A total number of points in a hand without an Ace, or where the Ace counts as 1 point.

Hit: To take another card.

"Hit Me": What players sometimes tell the dealer when asking for another card (even though a hand signal is required, and the verbal expression is unnecessary).

Hole card: The card dealers deal to themselves face down. The "mystery" card you won't see until you've played out your hand. Strategy for Beginners and Intermediates is based on the assumption that this card is most likely to be a 10, since nearly 1/3 of the deck – 16 of 52 cards — is made up of 10s.

The House: Another way of saying "the casino."

Insurance: A separate bet you're allowed to make, paying 2-to-1, when the dealer's up card is an Ace. If you place chips amounting to half your bet in the Insurance circle, you're paid an amount equal to twice your Insurance bet if the dealer indeed has a Blackjack.

Money Management: How you handle your bets. Secondary meaning: how you manage your money in coming out a winner or loser.

Negative Count: When the card count tells you that more high cards have been played than low cards. If this number gets high enough, you should begin to expect low cards to appear.

One-Hand Harrys & Harriets: The name the author gives to

players who come to your table in the middle of ongoing action, and play just one or two hands, often lousing up the flow of the cards. They are either bad players, or they might be shills (see below). Pay attention to their arrival.

Personality of the Cards: The author's term for the peculiar characteristics of the particular set of cards being used at the table. It refers to whether you might consider the cards "Great," "Good," "Neutral," or "Bad," as well any patterns that tend to repeat from shuffle to shuffle, and between shuffles. (Chapter 9.)

Personality of the Dealer Up Cards: The author's term for the behavior of each of the up cards, each of which has its peculiar tendencies in leading the dealer toward a particular winning total, or toward busting.

Pit Boss: The casino manager who's in charge of a certain number of dealers and lower casino bosses (floormen) who directly supervise the tables. They're stationed in an area encircled by Blackjack tables – the "pit."

Pitch Game: Where the dealer holds the cards, usually 1 or 2 decks, in his or her left hand and PITCHES them to each player, face down. The players then must pick up their cards (in one hand only) to play out their hands.

Placing a Bet: The act of putting the amount of chips you want to wager on the upcoming round, in your betting spot.

Positive Count: When the card count tells you that more low cards have been played than high cards. If this number gets high enough, you should expect the high cards to begin to appear.

Push: When you have a tie with the dealer's hand, neither winning nor losing any chips. You keep your bet. (The dealer typically knocks lightly on the table with the knuckles of his or her

right hand to indicate that you've both achieved a tie.)

Quick Ricks: The name the author gives to dealers who are brought in by management to unduly speed up the game to a ridiculously fast pace.

Round: The period of play from the first card dealt to the playing out of the dealer's hand.

Running Count: A card count you get by simply adding each card's card count value as it appears in the course of the game. This is what you use with the ***Blackjack The SMART Way*** **All-Inclusive Counting System.**

Second Baseman: The player that directly faces the dealer, in the middle of the table (in the fourth of seven seats).

Shoe: The open-top tray that holds cards in a blackjack game with 4, 6 or 8 decks.

Shoe Game: The alternative to the pitch game, where the cards, usually 4, 6 or 8 decks, are dealt face up from a plastic or wooden open-top tray called a "shoe." The players are not allowed to touch their cards.

Soft Hand: Any hand that contains an Ace.

Soft 17: When a score of 17 is made with the aid of an Ace. In other words, an Ace-6 combination. In some casinos, the dealers must continue to draw cards if their 17 was achieved this way.

Soft Total: A point total in a hand that contains an Ace, where the Ace is being counted as 11 points.

Shuffle Marker: A plastic marker in the shape and size of a card, of various colors, that's used both to cut the cards, and

then, by the dealer, to push into the stack of cards at certain point where he or she wants to stop play action and shuffle the cards again.

Silent 7: The nickname the author gives to the dealer's up card of 7, because, while the current wisdom is that it is a strong card for the dealer, it actually breaks more often for the player – either by busting or by achieving a weak winning score for the dealer. In fact, it causes the dealer to bust more than any other dealer up card, when the count is moderately or very negative (when 10s are overdue).

6-Unit Cheat-Proof Rule: One of the stop-loss levels advised in *Blackjack The SMART Way*, which tells you to *leave the table* if you've lost 6 or more betting Units after a dozen or less hands, upon arriving at a table, or with the arrival of a new dealer. Whether the result of rogue dealer cheating, or simply a downturn in the card cycle, it's time for you to leave the table. Invoke this twice in any one session and you should leave the casino.

Sizz: The term casino floormen and pit bosses use to describe a winning streak being enjoyed by one or more players.

Split/Splitting Cards: When you are dealt two like cards, say, two 2s, you are allowed (in most casinos) to divide those cards (after putting down an extra bet equal to your original bet) and start new hands with them. You tell the dealer "split" when it's your turn, while you put down the extra chips to cover the new hand. The dealer then plays each card as a new hand, giving you as many cards as you'd like on each card — with the exception of Aces; if you split those, you get just one extra card placed upon each Ace.

Stand: To "stand pat," not take any more cards, after receiving your first two cards.

Stiff: A hard hand that totals 12 to 16 points, which is in danger of busting with an extra card.

Surrender: Where the player decides his or her hand is so very poor and the dealer's hand so very strong that he or she wants "out" of a round of action. Upon saying "surrender" (as soon as it's the player's turn) – without making any signals – the dealer takes half of the player's bet (leaving the other half to the player), and discards the player's cards. (Not allowed at all casinos.)

Table Winning Percentage: The author's term for the approximate number of hands you win, in percent. You can do it through exact mathematics — dividing the actual number of times you've won, by the total number of hands you've faced, and then multiplying the result by 100. Or, an approximation is often just as useful. (See Chapter 9.)

Ten-pointers or 10s: Cards that either say "10," or are face cards, which are also valued at 10 points.

Third Baseman: The player who sits in the seat dealt to last by the dealer, immediately to the dealer's right (the left-most seat, from the player's perspective – see DIAGRAM A, page 55).

3-Level, Notch-Up, Notch-Down, Bet Management System: A 3-tiered betting system developed by the author.

Tip: Chips or money you give to the dealer, as in tipping a waitress. Also known as a "toke."

Tip Slot: The slot where the dealer deposits any tips. Dealers typically tap the tips (usually chips) loudly on the table before depositing them in the slot, to alert the floor managers. This is a check against dealers stealing chips they should not be taking.

Toke: A tip for the dealer.

Tray: Where the dealers keep their chips (the chips they use to payoff winning bets, or collect losing bets).

Tricky 2s: The nickname the author gives the dealer's up card of 2. While the current wisdom is that the 2 is a player-friendly card, it actually is the dealer's card, causing the dealer to achieve winning totals much more than it makes the dealer bust. Therefore, players playing by the old "rules" will lose to this up card more than not, if they don't wise up.

True Count: A card count you arrive at by taking the running count, and dividing it bythe number of decks of cards that remain unplayed. (Or, with some systems, the running count is actually divided by fractions of decks.)

Unit: The absolute lowest bet you will play. Usually, it coincides with the minimum at the table. If you're at a $5 minimum bet table, a $5 chip will be your "unit." At a $10 table, two $5 chips will be your basic "unit." (They don't give you $10 chips, or we'd say here "a $10 chip" would be your unit.) And so on. It's a way of simplifying how you think of your bets, and how you want to raise and lower them.

Up Card: One of two cards in the dealer's hand — the one that's face up.

X Factor: The name the author gives to a variety of factors that tell you how well you're doing and how well the dealer is doing, at any one particular table. The questions you must ask yourself to determine what the **X Factor** is at any one time, and provide the answers as to how to play your bets, and whether you should stay at the table or leave (see Chapter 9). They also tell you whether the table is "bad," "neutral," "good," or "great." In addition, it clues you in on what the **personality of the cards** is, and, with the resulting repeating patterns you notice, how to handle some of your card situations.

X Factor Indicators: Any one of a number of signposts that alert you as to how good or bad the table is for you. Some point you toward making higher bets and moving higher up within your **3-Unit, Notch-Up, Notch-Down Bet Management System**, other indicators tell you it's time for you to leave that table.

X Factor Questions: The questions that lead you to an understanding of what the **X Factor Indicators** are telling you.

Index

K

L

M

R

S

U

W

X

About The Author

The author of *Blackjack The SMART Way*, the audio book *Preparing YOU To WIN*, and the much-anticipated and back-ordered follow up to this book, *Cutting Edge Blackjack*, Richard Harvey is much in demand nationwide. Radio talk show appearances, blackjack seminars, and book signing events have taken him from one end of the country to the other, propelled by word of mouth excitement, which has spread like wildfire. Hundreds of enthused blackjack players have flocked to his wildly popular seminars and workshops. An expert blackjack player, teacher, researcher, theoretician, public speaker and writer, Richard credits his success at blackjack partly to the theoretical math he studied in college. A one-time resident of New York, Boston and Chicago, he now prefers the beauty of New Mexico (not to mention its many casinos, and proximity to Las Vegas!).